POKER WIZARDS

WISDOM FROM THE WORLD'S TOP NO-LIMIT HOLD'EM PLAYERS

WARWICK DUNNETT

POKER WIZARDS

WISDOM FROM THE WORLD'S TOP NO-LIMIT HOLD'EM PLAYERS

Daniel Negreanu
Dan Harrington
Chris 'Jesus' Ferguson
Marcel Luske
Kathy Liebert
T.J. Cloutier
Marc Salem
Mel Judah
Mike Sexton

CARDOZA PUBLISHING

Cardoza Publishing is the foremost gaming publisher in the world, with a library of over 200 up-to-date and easy-to-read books and strategies. These authoritative works are written by the top experts in their fields and with more than 10,000,000 books in print, represent the best-selling and most popular gaming books anywhere.

FIRST EDITION
Copyright © 2008 by Warwick Dunnett
- All Rights Reserved -

See page 352 for free book offer!!!

Warwick Dunnett images courtesy of Eagle Image, Dave Goudie

Library of Congress Catalog Card No: 2008927149
ISBN: 1-58042-227-6

Visit our web site—**www.cardozabooks.com**—or write for a full list of books and computer strategies.
CARDOZA PUBLISHING
P.O. Box 98115, Las Vegas, NV 89193
Phone (800) 577-WINS
email: cardozabooks@aol.com
www.cardozabooks.com

THE WIZARDS

CHRIS FERGUSON
Over $6,500,000 in career earnings and 5 WSOP bracelets.

DANIEL NEGREANU
Over $10,000,000 in earnings, 2 WPT titles and 3 WSOP bracelets

DAN HARRINGTON
2 WSOP titles and $6,500,000 in earnings

MARCEL LUSKE
One of Europe's best known players with over
$3,500,000 in earnings

KATHY LIEBERT
The #1 female money earner in tournament poker. 1 WSOP bracelet and
$4,000,000 in career earnings

T.J. CLOUTIER
Member of the Poker Hall of Fame, 6 WSOP bracelets and nearly
$9,000,000 in career earnings

MIKE SEXTON
1 WSOP bracelet, over $3,200,000 in earnings and more
than 43 WSOP cashes

MEL JUDAH
Career earnings approach $3,000,000. Holds 1 WPT title
and 2 WSOP bracelets

MARC SALEM
World-renowned mentalist and author on how to read people
and detect lies

WARWICK DUNNETT
Summary Chapter

Wizard

During the 15th century, the term "wizard" referred to a "philosopher, or sage." It was derived from Middle English *wysard* (from wys "wise" and the *-ard* suffix.) The semantic restriction to "sorcerer, magician" occurred in the 16th century. Colloquially, anyone who is especially adept at some obscure or difficult endeavor may be referred to as a *wizard*.

Poker Wizards is a compilation of interviews and insights from experts in one such obscure and difficult endeavor, the game of no-limit Texas hold'em.

Acknowledgements

Thank you to my fantastic children, Harrison and Jacqueline, for giving me a reason to make them proud.

Heartfelt thanks to my father, Don Dunnett (aka Aspen Bob), for all the hours of skillful editing he spent working on this book. Backed by fifty years of journalistic experience and an in-depth understanding of poker, he helped me craft my fledgling project into a much more fluid and readable work. Also, as only parents can, he along with my mother, Leila, continually made me feel as though this project was worthwhile through the hundreds of hours of rewrites that were needed to transform expert spoken words into readable prose.

Above all, thanks to my wife Gail who continued to have faith in my ability to see this project through to completion and for consistently being positive about its potential outcome. Thank you also to my publisher Avery Cardoza and agent Sheree Bykofsky for recognizing the merits of this project and believing in its author.

TABLE OF CONTENTS

Unless stated otherwise, all of the situations discussed by the Wizards in the Starting Hand Concepts and Specific Hand Strategy sections are assumed to be at a full table, during the third level of a tournament. The blinds are $100/$200, and you have an average stack of around $11,000 in chips. It is also assumed that the players are displaying a moderate level of aggression and appear to be playing reasonably well

Also, unless stated otherwise, odds for hand match-ups quoted in the book assume all four cards are from different suits and rounded to the nearest whole percent. In some cases, the total percentage may not equal 100% because of a possible tie.

The tournament winnings of the Wizards do not include results achieved after Spring 2008.

INTRODUCTION

In the following chapters, the world's greatest players explain how they weave their poker magic, get the most out of the game, and how you can duplicate some of their amazing success. All of the players who share their secrets in this book have a long-term record of profitability. Some are better known than others and many have opposing styles, but one thing is certain—these players rank among the world's poker greats.

How much would you pay for the opportunity to be coached for a hundred hours by a group of the world's best poker players? How many people would line up around the block for a chance to sit with Chris Ferguson in a quiet hotel room and talk about poker strategy? Enjoy a long lunch with T.J. Cloutier? Learn how to read body language from an expert such as Marc Salem? Receive inspiration from Dan Harrington over the course of an afternoon or get insider poker secrets from the likes of Daniel Negreanu, Kathy Liebert, Mel Judah, Mike Sexton and Marcel Luske?

To me, the opportunity to interview and record the thoughts of the Poker Wizards in this book was invaluable. Not simply because it gave me an opportunity to substantially improve my poker game and make more money, but also because of the opportunity to absorb the mental attitude of winners and great champions. It is a rare privilege to spend time with people who infuse you with the belief that you too can reach a level of achievement far beyond the norm. I hope that in reading this book, you will come away with that same inspiration and knowledge.

To become a poker wizard, you don't need to be athletic or born with a silver spoon in your mouth. The cards don't care if you're black or white, male or female, young or old, rich or poor, because poker is one of the world's great equalizers. Surprisingly, lots of people just rely on luck and don't make any effort to learn how to play correctly. When you know what you are doing and can bring a bit of wizardry to the game, you have a tremendous advantage over most of your opponents.

Fortunately for all of us, a select group of Wizards have agreed to pass on some of their priceless knowledge in the pages that follow. This book will allow you to capture some of their magic.

CHRIS FERGUSON

"Jesus"

Career Tournament Earnings Exceeding $6,500,000
Winner, WSOP No-Limit Hold'em Main Event, 2000
Winner, WSOP $2,500 Seven-Card Stud, 2000
Winner, WSOP $1,500 Omaha High-Low, 2001
Second place, $3,000 WSOP Pot-limit Hold'em, 2002
Winner, WSOP $2,000 ½ Limit Hold'em ½ Seven-Card Stud, 2003
Winner, WSOP $2,000 Omaha High-Low, 2003
Second place, WSOP $3,000 Pot-limit Hold'em, 2003
Winner, $2,500 No-Limit Hold'em Winnin' o' the Green,
Los Angeles, 2004
Second place, WSOP $5,000 No-Limit Deuce-to-Seven Draw, 2004
Second place, National Heads-up NLH Poker Championship,
Las Vegas, 2005
Winner, WSOP $10,000 No-Limit Circuit Event,
Harrah's San Diego, 2005
Winner, WSOP $10,000 No-Limit Circuit Event,
Harrah's Las Vegas, 2005
Second place, WSOP $2,000 Pot-Limit Omaha, 2005
Second place, National Heads-Up NLH Poker Championship,
Las Vegas, 2006
Winner, WSOP No-Limit Circuit Event,
Harvey's Lake Tahoe, 2007
Winner, NBC National Heads-Up Championship,
Las Vegas, 2008

Sitting Down With Chris

The man they call Jesus sits on the opposite side of the green poker table. Sinister-looking glasses cover his eyes and wavy brown hair escaping from a black cowboy hat drawn across his brow impedes what little chance you have of gaining knowledge from his expression. With hands propped under his chin, his face and head are unmoving, pointing forward and slightly downward so he can see both the other players and his own cards with ease.

Nobody at the table really knows what he is watching, yet your senses tell you he is absorbing every move you make. In vain you also wear glasses, hoping they will hide your innermost thoughts each time a card hits the table, but everybody knows he doesn't need to see your eyes to figure out what you may have. The few times you did bet, you made sure you were consistent in the way you pushed chips forward and did so with amounts that would not reveal too much information about your cards, but you've been playing too tight! You know it, and all the observant players know it. Betting rarely, and only with good cards, is like turning on a neon sign above your head. World-class players like Chris Ferguson use that information to exploit you with ease. Today is no exception.

It has now been a bit more than four hours and Ferguson is becoming more aggressive. It's clear that the majority of the people at the table are trying to survive by avoiding him, handing over small pots, waiting for the nuts before engaging in a conflict. His onslaught continues, and when opponents do connect and return his aggression Chris is able to back off before they extract enough reward. After a few more hours, his daunting stack has grown to form a barricade next to his left arm, and it has become impossible to ignore his omnipotent presence. As the tournament director breaks your table and passes out the new seat assignments, you try not to look too relieved. You shake the hand of one of the top tournament players in the world and thank the poker gods for a lesson you won't forget.

Most people recognize Chris Ferguson because of his distinctive black clothes, cowboy hat and long hair. What they may not realize is that he is one of the most accomplished tournament players in the world. He does present an appealing persona for the cameras, but if you play him, try not to forget that he holds a Ph.D. in computer science specializing in artificial intelligence from UCLA, is said to have a photographic memory, and is an expert in the field of game theory. Like Mike Sexton, Chris Ferguson also happens to be an accomplished dancer. Dana Smith, in an interview published on the web site Pokerpages.com, described him aptly by dubbing him, "a computer Merlin who works wizardry on the tournament circuit and makes mambo magic on the dance floor."

When not playing poker, Chris spends a lot of time working on FullTiltPoker.com, a website he helped create, and to which he has brought together many of the world's best players. This impressive website features nice graphics and lots of user-friendly options where one can play against top pros at lower-limit betting levels, or watch exciting high-stakes games between the likes of Chris, Erick Lindgren, Jennifer Harman and John Juanda. Each pro has a contractual obligation to spend a certain number of hours playing on the site each week, it therefore represents a great opportunity to play with the world's best players. If you don't want to play, you can usually find one of the stars to watch for a couple of hours, or pick up their weekly insights. When I was interviewing Chris he gave me a demo of the website and was having a great time playing with people at the 50¢/$1 level.

With well over $6 million in career earnings and five World Series of Poker bracelets to his credit, Chris Ferguson's intelligent, gutsy and persistent approach to tournament poker is a force to be reckoned with.

Let's hear what Chris has to say…

CHRIS FERGUSON

THE MAKINGS OF A POKER WIZARD

One quality that the top poker players have in common is that they're all extremely intelligent. Whether or not they have a strong educational background is not really important; they're all very, very smart people.

Above all, to excel in poker, you have to love being very competitive. It's got to hurt when you lose. But that competitiveness actually makes you. It is what drives and motivates you to become a better player. However, in poker you have much less control over the outcome than in many sports, so you must be willing and able to lose because no matter how good you are it is going to happen.

TOURNAMENT STRATEGY

The Secret of Adaptation

I do not think of myself as having a particular style because I adjust my play to fit my opponents. I think of my style as trying to give my opponents as much trouble as I can and make their decisions as hard as possible. I want to force my opponents to play a style they're not used to. If they're playing too many hands, I will make them pay to play. I am going to put pressure on them and make them shift to a style where they're going to want to see a lot fewer hands. So, in effect, I am going to play around them. If they're playing too few hands, once again I will put pressure on them and raise more often, but if they come into a pot, I'm more likely to let them take it. In essence, I'm saying, "Play more hands, steal the pot," because that is a style they're not used to.

If my opponent folds his blinds too often, I am going to raise him frequently. I am going to try to force him to play pots against me and defend his blinds more. Now, he is playing a game he is not comfortable with. If he defends his blinds all the time, I am going to tighten up slightly. I am going to tell him, "Well, you should throw those weak hands away because when I come in I have a good hand." I am forcing him to change his style to play a little bit more conservatively. If he is always raising me and trying to steal my blinds, I am going to start playing pots against him. I am going to punish him for raising me with those weaker cards by playing more hands.

If he does not want to play a lot of hands, and is not raising enough, I will let him steal my blinds. I'll only play my best hands. So again, in one sense, I am trying to force him to play a style he is not used to; or I am punishing him if he does not change. To me, that is a win-win situation. If he does not change the way he plays, that is fantastic because I am really taking advantage of him. If he does change the way he plays, now he is playing a game he is not used to. He is playing a style that he does not want to play. It is not his natural style and the fact that he is going to be slightly out of his element is going to be an advantage for me. So I think you could say my playing style is really geared to my opponents. I try to adjust to them as much as possible.

Forcing Opponents to Make Difficult Decisions*

One essential element of playing winning poker is forcing your opponents to make difficult decisions. That's why raising is almost always better than calling. It forces an extra decision on your opponents. To take this a step further, you'll win more money by forcing your opponents to make decisions when they're out of their comfort zones.

Here is an example. The opponent on your left is playing too tight before the flop. You want to punish him for this. The best way to do that is to raise more often and be more aggressive. Either you end up stealing a lot of blinds, or he adjusts his play. If you get the blinds, great! If he adjusts, even better! It's the best outcome you can hope for. If he starts playing more hands preflop, you now have a real edge. Anytime your opponent changes his preflop playing style, he's going to run into trouble later in the hand. A guy who usually plays nothing but very strong hands isn't going to know what to do with weaker holdings on the turn and river.

If a tight opponent raises in front of you, wait for a stronger hand to call. By playing tight when you are acting behind your opponent, you avoid losing money to his stronger hands. Again, if your opponent catches on, you're forcing him to play more hands up front, and you can outplay him after the flop.

---

*This section is an extract from one of Ferguson's lessons on FullTiltPoker.com, which provides interesting insights into how different pros think.

What about the guy who plays too many hands? If you're acting first, you want better starting hands than normal. Most of the value of a marginal hand comes from the chance that your opponent will fold immediately. If your opponent has never seen suited cards he doesn't like, the value of your marginal hand decreases because it's unlikely he's going to lay his hand down. He may win more pots preflop, but this is more than offset by the extra money you're going to make when you do see a flop with your stronger hands.

If a loose opponent raises you, you can call, or even raise, with weaker hands, and raise with hands you'd ordinarily just call with. By taking control of the hand, you can pick up more pots later. Again, you are daring him to change his style. If he doesn't, you're getting the best of it. If he does, he's a fish out of water, prone to making mistakes later in the hand.

It's important to have a lot of tools in your arsenal. First, it's helpful in being able to adjust to your opponents and force them out of their comfort zones. Additionally, it will enable you to take advantage of your own table image when you have already been labeled as a tight or loose player, and to adjust accordingly.

For example, Gus Hansen and Phil Ivey are known as extremely aggressive players. The only way they have been able to survive with that image is by being able to adjust to different opponents and to slow down occasionally, when appropriate. I have seen this happen sometimes just before an opponent starts reacting to their aggression. They're able to sense what is happening and change their games accordingly. Other times, they won't adjust much, and force their opponents to try and beat them at an unfamiliar game.

To best take advantage of your opponents, pay attention to everything, all the time, not just when you're in the hand, but especially when you're not in the hand. Every hand your opponent plays gives you valuable information about how he thinks, and how he's likely to play hands in the future.

If there's an expert at your table, watch how he plays. See what hands he expects to work, think about how he plays them, then try incorporating that style yourself. See how he pushes weaker players out of their comfort zone. Paying attention is one of the best ways to learn, and a great way to move up the poker food chain.

The Stages of a Tournament

I don't go into the different stages of a tournament saying I am going to play differently. I judge how my opponents play and I react to them. However, in the beginning, middle and late stages of a tournament, my opponents are going to play differently, therefore I'll play differently—but it is only in reaction to my opponents.

In the **early stages**, my opponents will probably be playing more hands. I try to start with a slightly better hand than they do because they will more likely call me down. It is tougher to bluff in the early stages of a tournament, but I will if the opportunity presents itself.

In the **middle stages** of a tournament, I am going to have opportunities to bluff later in a hand so I don't need a starting hand that is as good. It is not that the stage is so much different, but that my opponents are playing differently. If, however, I happen to be in the middle stage of a tournament and I am playing against a bunch of maniacs, I will tighten up. I will try to have a good hand if I think they're going to call me down. So it is really an adjustment to my opponents.

In the **later stages** of a tournament, players tend to tighten up. If I am the first one to act, I can come in slightly weaker because I don't expect to be played with as often as I would in the earlier rounds. In the later rounds, if someone comes in, I am going to give him more respect because my opponents are not playing as many hands. Again, it is really an adjustment to the way they're playing.

The only time I adjust for a particular stage in a tournament is when I am very close to the money and have a short stack. Then I'm really trying to get into the money. Once I have achieved that, I play more conservatively than I normally would because a tournament is actually a contest to see how long you can last and not a contest to see how many chips you have at any given point.

Intellectualizing Gut Feeling

Gut feeling—intuition and reading your opponents—is important in a poker game. Subliminal input is a good way to describe gut feeling. It is something that is very hard to quantify. Once you quantify it, it is not a gut feeling anymore. Once you understand why you feel that way, it is an intellectual decision. I would rather make the correct intellectual decision than go with my gut.

Gut feelings can be wrong, so you have to be able to adjust them. For example, if my gut feeling is wrong five times in a row where I thought an opponent was bluffing, I have to understand why I thought he was bluffing. If I don't figure that out, he is going to keep taking advantage of my gut feeling until I intellectualize that feeling. Why did I think he was bluffing? What is he doing? Oh, maybe he has a big hand when he does this. Or perhaps you could also argue that my gut feeling will adjust. Eventually that will happen, but I think it happens faster if you intellectualize it.

I also use my opponents' gut feelings against them by making them think something that is not true. I do this by putting an idea in their mind that is false.

Common Tournament Errors

I think people overadjust for tournaments because they're too worried about going broke. When they get a small stack they play too weak. Even middle stacks often don't play enough hands. They would play a lot more hands in live action. In a sense, it is right to slow down a little bit because as I said, you are rewarded for how long you last in a tournament, but many players incorrectly slow down too much.

Mathematics and the Decision-Making Process

Mathematics has a huge influence on me in the sense that when I prepare to play a game, I understand the math. If I play a hand and don't know the math, I will go home and study so that the next time I see that situation I will know what to do. Mathematics has a huge amount to do with my preparation, but am I naturally doing the math at the table when I am making a decision? Not normally.

There are times, of course, when you'll make some calculations. For example, if your opponent has moved all in, you have to calculate whether or not you have the correct odds to call him. What kind of hands can I put him on? What is my chance of winning if I call? Then I am going to do some math. Apart from that, there really are not that many math calculations involved in the actual play of the game. For me the math comes in preparation at home when I am analyzing different situations.

AGGRESSION

Being Aggressive at the Right Time

The question of how aggressive you actually need to be is not easy to define. Making the right bets are a lot of what being a great poker player is all about. You have to be aggressive, but at the same time, you have to be able to lay down a big hand. It is very hard to find people that can do both of those things successfully. Just being aggressive is not going to do it. You really have to know what you are doing. It is picking your spots, being aggressive at the *right* time that is important.

In the later stages of a tournament, when I am close to the money and have a big stack, my opponents are not going to want to gamble with me because they risk going broke. I can put a lot of pressure on opponents with weaker hands at times like that. Just before the money is a great time to become most aggressive. When I make the final table my aggression can kick in again if I have a big stack.

In those situations it doesn't mean I am raising every hand. I just raise a little more often; they're subtle changes. If we are one out of the money, and the big blind risks going broke, I'll often raise with any hand. My opponent can know I haven't even looked at my cards and he's still going to fold most of the time because he won't want to gamble. I am not trying to fool him by raising. I just know he is going to act in his own best interest, and his own best interest is to fold most of his hands.

Top Players Call Less Often

Amateur poker players prefer calling as opposed to raising or folding. If they have the worst hands they will fold; if they have the best hands they will raise; but with average hands they will just call. The top players play differently; they do a lot less calling. They will fold more hands and they will raise more hands. They put pressure on opponents by raising back as opposed to calling.

If people limp in front of me, I might limp in as well—I am not raising every time I play. Of all the players at my table, I am usually the one raising the most. But if I am the first one into a pot, I never call. I either raise or fold.

Preflop versus Post-flop Play

Many books describe good preflop strategy. Actually the number of situations that occur preflop are vastly limited. You only have two cards, and there aren't that many different bets you are going to see from your opponents. As a result, preflop play can become very repetitive. On the other hand, post-flop play is an art, and can be much more interesting.

After the flop, you must be able to adjust to a lot of different situations. Now, not only do you have the flop cards to consider, you also obtain a lot of information about your opponents' cards based on their actions, and are forced to adjust to a multitude of different situations. Because post-flop play is tougher and requires a lot more skill, it's where the really good players are able to distinguish themselves from the rest of the pack.

STARTING HAND CONCEPTS

> Unless stated otherwise, all of the situations discussed by the Wizards in the Starting Hand Concepts and Specific Hand Strategy sections are assumed to be at a full table, during the third level of a tournament. The blinds are $100/$200, and you have an average stack of around $11,000 in chips. It is also assumed that the players are displaying a moderate level of aggression and appear to be playing reasonably well.

Early Position

In early position, I normally only enter the pot with the premium pairs, and high cards such as A-K, and A-Q. On occasion, I will also play A-J, plus the lower pairs down to 7-7.

Middle Position

When in middle position, I can fool around a little bit more and normally play any good ace. I will also play any suited A-J, K-J, K-10, two reasonably high cards, some of the suited connectors, and any pair.

Late Position

In late position with no one yet entering the pot, I can play around a lot more, sometimes even with king high.

Misrepresenting the Strength of Your Hand

Before the flop, I am misrepresenting my hand only a very small amount of the time. Very rarely, I may raise in early position with a hand such as 7♣ 6♣. Once in a blue moon, I'm going to reraise a guy with a J-10 suited. In my mind, I really don't think of it as misrepresenting myself. I could tell you that one out of every 100 times I'm going to raise you with that hand and my opponent could know that. I'm not worried that he knows that I'm capable of doing that. If he thinks I do it all the time, he's in big trouble because I have news for him: I don't. Most of the time I wait for premium hands. I play far fewer hands than many of the more aggressive players do.

When Players Have Already Entered the Pot

If someone else is in the pot, you have to consider what position they come in from. If they bet from first position, they're saying, "I've got a hand that can beat eight or nine other opponents," so you normally assume they have a strong hand. However, if you're on the button and the player raises from the cutoff (one seat in front of the button), now your A-9 is playable. A-9 is unlikely to beat the worst hand they would raise with from first position, but could easily be a favorite against a late-position raiser. But if I'm on the button and nobody else has entered the pot, I'm going to raise close to 100 percent of the time with that A-9.

The Continuation Bet

If somebody behind me calls my raise preflop from the big blind, I'll almost always make a continuation bet on the flop. If he calls from behind in better position, I just have to go with the flow; I don't necessarily have to make a continuation bet.

Playing Marginal Hands

On occasion, I like to call in marginal situations with weaker hands just to say to my opponents, "Hey, don't fool around, I'm willing to gamble." It's important to have an image where opponents know you can't be bullied. But I'm not going to give up a lot of money to do that either.

SPECIFIC HAND STRATEGY FOR NO-LIMIT HOLD'EM TOURNAMENTS

A-A

If I make a standard raise and I am reraised all in, I am definitely calling with A-A. You can't ask for a much better situation. If my opponent gets lucky and makes a set or some other winning hand, that's just the way it is. In the very likely scenario that I win the hand, my stack will become twice as large and my long-term advantage will be amplified.

I believe slowplaying A-A preflop is a mistake because it invites multiple callers behind you, which is exactly what you don't want to happen. When you're in a multiway pot, pocket aces lose a lot of value. A lot of people think that they can make more money by slowplaying A-A from an early position in the hope they will be raised and can reraise, but I disagree. I believe that the best way to make a lot of money with A-A is to raise and then have somebody reraise me. At that point, I can decide whether to slowplay my A-A by just calling my opponent's bet, or come back over the top for another raise.

If your opponent calls and sees the flop with you, you have to pay attention to the situation. If you bet on the flop and get called, bet the turn and get called, and bet again on the river and get raised, you can be sure that your aces are no good. Three bets of around two-thirds the size of the pot is really the most that you want to invest with aces in that situation, not four bets or more. Therefore, checking on one of the earlier rounds can sometimes be a very good idea to minimize your loses if you think an opponent may have hit the flop in a big way.

Of course, some flops are a lot scarier than others and you can't afford to play A-A slowly. But when you can, the following reasons are why it sometimes makes sense to check A-A on the flop or turn:

1. You can often minimize your losses, or achieve a reasonable gain by limiting the pot to two or three bets.

2. If your opponent hasn't flopped something like two pair or a set, checking your aces once after the flop is probably not giving your opponent as many outs as you may think. If he made a pair and has an ace kicker, he only has two outs against you. If he has an underpair he also only has two outs. If he paired one of his cards, and his other card is not an ace, he has five outs. The only time he really has more outs than that is when he has a flush or straight draw.

3. If your opponent did actually flop two pair or a set, once again, you are not giving anything up by slowing down because you are behind in the hand anyway. By slowing down, you are actually minimizing your potential losses somewhat.

4. You can also occasionally induce your opponent to bluff and give you an opportunity to win extra chips that you wouldn't have made by betting.

K-K

Let's say I raise to $600 from up front with pocket kings and another player reraises to $10,000 and puts me all in. I'm calling the all in bet with K-K, and here's why. If he has A-A, he was supposed to raise me to about $2,000, and I would then reraise again. We're probably going to get our money all in anyway.

He's made a mistake if he played aces by just going all in like that: What if I didn't have kings? If he played them correctly, and I had Q-Q, J-J, or 10-10, I might reraise him. Now he's going to get me off my hand, right? And what that means is that if he'd played his A-A correctly, he would have made more money if I had Q-Q, J-J, or 10-10 because I would have reraised him instead of folding.

Now think about all those other hands he may have, such as Q-Q, J-J, or A-K. If he played those hands correctly and just made a small raise instead of moving all in, I would come over the top and he may have been able to lay it down. Again, he could have saved a lot of money if he had played the hand correctly. No matter which hand he has, he is making a mistake by going all in, and I will take advantage of that error as best I can.

A-K

With A-K during the third level when I am first to act and there are no antes, I'll bet around two times the big blind. I'll make it a very small raise. If there are antes, I will make a raise of around three times the big blind. If I'm reraised—let's say I raise three times the big blind and somebody comes back over me with a bet of two times the pot—I might come back over the top if I don't have a huge stack. It depends on the size of my stack relative to the blinds; that's what it all comes down to. If I bet $300 and an opponent makes it $1,000, and I have $3,000 or $5,000, I am moving all in. If I have $10,000, I may just call.

Basically, I'm going to be out of position later in the hand, so my opponent will have the advantage of acting after me in all future rounds. If I go all in and we have all the money in the center, that player's positional advantage is worthless. I also think I've probably got the best hand because A-K is one of the best hands I'm going to raise with up front. I also may raise with A-Q, and from the third seat, I might raise with A-J. A-K is pretty strong relative to the hands that I might have in one of the first few seats. If I start folding that, I'm actually asking my opponents to just come over the top of me whenever I bet. You also know that even if your opponent has a high pair and decides to call you rather than laying down his hand, you still have a reasonable chance of winning by hitting an ace or a king.

Preflop Matchup

A-K unsuited against Q-Q preflop has approximately a 43 percent chance of winning if the hand is played to the river. However, there is a 68 percent chance of not seeing another ace or king on the flop. A-K against K-K still has nearly a 30 percent chance of winning by the river.—WD

If you just call his reraise with a short stack, you also put yourself in a tough spot when the flop doesn't come with an ace or a king. I'm thinking ahead about what I am going to do on the next betting round. When you have a larger stack, the decision to get away from the hand is a lot easier when you don't hit your cards on the flop—you're not leaving a large portion of your chips out in the middle.

If I move in preflop, I'm removing my tough decision and giving it to my opponent. If he has A-A or K-K, it's not as hard, but if he has a hand such as 10-10 or J-J, he really has to think. With a pair of sixes he doesn't have a hard decision: He's just going to throw his hand away.

I wouldn't just call preflop because my A-K may be the best hand or I may be able to get him to lay down his pair. If I get him to lay down his 6-6, he has laid down the best hand. Sometimes you can get him to lay down an A-K because he is assuming you would probably just call the reraise if you had A-

K or A-Q. Alternatively, if I have a huge stack, I might just call after his reraise and see if one of my cards comes on the flop.

I would be less likely to move in with a bigger stack because I'm only going to win his $1,000 plus my bet and the blinds. I don't want to risk $10,000 to win that because he might actually have A-A or K-K. If so, he will call. Now, why don't I make it $3,000? Again, he's going to move back over the top of me with aces or kings and I'm going to have to lay it down. That's not going to be something I want to do at that point. With a big stack I'm going to have a tough decision no matter how I play it, unless I flop an ace or a king.

A-Q
Let's say I have a small stack with $1,800 in chips left and get dealt A-Q. The average stack at the table is $3,500. The blinds are $100/$200 with ten players and an ante of $25, so there is $550 in the pot. If I'm second to act before the flop, I'm going to move all in. If I just make a raise of three times the blind I'm committed at that point because I'm putting in a third of my chips. Any time I put in a third of my chips, the rest of them are normally going in. You can think of it as trying to avoid a hard decision. If I make it $600 and someone moves all in over the top of me, I'm not going to like it. I may have a coin toss. Do I call? Do I fold? My preference in that situation would be to move all in rather than make a raise.

Any time you make an aggressive move, you are often saving a little bit of a headache later. For example, if I have 5♣ 4♣, maybe I'll make it $600. If I have A-A maybe I'll make it $600. There is a good reason for not moving all in with those two hands, because now if an opponent comes over the top of me I have an easy decision. I'll fold with the 5♣ 4♣, and I'll call with the A-A. Therefore, in those two situations I don't need to avoid a hard decision later by moving all in. Of course, I don't normally condone raising with a 5-4 suited in early position.

It's something you should do very rarely, because it's not a very good hand.

J-J

I try to avoid difficult decisions, but there are a lot of hands where you're just not going to be able to help it. With J-J in early position you're going to raise. If they raise you back, you have a hard decision; you have to play the player.

With J-J in early position, I might make a very small raise. In middle position, I might make a smallish raise and in late position make a medium raise, maybe two to three times the big blind. I'm certainly going to play the hand. If I raise in late position with J-J we're going to get a lot of money in the pot if I get reraised. If I'm making the raise from one of the first few seats, you're not going to get that much more from me because I'm so tight from early position.

If a solid player makes a substantial raise from up front, I would probably just call from late position. If I reraise, he's only going to call me with hands that are stronger than mine, and perhaps A-K as well. If an ace flops and he makes a sizable continuation bet, I'm in a lot more trouble than if a queen flops; I'll have to really look at the situation. If the overcard instead is a queen, and he bets, I'm either going to call or raise. With a raise, you'll find out where you are straight away. With a call, you're potentially inducing a future bluff. It's a very hard way to play, but there are players against whom you should play that way. If you're playing against a person who's just raising a lot and is going to keep betting no matter what he has, calling is not a bad move. You're telling the person, "Hey, I'm going to play in such a way that you're going to have stop doing what you're doing. You'll have to play a game that you're not used to."

But as I said, just calling the other player's raise is a very dangerous way to play the hand because he's probably going to have at least one overcard. Just because this guy is aggressive doesn't mean he won't have aces, kings or queens.

10-10

A pair of tens is a similar hand to jacks; you play them much the same way. If a reasonably tight player raises three times the big blind from an early position and everybody folds around to me in the big blind with a pair of tens—say we both have average stacks—I would probably just call. I really expect my opponent to bet on the flop so I'll just call, see the flop, and then decide if I am going to raise him or not.

Let's say the flop comes 5-5-9 rainbow; I'm not really worried about draws. I'm going to check and he's going to bet. It is a tough hand, because it can be played many ways. I don't think I'm going to fold here because he's kind of forced to bet, so his bet is not saying a lot. He's not necessarily saying that he has an exceptionally strong hand by betting. He's saying that I probably have a weak hand, that he's the one who raised from first position and had to face nine guys when he did it. He's kind of saying, "You didn't have to face nine players, you only had to face one and you didn't have to put as much money in as I did because you already had some money in the pot. You only had to put in two-thirds of what I had to put in." He may just be saying that he thinks he has a stronger hand and is making a typical continuation bet.

In this situation, I could either call or raise. If I call, I can choose to bet out on the turn. That's not a bad way to play because it is what most people would do if they flopped a set. However, I'm still not that proud of my tens because he can have A-A, K-K, Q-Q, or J-J. There may be a 25 to 35 percent chance that he has the overpair. I would still be a little bit worried about it. I don't like giving up free cards, so reraising sounds a little bit better to me than just calling.

Small and Medium Pairs

From early position I'm going to throw away my small pairs. If I have a medium pair such as 9-9, 8-8 or 7-7, I'm probably going to make a small raise, but if anyone reraises, I'm out of the hand unless it doesn't cost much more to see the flop. Then I'll call to try to flop a set. In middle or late position, I'll probably raise with any medium pair. If I am first to act, I'm always coming in for a raise. I'm never going to limp in unless there are callers ahead of me, and then I may call. If I have a huge stack, I might fold.

For example, if we're early in the World Series of Poker and the blinds are $25/$50 with a $10,000 chip stack and I've got 2-2 with a lot of players limping ahead of me, I would likely fold because I want to avoid a possible set-over-set situation. If the blinds are $100/$200 and I have $10,000, I'll limp in because I am trying to win around $1,000 by calling. If the blinds are just $25/$50 the risk-reward situation is not as favorable. I'm actually more worried about set over set if I have a relatively large amount of chips, because they can put a huge dent in my stack if I lose.

6-5 Suited through 9-8 Suited

I'm not a fan of suited connectors, so I'm normally going to toss them. However, in late position when everybody has folded to me, I'll raise with them. I will also occasionally raise with them from early position, but very rarely.

I just don't understand the love affair some players have with suited connectors. I don't play them that often. Suited connectors are not as much of an underdog as many people think, but I would rather have a pair of deuces.

With a small pair, mathematically I'm a favorite against A-K. With suited connectors I am an underdog. Against an overpair, 8-7 suited and 2-2 have similar probability of success, but when you do flop a set with your 2-2 it has a lot of value to it.

With suited connectors it's rare to flop a straight or a flush; if you catch something, it is normally going to be a draw. What do you do then? Well, you're going to play around, you might bluff, but you haven't made your hand yet. You'll more frequently flop a set with a pair than you'll flop a straight or flush with your suited connectors.

HAND MATCHUPS

Probability of success if played to the river. Odds are rounded to the nearest whole percent. Unless stated otherwise, assume all four cards are of different suits.

		Win	Lose
8-7s	versus A-K	42%	58%
2-2	versus A-K	53%	47%
8-7s	versus K-K	22%	78%
2-2	versus K-K	18%	82%

> ## FLOP PROBABILITIES
> **The probability of flopping a set when holding a pair**
> 11.7%
>
> **With 8-7 suited, the probability of flopping:**
>
> | | |
> |---|---|
> | Four to a straight | 26.2% |
> | Four to a flush | 10.9% |
> | Two pair* | 2.0% |
> | Straight | 1.3% |
> | Flush | .8% |
>
> *Using both your cards

GAME THEORY

Many people think that understanding the math in poker is limited to understanding probability and pot odds. Knowing the probability that one hand will beat another and understanding what odds the pot size is offering is a very small part of what mathematics can tell you about the game. The mathematical field of game theory actually tells you how to play hands. According to game theory you should bluff with a certain frequency with certain hands. It can also tell you a lot more than people would expect.

Game theory is a field of mathematics that deals with decision-making in a competitive environment. In the case of poker, you are playing against numerous opponents and have to make decisions based on the decisions you believe your opponents are going to make. When there are forces out there that are trying to prevent you from doing what you want to do, game theory can help you understand how you should react to those forces and how they should react to your actions. These forces are generally understood and are going to act in their own best interest.

Poker involves a lot of game theory, which is very hard to expand on in a short paragraph or two. I have researched the subject extensively, and what I can say is that there is a lot of relevance to poker, such as how often you should bluff, and how often you should call. Even if you have just lost ten hands in a row, it doesn't change the fact that a particular action is the correct move to make.

A Simple Example of Game Theory

If you create a game by assigning a number to each of a group of players instead of a poker hand (let's say a number from 0 to 1, such as .9743), with the person holding the largest number having the strongest hand, and then add betting, it starts to look a lot like a poker game. From the prospective of game theory, you can derive certain mathematical truths about the way you should play this particular game.

Coming to the same conclusions in a real game of poker is a little bit more difficult because there is a relationship between your cards and your opponent's hand. The relationship between the commonality of the cards in poker is hard for game theory to deal with. However, if we extract the influence of common cards, the two games—the hypothetical one and poker—would be somewhat similar in the way they should be played.

How Often to Bluff – The Principal of Indifference

The 'Principle of Indifference' in game theory as it relates to poker is very important. It basically says that you should play to make your opponent indifferent to his most likely play. I try to bet my best hands for value and my worst hands as a bluff. If my opponent has a great hand, he is going to call me. If he has a terrible hand, he is going to fold. But when he has a hand somewhere in the middle, I want to make him sweat. I don't want him to know if he should call me or not. I do that by playing in such a way that he will do equally as well if he calls or folds with all those average hands.

If there is $100 in a pot and I bet $10 into that pot and he calls me, he is only risking $10, but stands to win $110. He is only going to beat me if I'm bluffing and he is going to lose if I have a good hand. When I'm not bluffing he is going to lose $10 in this case. Therefore, if I were to bluff once for every eleven hands that I have, over the twelve hands he will break even if he calls me every time. If he folds every hand, he is also going to break even. Of course, he would also lose or gain any money that he already had invested in the pot. In this example, if I were to bluff with that frequency, he would then be indifferent; he wouldn't know whether or not to call me.

Why do I bluff at all? Because I don't want him to fold all of those average hands to my better hands! He is actually supposed to call me with a lot of average hands to make me indifferent to bluffing a lot.

In the case where I am betting $10 into a $100 pot, I'm bluffing infrequently. That is a situation you may face in a limit hold'em game. In no-limit, you are going to bet much more. This is the reason that no-limit is much more of a bluffing game, because you're able to bet $100 into a $100 pot. If he calls, he wins $200 with these middle range hands. He is risking $100 to win $200, which means that instead of bluffing one out of every twelve in the previous example, I should be bluffing one out of every three. In other words, for every two hands that I am betting, I should bluff one more if I want to make my opponent indifferent to calling me.

In theory, if you are betting $50 into a $100 pot, one out of every four bets should be a bluff. Another way of saying that is that for every three good hands you have, you could bluff with one bad hand.

If I never bluff, my opponents are going to figure that out and only call me when they have a hand that they think can beat me. Therefore, I am only losing money with my good hands because I only get called when I am beaten. If I bluff too often, I will get called too often, and end up losing more money with my bluffs than I make from my good hands.

Bluffing Opportunities in No-Limit Hold'em

Bluffing is a big part of the game in no-limit hold'em. I don't look for bluff situations; I think it's dangerous to go out and look for them. They have to find you and they have to be the right situations.

A typical bluffing opportunity that occurs is when I've represented a big hand, but don't actually have one. Often, on the river, I may be forced to bluff if I want to win the pot. An example would be if I have a straight draw and the flush draw gets there. If I bet again, my opponents may think, "Oh! Maybe he was showing strength but he actually had the flush draw!"

Why would I play a straight draw that way? Well, because I might hit it and really get paid off or I might be able to bluff on the river. It's also nice if a scare card comes when I've got nothing. That's often the time to bluff.

Here's another example. Let's say I'm heads-up against another player, he raises preflop, I reraise with the J♦ 10♦ as a bluff, and my opponent calls me. If he checks to me after the flop, normally I'm going to bet. If the flop is A-4-4 there will be no question that I'm going to bet, because I can represent I have the ace and get weaker hands to fold. My J♦ 10♦, is a horrible hand, but with a flop like A-4-2 or A-4-4, I can represent hands he has to lay his cards down against. I don't like coming over the top with a J-10 suited too often because it forces me to risk a lot more than my initial bet.

TELLS

I really don't like discussing the specific mannerisms that I look for in tells because I will be giving my opponents a key to deceiving me, though I would suggest people read the best book out there on the subject, *Mike Caro's Book of Poker Tells.* I think that is a fantastic place to start.

The normal tell that I discuss with people is the strong-means-weak tell that Caro talks about. Often, players will act strong when they're weak and will act weak when they're strong. In fact, this is something human beings do without even being aware of it. It is a subconscious action. We are preprogrammed to deceive in a subconscious way. When people have a big hand, they shrug their shoulders, toss their hands in the air, and their mannerisms often say, "I don't like this hand very much," yet they go ahead and raise!

When players are bluffing and want to appear strong, they do this subconsciously by placing more force behind the bet and slamming their chips on the table. They're thinking, "I want to get this guy to fold, I want him to think I have a big hand." They're not actually thinking, "Oh, I want to slam my chips on the table, I want to make a forceful bet," or "I want to stare this guy down." They do that subconsciously.

Tells can be very effective, but it is important to distinguish whether your opponents' actions are subconscious or deliberate. If somebody is doing these things consciously then it can have a very different meaning. Perhaps they even read about it and are intentionally giving off false tells.

PLAYING ONLINE

The Benefits of Learning to Play Online

I have been playing online since 1989. People don't know this, but online poker has been around since then. I was playing on a site called IRC poker, which stands for Interactive Remote Chat. IRC was a fantastic way to learn the game. It was basically a regular chat room, but there were programs that would interact with and deal cards for the players, take care of all the betting, and everybody's bankroll. These bots knew how much money everyone had and the information was kept on a database. I really credit IRC for teaching me how to play poker even though there was no money involved.

Money is not what motivates me to play poker anyway; it is pride, the ability to outplay and outthink my opponents! It isn't about the money for many people, it's about the challenge. When I play basketball, I am not lying back because there is no money involved. I am going all out, I enjoy the competition, that's what it's all about. IRC kept statistics, and eventually added tournaments with a tournament leader board. That really motivated me to play extremely well. There were some very good players there, just playing for fun, but they were definitely trying to win.

Some players are scornful of Internet players. They'll say things like, "Oh, he is just an Internet player," as though he is not a real poker player. "He only knows how to play on the net. He doesn't know how to play face-to-face like a real man knows how to play." But people are starting to learn that these Internet players are really, really good. Look who won the World Series in 2003 and 2004. Both champions qualified on the Internet. In fact, I think Chris Moneymaker had never played in a live tournament. He had only played on the Internet. I remember watching him when there were maybe four or five tables left, and he really came across as a professional player.

One of the reasons that Internet players have done so well at the World Series of Poker is that they have been able to play so many hands online and gain a lot of experience. When I was playing heads-up on IRC poker in the early '90s, I would play 300 hands an hour heads-up. In a cardroom, you may get a maximum of sixty hands per hour. Therefore, online, I can learn more than five times as quickly. In ten hours I could play 3,000 hands. It would take a player a week to play 3,000 hands in a casino.

Internet players become really good at playing what I consider pure poker. There are tells online, believe me, and they're actually pretty effective, but there are not as many as there are in live action. That's a real difference between live action and Internet poker because tells can become a crutch. People will rely on them to make their decisions. "Ah! I'm going to make my decision based on a tell instead of the cards." But you can't do that as much on the Internet. When you're looking at a computer, you have to make the majority of your decisions based on your cards and on the way your opponents are playing. That's incredibly powerful. People can give off false tells in live action, but betting patterns never lie. If your opponent raised before the flop, that is a truth, and it gives you a lot of reliable information about what he is holding.

Players in live action often overuse tells. If they just ignored them, they actually might become much better players. The Internet players learn how to play the game online. Then, when they go into the casino environment where you can add tells on top of that, it can be a powerful combination. It's actually the fact that they're adding the tells later that makes them much stronger players.

Bluffing Online
Players are more likely to bluff online, but again that's an adjustment you make to your opponent. It doesn't matter if

my opponents are bluffing in the cardroom at the Bellagio or online. If they're bluffing a lot, I am going to call them on it.

The Benefits of Multitable Play

For some players, being able to play multiple tables at once has several benefits. They can play hands a lot faster and can learn a lot faster as well. It's also great for players who just want action. When they go into a cardroom, they're playing way too many hands. That is one of the biggest mistake people make, especially beginners.

When you play online, if you want a lot of action, you don't have to sit at one table and play every single hand and play horribly. A person can sit at four tables, play 20 percent of the hands and be playing fantastic poker. Maybe he will be a little distracted, but at least he's not throwing money away playing every other hand. Playing multiple tables can actually make a player better. I have a very large screen at home and I can fit eight tables on it at once. They only overlap a little bit and I can see my seat on each one of them. On my laptop I'll only play two at a time.

Some people have a problem playing multiple tables because they tend to lose their sense of how the opponents are playing. That's true to a certain extent, but you'll pick up the obvious cases. You'll miss some information, so you are not always going to play as well. If you're not there for the action, then you'll play better at one table than at two. Will you make as much money playing multiple tables? Maybe you'll make more, maybe you'll make less. It depends on your skill level and style.

PSYCHOLOGY

Periods of Self Doubt

I don't really have periods of self doubt in poker. You have to look at your results over the long term, not the short term. My results are there over the long term, and I am fortunate because my style is based in mathematics. I can go back and see the way I've been playing and see that it is real.

Tilt

In handling frustration, and avoiding tilt, remember that in a poker tournament you have all the time in the world. If you have just taken a bad beat and lost a lot of chips, you have to refocus. You are now in a different situation than you were a few minutes ago. If you play the same game you did when you had a big stack, you're making a mistake. You have to count your chips, see who has a comparable stack, and who still has a smaller stack that you can push around. Just as important is realizing who can push you around, and whether you need to tighten up a bit because of your new stack size.

Sometimes it can also be frustrating when you're forced to lay down a number of big hands in a row because people keep coming back over the top of you. Once again, you have to be patient in those situations. Sometimes you have to lay down good hands over and over again, and you have to do it without going on tilt. You have to keep reminding yourself that just because the person who keeps reraising you is aggressive, it doesn't mean that he can't have a great hand!

When I do find certain players who consistently reraise me, I will look for situations where I can play back at them, but I am not going out of my way to do it. If the dealer doesn't give me any hands, there is nothing I can do about it. If I get a pair of deuces, I may play, but I'm not going to take a stand with a 10-3. Some players will, but I prefer to have some reasonable cards when I start to play back at the person. Eventually he is going to realize that I know he is just playing around with me and he will shift gears. Then he is likely to wait for some good cards before he does it the next time.

Above all, when things are going badly, take a few moments to understand your current situation and forget about the past. Frustration gets to all of us; fortunately I have played for enough years to know when it is starting to affect me, and I know how to deal with it.

MONEY MANAGEMENT

Money management all comes down to a daily basis. You can throw the weekly and yearly basis out the window. Just never bet more than you can afford to lose.

Let me tell you a story about money management. I always had this love for playing poker online, and even though a lot of people wouldn't understand it, originally I was never playing for any money. In the early 2000s, I decided to rekindle my love of playing poker. I put $1 into an online poker site with the idea that I wanted to turn that dollar into $20,000 without going broke. Unfortunately, I lost that first dollar, but I started again with a second dollar.

I started playing the smallest games I could find online, carefully nursing my stack. I would buy in for 10¢ into a 1¢/2¢ blind game. When I'd get up to 20¢, I'd cash out because I couldn't afford to risk my 20¢ and then would buy into another game for 10¢ again. My goal was to never buy in for more than 5 percent of my bankroll. If I ever had 10 percent of my bankroll at the table I'd leave, cash out and then buy into another game. I slowly moved my way up to higher levels. Even though I played the 1¢/2¢ limits for a long time, I eventually moved to the 5¢/10¢ buy-in games, then 25¢/50¢, $1/$2 and so on up to the $10/$25 level. It took me a long time to get from the $10/$25 game to the $25/$50 level, which was the biggest game they had. Under my bankroll requirements I needed $10,000 to be able to buy into the top game.

The really tough thing was that I took three or four shots at the larger game. I'd build my bankroll up to $10,000, then buy in and lose. Then I had to go back to the $10/$25 game. I'd play that, build up my stack by playing the smaller game until I'd get back up to a $10,000 bankroll again, bingo, buy into the $25/$50 and lose again. So four or five times I got my head smacked back down to the lower level.

When playing poker, you're going to go on winning streaks and you're going to go on losing streaks, but if I lost half my bankroll I would go back down to a lower level again. That's very hard to do, but that was the challenge I set for myself. I wasn't going to break my bankroll requirement rules. There is a lesson here: No matter how good you are, you are going to experience losing streaks and may have to drop back down to a lower level to build up your equity again.

Turning $1 into $20,000

Chris not only reached his goal of turning $1 into $20,000, but in 2006, he decided to start with nothing on FullTiltPoker.com and eventually earn $10,000. He reached that goal in 2007 by playing freeroll tournaments until he earned some cash. Then he employed his money management rules and skillful play to reach his goal. —WD

Bankroll

The tournament lifestyle is not cheap. During a typical year it costs me over $300,000 to play all the tournaments I enter. That's a lot of money, so when someone sees me on TV winning $120,000 they don't always understand the whole picture. That $300,000 is only my cost for playing the major tournaments like the $10,000 buy-in televised events. I also play everything at the WSOP.

Recommended Bankroll for Playing $1,000 Tournaments

If an extremely good player wanted to play $1,000 tournaments, he would need at least $100,000. If he's only a very good player, he would need $200,000.

Tournaments are very different than live action. You need a much larger bankroll to play tournaments than live action because you have huge variance. I've gone a year and a half without winning a tournament, and I've gone six months without any major cashes. That's just going to happen when you play tournaments exclusively for a living. Over that year and a half I probably broke even, but spent around $300,000 on buy-ins. There was a six-month period when I was probably down $100,000.

I've even been through periods where I played around 30 tournaments in a month and only made the money a couple of times. That's very hard on a player.

Pro Expectations: Making Money

If there are 500 entrants in a tournament, an average player will win one out of every 500 and make nine out of every 500 final tables. If they pay 45 spots then he'll make the money 45 out of every 500 times; it's pretty much 10 percent of the time that he will make the money. That's an average player.

A good player, who is one of the top fifty in the world, may double the average success rate. In the smaller fields, such as the $10,000 to $25,000 buy-in tournaments, it's not going to be a lot more than 50 percent better than the average because the players will be tougher. In the strong fields, it's tough to make a lot of money. At the main event at the World Series, a top player may do six or seven times better than an average player.

FINAL WORDS OF WIZDOM

For Players Who Want to Turn Pro

Turning pro is not something that you decide to do; it just happens. If poker is your passion and you play a lot, you should get better at the game the more you play. If over a long period of time you find you are making more money playing poker than you are at other things, then you've already become a pro. In other words, don't quit your job or school because you want to be a professional poker player. If you're good enough, it will happen naturally, not by design. The only reason to give up your day job would be if you were already a pro. I certainly wouldn't recommend that anybody quit school to become a pro no matter how good they are.

WD: I watched Chris play online at FullTiltPoker.com in a 50¢/$1 no-limit cash game. It was fascinating to hear him narrate the reasoning behind the aggressive plays that he was making and watching him play at a skill level that I had never even thought about before. His actions often bore little resemblance to the cards that he held. They were related more to what he thought his opponents were thinking that he had and what they were thinking he was thinking about them! Despite thousands of hours of online experience, my own game took a quantum leap after briefly seeing Chris constantly impose tough decisions upon his opponents. It represented a huge leap of understanding and profitability for my game.

After spending a couple of hours sitting with Chris, the time to complete our discussion came with a call from one of his fellow players who was in need. His focus on poker suddenly shifted to a genuinely compassionate air of friendship as he started to figure out a way to help. It was time to go.

Much to my surprise, when I met with Chris for our follow up, he spent an additional four hours with me going over the wording to make sure everything was absolutely correct in his chapter. His overwhelming passion for the game translates to excellence on a playing field overflowing with lesser talent. It comes as no surprise that Chris Ferguson has achieved such consistent success as one of the world's best tournament players. Even though the standard of play continues to improve, I am sure he will dominate the game well into the future.

DANIEL NEGREANU

"Kid Poker"

Career Tournament Earnings Exceeding $10,000,000

Best All-Around Player, Foxwoods World Poker Finals, 1997
Winner, Commerce Casino Heavenly Hold'em Main Event, 1997
Winner, World Series of Poker $2,000 Pot-Limit Hold'em, 1998
Winner, California State Championship Limit Hold'em, 1998
Winner, United Sates Poker Championship Main Event, 1999
Winner, WSOP $2,000 Limit S.H.O.E., 2003
Winner, WSOP $2,000 Limit Hold'em, 2004
Poker Player of the Year Award, *Card Player* Magazine, 2004
World Series of Poker Player of the Year, 2004
World Poker Tour Player of the Year, Season 3
Winner, WPT Borgata No-Limit Poker Open, 2004
Winner, WPT Five Diamond World Poker Classic II, 2004
Winner, WSOP No-Limit Circuit Event, Robinsonville, 2006
Second Place, WSOP Tournament of Champions, Las Vegas, 2006
Third Place, WPT Five Diamond World Poker Classic,
Las Vegas, 2006
Second Place, WPT World Poker Open, Tunica, 2007
Third Place, WSOP No-Limit Hold'em Shootout, Las Vegas, 2007

Author

Hold'em Wisdom for All Players
Daniel Negreanu's Power Hold'em Strategy

Sitting Down With Daniel

If you have ever wondered what the bright kid next door who quits school, goes out into the world and makes it big looks like, the next time you see poker on TV, focus on Daniel Negreanu. He has risen to the top of the poker world using a combination of guts, intelligence, perseverance and an enormous ability to understand the people around him. When you speak to Daniel it is immediately clear that he is a very motivated and extremely bright individual. However, by looking at him you would never know that he is one of the most successful poker players in the world. Perhaps my admiration for his achievements was so immense that I expected an aura of greatness to surround him when he first walked into the courtyard where we met. What I found most striking about Daniel was that, for all his achievements and ability, he is a very unassuming and seemingly ordinary person.

Daniel has a great deal of natural talent for the game that cannot be easily duplicated. However, he attributes a lot of his success and past failures to his state of mind. Absorbing the Negreanu story allows you to understand that believing in yourself is one of the most important ingredients for success in poker. I came away from my time with Daniel with the distinct belief that every poker player who is willing to strive for greatness, has the correct mental attitude toward the game, and is able to work hard and focus, will be able to duplicate *some* of his success.

The son of Romanian immigrants, Daniel was born on July 26, 1974 in Toronto, Canada. His parents emigrated only a few years before his birth in the hope that they could provide a better life for their family. They worked tirelessly to give Daniel and his brother the opportunity to grow up in a stable environment with a roof over their heads and access to a good education. According to Daniel, they always encouraged him to strive for success and pursue the things that he loved most in life, so it may not have come as a shock to them when their son announced only months before graduation that he was going to be playing cards instead of finishing high school.

For a couple of years, he followed his passion in Toronto and made enough money to survive, slowly building his bankroll and gradually developing the tools he needed to be a more consistent winner. By the time he was 21, with a proven track record of profits from back room card games, Daniel had made the decision to move to Las Vegas and try his hand at the big time.

When you take a close look at the history that lies behind most success stories, you inevitably find evidence of multiple failures overcome through determination and a will to succeed. Daniel's initial foray into the nonstop action of Vegas was no exception—a string of loses eventually forced him to return to his hometown to regain confidence and rebuild his bankroll. Within a year, still determined to succeed, he returned to Las Vegas a second time and started playing small- to mid-level cash games to make ends meet while working his way up to higher betting levels.

A few months after returning to Vegas, when only 22 years old, Daniel faced a major personal challenge with the passing of his father. The loss of his friend and role model only served to make him more resolute. Daniel was determined to prove himself. He traveled to the East Coast to compete in the Foxwoods World Poker Finals and achieved his first major recognition. He won back-to-back limit hold'em tournaments at Foxwoods and placed so consistently in the other tournaments that he was named best all-around player at the competition. That same year, 1998, he also won the Heavenly Hold'em event at the Commerce Casino in Los Angeles, and then continued his success in the World Series of Poker, becoming a bracelet holder at age 23 by winning the pot-limit hold'em event— at the time, the youngest person to ever win one of the coveted bracelets.

If you were lucky enough to get to know Daniel Negreanu, you would come to realize that he is an anomaly in the world of poker. His makeup is centered on wholesome values, a desire to improve, and a respect for the people around him. I did not expect this from one of the hot young guns of poker. Daniel went through a period of indulgence when he was younger, but his attitudes toward life and religion were unexpected.

Daniel is the author of *Daniel Negreanu's Power Hold'em Strategy*, a must-read for players who want to maximize their poker potential.

DANIEL NEGREANU

If you want to get a more in-depth understanding of the way this amazing person thinks, you can also do so by reading his blogs on fullcontactpoker.com and his informative articles in *Card Player* magazine. He is also currently an online pro at pokerstars.com.

Let's hear what Daniel has to say…

DANIEL
NEGREANU

THE MAKINGS OF A POKER WIZARD

In order to be just a good poker player, you must have people skills, some math knowledge and good intuitive ability. These are the same attributes that make you successful in most types of business endeavors. However, the best poker players are not simply intelligent people, they have a particular type of intelligence. You have to be pretty smart to be good at poker, but I don't mean doctor smart or lawyer smart—you have to be street smart.

Feel is also what separates the great players from the average ones. It's a good sense of when you can make a particular play. Let's say you're bluffing. You've got to find the right situation where people will believe what you are doing. You can't just throw a bluff out there. You have to do it in such a way that people say, "Okay, he must have this hand, because of this and this." But to know when that happens is all about feel, and the ebb and flow of the game. This intuitive sense is something that many players don't have, making them very static players who are easy to read.

A good player knows when he should or should not make a particular play. How? It's just by feel or instinct or gut; they all have the same meaning. It comes from the subconscious. For example, a guy will bet the river and I have a decision about whether or not I should call him. I don't know what he has, I'm not sure at all and I don't know what to do. In that case, I will go with my first instinct. My subconscious has seen this move one thousand times before and is telling me something. I don't know why, but a voice is saying, "Okay, something smells fishy about that bet. He's bluffing!" So if I can't figure out any better reason, I'm going to go with whatever my subconscious is telling me.

Important Qualities of a Successful Player

The one quality that I think is definitely the most important in being a successful player is having good people skills. By that, I mean the ability to tell what type of people you are dealing with. When I meet people, based on what they're wearing, based on the way they talk, the way they're sitting and the way they're standing, I have a feel for what kind of person they are. Once you know these types of things, it is much easier to understand how they'll think at the poker table because, really, a leopard doesn't change its spots. A conservative guy in business is going to be a conservative guy at the poker table. This is all a part of just reading people and understanding whether or not they're honest. I'll even ask a person what he does for a living. If he says he is a lawyer, I'm going to be thinking, "Watch out for that guy!" Good people skills are what separate the best players from the rest of the pack.

The second most important quality is an aggressive personality. In a sense you have to be "ballsy." Weak and timid just doesn't work in poker.

Third is discipline. All the other talents and qualities are great, but if you don't have the discipline to have faith in your system, you just lose it when things go bad. And if you don't have emotional control, all your other skills are useless.

The last quality is having a fundamental knowledge of the game, which is the easiest part. You can obtain that knowledge from reading books and understanding concepts, such as you're even money in a hand, or a two to one favorite—just simple things like that. That's the book stuff, which is easy; anyone can do that.

My Start in Poker

By the time I was *officially* a "professional poker player"—a term I find very strange—I had already been one for several years. I just never made the decision to say, "Okay, I am a pro." I was probably 22 or 23 years old when I woke up one morning and said, "I guess this is what I do for a living," but I had never really been conscious about it before that. I would say that I started playing poker on a regular basis at about 18 years old. That's all I did for money, so I guess that made me a pro.

TOURNAMENT STRATEGY

Basically my motto is, "Don't do anything stupid." The one key adjustment that has had the most substantial impact on my game, especially in tournaments, is that I wait for my opponents to make a mistake. That seems like a simple thing to do, but there's more to it. I wait for them to crack. I'm not going to be the guy you see saying, "I made a bad read, oops!" or "I just took a bad beat." You messed up, that's what you did! You didn't wait the other guy out. I'm confident enough now that if I play somebody heads-up or whatever the scenario, I can wait him out until he has to gamble and make a mistake.

Be Unpredictable

The way I push my opponents to make mistakes is by staying unpredictable. To use a boxing analogy, what I'm doing is throwing lots of jabs, but I'm also keeping my guard up the whole time. Then, when the guy throws his wild punch, his chin is available and I just give him an uppercut and knock him out. Basically, opponents get frustrated by this jab that keeps coming at them nonstop, and eventually they want to counter with some wild rabbit punching. That's when they open themselves up and get destroyed.

Reading People and Situations After the Flop

One of my basic strengths is reading people well after the flop. By the turn card, I generally have a good idea of what is going on, based on what I know of my opponents, what they're capable of, and what they're likely to have in a certain spot. Then I'll know when to continue and when to bluff. I'll also know when to back off and not make big mistakes. I don't mind making some little itty bitty errors, but it is important not to make the big mistakes that cause a lot of the other players to blow up. For example, they have this big stack and all of a sudden go all in on some stupid hand and end up saying, "Why did I just do that?" I don't think that you've ever seen me in a situation where I've had a big blow up and just given my money away.

Playing Cards versus Playing People

If you're starting out as a beginner you're going to play your cards, but if you're a pro, you play the people first—the cards are completely secondary. You're just playing situations and people. Obviously, you also need to depend on the cards and must understand the fundamentals of the game and be able to read the situation properly. To some degree, there are stretches in a tournament where you're just going to go on autopilot and play your cards. Later, you'll use knowledge of your opponents to play your cards better. So in a sense, they do go hand in hand. One can't live without the other.

Ego

Every great poker player has a tremendous amount of self-confidence in his own ability. However, if he lets it go too far, he can be blinded by his own ego and make critical errors. You have to be able to look outside yourself and recognize when you are not playing better than your opponents.

Some players keep losing over and over again and continue to think they are unlucky. Their ego blinds them to certain situations. That's dangerous for a poker player; people with big egos often attribute their losing to bad luck or blame the dealers, silly things like that.

COMMON TOURNAMENT ERRORS

The Turn

You often see people make huge mistakes on the turn because it's simply the most difficult street in hold'em to play. The turn is really what separates the men from the boys because it's the most critical point of a hand. It is where you decide whether you're going to move forward or not. The biggest mistake that I see from a lot of players is that they become too meek and passive on the turn. They become paranoid. Say they bet the flop and somebody calls and now the turn card is a queen. If they have two jacks and the person ahead of them checks, they often just check also and give away a free card when they should be betting.

Bad Bluffs

To set up a bluff, it's important to do so before the flop, on the flop and on the turn. Too often I see people playing a hand in a weird way: All of a sudden on the river, after an unrelated card such as a deuce comes off the deck, they make a big bet that makes no sense. You're expected to believe that it suddenly helped them!

Any time you make a bet that makes people think, "What in the world is that?" it's usually not a good thing. People are trained to call more often than not whenever they see something suspicious. If it's a strange bet, you're far more likely to get called.

AGGRESSION

An Aggressive Style
My approach to the game, which I think is the optimal one, is an aggressive style similar to that of Phil Ivey and Gus Hansen, but still a little different. I think Gus is a bit overly aggressive and Phil takes bigger risks on the turn or the river than I think are necessary.

Another top player with an aggressive style is John Juanda. He is absolutely a master at understanding when people are getting frisky. He knows when they want to raise. I've watched him do this and it really amazes me. For example, there was recently a player at our table that didn't play a hand for three rounds. All of a sudden, the player raised from first position. Juanda chose him to move all in against. I said to myself, "What in the world are you doing? That seems to be doing things backwards."

I asked John after the hand why he would raise a guy who was playing so tight? Juanda said, "Well, I knew he was getting desperate and was going to use his image to make a raise."

Juanda was right. The guy folded his hand. John had sensed his weakness before the flop. He can look at a person and say, "Okay, if I move all in, and he doesn't have A-A or K-K, then he won't call." That's his biggest strength. Every time I do it, they seem to have aces!

When to Be Aggressive

When you should be aggressive is totally dependent on the type of players you're up against. You have to be willing to adapt to each situation. You might be at a table where strategy A works, but then you get moved to another table where it would be the worst possible strategy. There is an ebb and flow in poker that is similar to football. If the defense is playing the run, you pass. If the defense is playing the pass, you run. If the table is playing too conservatively, you want to play aggressive poker. However, if they're all really aggressive, then you need to sit back and set traps for them. You have to be a chameleon and adapt to the situation rather than just saying, "Okay, I'm going to be aggressive."

What I usually do is map out my table and look for trouble spots and easy spots. Some players are very conservative. That's a good opportunity to start raising because they're less likely to defend their blinds. Conversely, if they're aggressive players, you'd want to avoid raising their blinds. The key targets you want to have when you're being aggressive are predictable players.

Suppose a conservative player raises from an early position and you call. If the flop then comes with three random cards and he checks, you often have a good opportunity to take the pot from him or to find out what he's doing. You know he's conservative, so he's either trapping you or he has an A-K and he won't call you. Right there, on the flop, you can find out what he has very quickly. More often than not, he won't have A-A or K-K. If he does, you'll know soon enough.

How to Defend Against Aggressive Players

The great thing about the style that players like Gus, Phil Ivey and I play is that there is no secret formula to beating it. A few years ago when playing in a tournament against Gus Hansen, Howard Lederer thought he could come up with a strategy that would defeat his aggressive style. Gus destroyed him. Howard tried to make an aggressive preflop strategy work. Gus was raising small and Howard would make big overbets. Well, that didn't work out too well because on the occasions that Gus picked up a good hand, Howard was risking his whole tournament on those plays.

The only thing you can do against players like Gus is play flops with them and outwit them after the flop by using position. If you have position on a really aggressive player you need to call him before the flop with a lot more hands than you normally would, maybe call him on the flop and stay with him till the river. If you saw me, Gus and Ivey at the same table, you'd end up seeing one person raising, the other two calling, and everybody just pussy-footing around on the flop, taking a little jab or a little step. Nobody is putting in big chips. The bottom line is that, if we continue for an hour playing every hand, the rest of the players at the table are just anteing off. We're all going to increase our stacks while the others die a slow death. You have to step up to the bully! However, I wouldn't say that a big preflop move going all in is very effective because the price you pay is simply too big.

An Evolving Strategy in Today's Environment

If you look at a lot of the old-school players who did really well in the 80s and 90s, you'll notice that they don't win quite as often today because the game has changed. It's evolved. You can now get seven years of experience in one year playing online. The Internet players have become good very quickly and have revolutionized the way the game is played. Today, you get these kids who reraise, make moves, and use lots of plays. You have to completely adapt to that type of play.

Taking Advantage of Bad Players Early

The key thing you need to think about on day one of a big tournament is this simple fact: If there are 400 people, the majority of the bad players are going to go out on that day and somebody is going to get those chips. I want them! Because of that, I am willing to take a few chances.

I'll give you an example of a hand that clearly explains my strategy and what I was thinking in a recent tournament. We had $10,000 each. It was the very first level and the blinds were $25/$50. This really new player, who I knew wasn't very good, made it $150, and one of the other players called. I was in the small blind with the Q♥ 4♥. This isn't a hand you'd normally call with because it doesn't have much potential, but knowing how weak this guy was, I thought, "Why not call for a buck and a quarter?" So I called $125 more.

The flop came 7-4-4 with two spades.

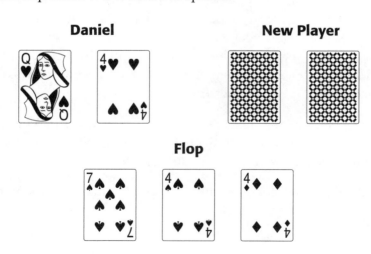

Daniel

New Player

Flop

I checked and was hoping somebody would bet. The first player bet $200, which was a good sign. I was thinking that perhaps he could possibly have Q-Q or K-K. The next player called and I raised it $300 more to $500. The first raiser then went all in for the whole $10,000! The next player folded and I was thinking to myself, "If this was a great player, I would fold my Q-4 because he's going to have A-4 or 7-7 here, but it's this rookie who doesn't know any better." If he did have a hand like A-4, why would he go all in? It just made no sense for him to overbet the pot so much. It clearly seemed to me that he had a hand like two scared queens. To me, his all-in bet was a sign that he just didn't want me to outplay him.

I said, "Do you play on the Internet?"

He responded, "Yes, I do."

I called instantly when he said that. He then turned over 9-9.

A lot of online players play preflop poker and are not really good at playing after the flop. Only a player who's been around for a while can really understand post-flop play. A lot of the tournaments that people play online have such big blind ratios that everybody just goes all in. Knowing that he was not a very seasoned player helped me to understand why he risked his whole $10,000 to win a very small pot. His background was an important part of the puzzle.

Most players would not have had the opportunity to win that money because they wouldn't have played the Q-4 of hearts in the first place. There was very little risk for me!

As it turned out, I got all my money in, he hit a 9 on the river, and I went out!

SPECIFIC HAND STRATEGY

> Unless stated otherwise, all of the situations discussed by the Wizards in the Specific Hand Strategy section are assumed to be at a full table, during the third level of a tournament. The blinds are $100/$200, and you have an average stack of around $11,000 in chips. It is also assumed that the players are displaying a moderate level of aggression and appear to be playing reasonably well.

A-A, K-K

Let's say that it's early in a tournament and I have just been moved to a new table of unknown players with average stacks. I get dealt a big premium pair, aces or kings, under the gun. If I am first to act, I'm generally raising about two-and-a-half to three times the blind. If the blinds are $25/$50, I'm going to make it $150. If the blinds are $50/$100, I usually make it $250. I will keep it consistent. I am doing that with 8♣ 7♣, I'm doing that with 9♦ 5♦, and I'm doing it with aces. If I did anything differently with the A-A, people might catch wind of it.

However, I will sometimes limp with the aces if I feel like the table is right for it. I limp a very small percentage of time to mix up my play, but normally I'll make a standard raise.

Q-Q

Here's another situation early in a tournament, but this time I have queens. I make a standard raise, then a loose-aggressive player reraises me all in. How I play here depends on a couple of things, primarily whether or not the decision would actually break me.

If I have $10,000 in chips and he has $6,000, it's a no-brainer to call; but if I have the $6,000 and he has the $10,000, it makes calling a little more difficult. In order to win these big-field tournaments today, you have to be willing to take some risks. If you know you have the best hand you should be calling. Phil Hellmuth is a perfect example of a guy who, at the time this section was being written, isn't doing that. He's taking it to an extreme, saying "I know I have you beat; I know I have the best hand, but I'll keep folding."

All these young kids, these great Internet players know this, so they keep raising him before the flop because he has already said that he's going to keep folding. You don't want that kind of an image! You can't let people know that you are willing to fold in that situation; they will take advantage of it.

It's powerful to have an image like Gus Hansen's. Gus will raise with K-K or Q-Q. You can move all in and he'll still call you. How do you defend against that? It's tough. So people end up playing into his hands or saying, "I don't even want to get involved with him, I think I'll just get out of his way."

Early Tournament All Ins: Take a Risk?

Over the long run many skilled tournament players will have a big advantage in a tournament because of their superior ability. Some professionals will often shy away from an all-in confrontation earlier in the event unless they're a clear favorite. The theory is that by calling in a coin flip situation such as Q-Q versus A-K, they're giving up a big skill advantage that can be used later. —WD

A- K

When you watch poker on TV, you'll often hear the commentators refer to A-K as a monster hand. It is often grouped with hands like A-A, K-K, and Q-Q. This is a mistake. Sure it's nice to look down at your hole cards and find an A-K, but more often than not, if you end up playing a big pot with this hand, you are statistically behind. The most likely situation is what would be called a coin-flip situation, where the outcome is close to 50-50. For example, rounded to the nearest whole number, 2♦ 2♠ is a 53 to 47 percent favorite over A♥ K♣.

Even a lowly pair of deuces is a favorite over the powerful Big Slick. Big Slick is even worse off against some of the premium starting hands it will often be up against. Here is how A-K does against the top five pairs:

Hand Matchups

Probability of success if played to the river. Percentages are rounded to the nearest whole percent. Assume that all four cards are of different suits. In some cases, the total percentage may not equal 100 percent because of a possible tie.

	Win	Lose
10-10 versus A-K	57%	43%
J-J versus A-K	57 %	43%
Q-Q versus A-K	57%	43%
K-K versus A-K	70%	30%
A-A versus A-K	92%	7%

So, as you can see, when Big Slick is up against these premium pairs it is hardly a coin flip, especially against the two top hands (A-A and K-K).

Of course, your opponent won't always have a pair and when he doesn't, the A-K does start looking like a monster, especially if your opponent has an ace or a king in his hand. If your opponent held K-Q or A-Q, for example, you would have him dominated, meaning that he would only have one live card available to outdraw you. In that case, your Big Slick would be a substantial favorite as you can see by the following chart:

Hand Matchups

Probability of success if played to the river. Percentages are rounded to the nearest whole percent. Assume that all four cards are of different suits.

	Win	Lose
A-K versus A-Q	74%	26%
A-K versus K-Q	74%	26%

Being up against A-Q or K-Q is the ideal situation with a hand like Big Slick if you happen to find yourself in a big pot. There is one other group of hands that your Big Slick might match up against that would be interesting to look at—two live cards that are suited:

Hand Matchups

Probability of success if played to the river. Percentages are approximate, based on 2.5 million deals and rounded to the nearest whole percent.

	Win	Lose
A♥ K♣ versus 8♦ 7♦	58%	42%

That should give you a little statistical background on this enigma of a hand. In some cases it is quite strong, while in others it's vulnerable. So, knowing this, the key to playing A-K before the flop is to avoid getting involved in big pots when your entire stack is on the line. Too often, when your opponent is willing to put all of his money up against you, he'll have the dreaded A-A or K-K, which would make you a substantial underdog to win the hand.

If you find yourself in a no-limit hold'em tournament looking down at Big Slick, you want to be aggressive with it and attack the blinds. However, if you receive any resistance from your opponents you should seriously consider folding the hand and waiting for a better situation.

A few things to think about:

1. **How many chips do you have?**
   If you are short-stacked and need to win a big pot to get back in the game, you should probably be very aggressive with Big Slick and go all in! However, if you have a good stack of chips and another player at the table raises you big time, then you likely don't need to get involved in that marginal situation.

2. **How do your opponents play?**
   This is a very important consideration when deciding whether to play Big Slick. If you're reraised by the Rock of Gibraltar, a player who is extremely conservative, you can be pretty sure that he has a pair, one that just might be A-A or K-K. On the flip side of that, if your opponent is wild and reckless, your Big Slick might be in great shape against a hand like A-J or K-10.

The important thing to understand about Big Slick is that it's a drawing hand. Now if it's suited, it is the most powerful drawing hand you can be dealt in Texas hold'em. It is usually only good if you pair your ace or king or get lucky enough to make a straight or a flush.

J-J and 10-10
Middle pairs are especially tricky hands for people who don't play well after the flop because they're so flop-dependent. While jacks and tens are good hands, you can get so many bad flops. If the flop comes with an overcard, you're in no man's land. If you're not good at reading hands after the flop, your best approach with jacks or tens is to make big bets before the flop and get people out. You want to play these pairs preflop. I can call a guy when I have two tens, or just limp with J-J and see a flop. That's okay for me to do because I can determine whether or not the jacks are good after the flop. For beginners and average players, that strategy can be suicide.

Suited Connectors
I'll often play suited connectors, but I won't normally raise a lot with them. For example, if the blinds are $25/$50, I'll come in with a 6-8 suited for $150. At other times, I'll limp in for $50. But when there are enough chips in play and the implied odds and stacks are deep enough on day one, it's well worth playing those sorts of hands, especially when you're only risking something like 1.5 percent of your stack.

On day three, later in the tournament, calling a standard raise with those hands could represent something like 25 percent of your stack. You can no longer play J♥ 9♥ or 6♣ 8♣ and hands like that. You have to make the conscious decision to mix up your play a little bit and move away from post-flop poker to a greater emphasis on preflop strategy.

Let's say that I raise preflop with 9-7 suited, get a caller, and the flop comes with a 9 and two random unsuited low cards. How I play is based on what I know about my opponent.

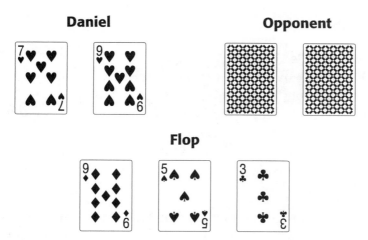

Daniel   Opponent

Flop

Let's say I raise in first position and I know the player on my left reads books. So the book guy calls my under-the-gun raise. Well, right now I know he has either a pocket pair or a good ace. It's as clear as day. That particular type of player won't call with Q-10. He won't call with 8♣ 7♣ either, so it's pretty easy to read his hand. Against that player, if the flop comes 9-3-2 or something like that, I'm obviously going to bet.

Even if the flop has an ace without the 9, I can bet it because if he has two nines or two tens, he's going to be afraid of the ace and I'll be able to steal it. If he calls, okay, I abort the mission, because obviously I know he has an ace.

Now let's assume that there is $400 in the pot, and I'm going to make a continuation bet representing the ace. I'm going to bet $225 to $250, about half the size of the pot, or just less than half. That's one of the things that I'm a big proponent of. I call it "small ball," but it means small-bet poker. It's much more controlled and less chaotic than making big, extravagant bets. I can learn as much information for $225 as I can for $275, so why bet $275? Why bet $300? Why bet $400? I would prefer to save money in case I'm beat.

TELLS

Physical Tells

When people have a really strong hand, they'll often look at the flop and if they really like it, the first thing they'll do is glance down of their chips. That is subconscious and hard to avoid. It is a well-known tell, yet people still do it. It's not something that a person can really control that well. Maybe you can for a while, but if you play for twelve or fourteen hours, it is easy to get lazy and sloppy.

Arm extension is another tell that Mike Caro wrote about in his book, *Caro's Book of Poker Tells*. When people are bluffing they're often much more forceful, so that arm will extend all the way and they'll splash their chips into the pot. At other times they might slide the chips into the pot.

What you need to do when you're looking for tells is to look for anything unique, because everybody is different. Some will be actors, and some will try to misguide you. It's your job to figure out what type of person your opponent is. Any time you see something out of the ordinary just put it in your memory bank and try to remember what it meant.

The Poker Face

I once wrote a column about the misconceptions players have about tells that I titled, "Truth about Tells." People often say that they can't play poker because they don't have a good poker face. If a poker face is necessary, I'm in trouble! I'm always making strange facial expressions. Phil Hellmuth will try to tell you that he can see through your soul. He can't see through anything. It's this big myth that pro players want to tell people to scare them. If I told you that I could tell what you were thinking by the way your ears wiggled, would you believe me?

If somebody is sitting there and looking straight at the cards, what are you getting off that? I mean, really, you can't see through that person's soul. When you get people to talk and open them up a little, they'll give you more.

Betting Patterns

I mostly look for personality tells. These will help dictate betting patterns, which are far more important than physical tells. For example, if I know that somebody is an honest person in general, I know that his betting patterns will be honest as well. If I know that a player is a really tricky, shady kind of character, I expect that his betting patterns will be the same. It's more about personality than how someone plays A-J in early position.

PLAYING ONLINE

Because of my association with PokerStars.com I spend quite a bit of time playing online. I also understand that there is a new wave in poker and online players are really learning a lot in a short period of time. Rather than take the old-school approach and assume that these kids didn't know anything, I decided I wanted to learn how they thought. By playing online I get a feel for the differences in the way online players approach the game, which has especially helped me in tournaments. Players who don't do this will be surpassed.

Online Play versus Live Games

Many players tend to be a lot more confident online than when they're in a live game. As far as the style and approach are concerned, people call more often online because they have less information than in a live game, which sometimes makes it harder to bluff. You can spot betting patterns and things like that, but when push comes to shove and you make your bet on the river, you'll get more calls on those bets. You don't know what you're up against if you're dealing with some crazy guy unless you've really studied that opponent. Another key difference is that online poker teaches you to value-bet more often rather than bluff. Because online players tend to call, big bets are simply less effective.

PSYCHOLOGY

State of Mind

Your mental state of mind is absolutely the most important factor in being a successful player. It's amazing how much of an effect your state of mind has on your play. You don't realize it when it's happening, but your outlook on your game is affected by what is going on in your life. You might think you're playing well, but really, you're not using your whole brain because part of it is busy worrying or reminiscing about other things in your life. That lack of focus can affect anyone so it is very important to make sure you have a positive state of mind when you play. When things are going smoothly and your health is good, it won't be a coincidence that you'll just "happen" to do well at poker.

Dealing With Dry Spells

Although I have never had many issues going through losing periods, I know others who have. You really have to look at bad runs from outside yourself. You have to be realistic and understand that losing is going to happen. Also understand that in tournaments, the luck variance is very high. You figure that you want to make the money at least 20 percent of the time. A modest goal would be 15 to 20 percent. Losing eight straight tournaments is statistically probable. Rather than thinking how unlucky you are, just realize that it is going to happen again and again, sometimes for even longer periods of time. If you come to the game with that approach, it's less scary.

DANIEL NEGREANU

Going Through Difficult Times

In 1999, I had a great year, but as a result of my successes, the following year turned into a disaster. I had made money and didn't know what to do with it, so I would play golf, go out with the boys, and have some drinks. That is what I did for a year. We would go to dinner and have a couple of bottles of wine, a Bailey's coffee and some Coronas, then go to a poker room. A bit drunk, I often would blow $20,000 or $30,000, and not really care because "it was only money." I did that for a year and then ran out of cash. Afterwards, I was very disappointed, knowing that I had worked so hard in poker to get to a certain point, just to lose it all because I was being lazy.

When things are going badly, you're broke, but more importantly, your spirits are broken. You grind all the way up to a certain point and then after you fall, you know that you have to go all the way back up again. Each time it gets harder and harder. I have friends around forty-five years old, who built up a million-dollar bankroll, went broke and then did it all over again. How many years can you do that for? Nevertheless, I would not trade what I went through in 2000 for the world because I learned so much from it.

Mental Stability and Poker

I had too much anger in me when I was younger. Negative feelings like that are distractions. I was judgmental, boastful, had too much pride, just about all the bad character traits that you can have. I struggled with those just like anybody else, and sometimes they would consume me. In the poker world there are a lot of politics and I got caught up in that a little bit.

However, several years back, as a result of my ex-wife Lori's influence, I came to a realization that helped me become a better person. In the movie *As Good As It Gets*, Jack Nicholson's character says to the woman he loves, "You make me want to be a better man." I think that is exactly how I felt when

I met Lori. I believed that she didn't deserve a bum like the person I was in the year 2000, or a guy who couldn't get his act together. I wanted to be the "somebody" she deserved. When you are happy it is easier to focus on what is important. As it turned out, improved poker results also came with my desire to be a better person.

Proudest Poker Achievement

The one poker achievement that I am most proud of in my career is winning the Player of the Year award in 2004 because it encapsulated so many great moments over the whole year. The World Series was a great run and winning the Bellagio event at the end of the year was also wonderful. There were many great points I could look at and say, "This was the pinnacle," but combining the whole year in that award was just the greatest moment of all for me.

Prior to 2004 I was always among the top players in the Player of the Year rankings, around seventh or eighth. In 2000 and 2001, I was just going through the motions. I wasn't putting in my best effort. But in 2004, I decided that if I was going to play, I was going to play well; I wasn't going to fool around any more. I focused more energy on really trying to do my best and my results showed it. That kind of realization just comes with age and maturity, I guess.

Although I did make some strategy adjustments, it was more taking care of myself than anything else. Previously, I'd often play tournaments on no sleep after being out with the guys till four or five in the morning. Now, I make sure that I mentally prepare for a tournament a day or two in advance and am well rested.

MONEY MANAGEMENT

Bankroll Requirements

If you're a losing player who isn't good enough to compete at the level you're playing at, it doesn't matter how big your bankroll is, you'll eventually lose it all. To a large extent, a person's bankroll requirements depend on how willing he is to go broke. I'm not big on exact numbers, but realistically, if you are a winning player participating in $1,000 buy-in events, $50,000 should be enough. If you had $30,000 or $40,000 and you lost half of it, you'd probably want to save the other half. If you go through $50,000 straight playing $1,000 events, that's either really a bad run, or you're not quite as good as you thought you were.

Daily, Weekly and Monthly

Money management is one of the major struggles for most poker players because the lifestyle doesn't lend itself towards stability. If you work a regular job Monday to Friday, you know how much you are going to make each month and can budget appropriately. Tournament players are often broke for a couple of weeks, suddenly win $40,000, and go out and spend it. Then they play six more tournaments and they're broke again! Many of them really don't have any sense of stability.

A few years ago, before so many million-dollar events were available, you could look at the top-20 list and see that perhaps five of the players were not broke or being staked by other players. The guys playing in the cash games had a more stable life and a stable income. They all had money.

I would advise anybody who is serious about becoming a professional poker player to do it the good old-fashioned way, through the side games. Cash games can provide a much more steady diet of money. If you're going to try to play tournament poker for a living, you're going to face many money management obstacles because it takes so long to get there.

Pro Expectations: Making the Money

In 2004, I had an exceptional year. I played about forty events and made eleven final tables, which is a high number. More realistically, my personal expectation is to make about one final table out of every eight or nine tournaments that I play because the fields are so big now. On average, a good player should expect to make the money around 25 percent of the time. However, in the huge WSOP events, where a thousand or more players compete, it is often difficult for players to even make the money.

FINAL WORDS OF WIZDOM

If you want to get serious about poker, take it slowly. People often try to rush themselves and get to the next level too quickly. Go at your own pace and don't be jealous of other people who are getting there more quickly than you are. Luck is involved and that often determines how quickly or slowly you'll achieve your results. Poker is not going anywhere. Get your feet wet playing online, and practice a lot. And always remember one thing: If you find yourself thinking inside the box, you are trapped. Always be willing to create new ideas and fool around with things. Experiment. You never know what you can learn.

DANIEL NEGREANU

WD: Daniel Negreanu is such a charismatic, intelligent person that I could have happily spent days listening to his theories on life and poker. I have studied his books and read his online blog on a regular basis to keep up with this poker great. If you found this chapter interesting, I recommend you do the same. Negreanu has a wealth of insights to offer those who are willing to study.

If you want more Daniel Negreanu, play with him on PokerStars.com, and get his books: *Hold'em Wisdom for All Players* and *Daniel Negreanu's Power Hold'em Strategy*. Both books are great reads for anybody who is serious about improving the way he plays.

DAN HARRINGTON

"Action Dan"

Career Tournament Earnings Exceeding $6,500,000

Sixth place, WSOP Championship Event, 1987
Winner, WSOP Championship Event, 1995
Winner, WSOP $2,500 No-Limit Hold'em, 1995
Winner, Four Queens Poker Classic, $5,000 No-Limit Hold'em, 1995
Winner, Festival of Poker £1,500 No-Limit Hold'em,
London, 1995
Third place, WSOP Championship Event, 2003
Fourth place, WSOP Championship Event, 2004
Second place, WPT Doyle Brunson North American Poker
Championship, 2005
Winner, WPT Legends of Poker Championship Event,
Las Vegas 2007

Author

Harrington on Hold'em Volume 1: Strategic Play
Harrington on Hold'em Volume 11: The Endgame
Harrington on Hold'em Volume 111: The Workbook

Sitting Down With Dan

If it were not for his trademark green Boston Red Sox cap and the perpetual crowd of autograph hunters that surround him, a casual observer would be unlikely to pick Dan Harrington out of the crowd at a poker tournament. Understated, quiet and casual are terms which aptly describe his general demeanor, but as soon as he speaks it is apparent that this WSOP bracelet holder, author and successful businessman is anything but average.

An extremely gifted and bright individual, Dan Harrington was born in Cambridge, Massachusetts in 1945. He earned an undergraduate degree from Boston's Suffolk University and then attended Suffolk Law School. While a student at Suffolk he found time to learn the game of poker and, coincidentally, played with the likes of Bill Gates, who was attending Harvard at the time. He was also reportedly part of a team that used MIT mathematical formulas to calculate roulette odds and beat the casinos until seriously discouraged from doing so by the Sands Casino in New Jersey.

After graduating, he worked as a bankruptcy lawyer for nearly a decade in Boston before leaving the field to explore other business opportunities that might offer more personal satisfaction. Even when he was working as a lawyer, his love of competitive intellectual games continued. He was the Massachusetts State Chess Champion in 1971 and also gained a reputation as a world class backgammon player. Although clearly possessing the ability to do so, Dan decided not to play backgammon professionally when the organizers of a tournament failed to pay the $27,000 he earned for his first-place finish.

In 1980 he moved to Philadelphia and regularly caught the train to New York to play poker at the Mayfair Club with Howard Lederer, Erik Seidel and Steve Zolotow. And in the early 80s, he started traveling to Las Vegas a couple of times a year to play poker.

His first recorded tournament poker payout was in 1986, and in 1987 he entered his first WSOP championship event, finishing an impressive sixth when his A-Q lost to the A-6 of his opponent. Though disappointed, Harrington received $43,750 for his finish and took home his first—but not his last—major poker prize from the WSOP. That win marked the beginning of a part-time poker career that has earned payouts totaling more than $6,500,000.

Poker, chess and backgammon are not the only areas in which Dan Harrington excels; he also considers the real estate market and stock market as "just other games" which offer winning opportunities. His passion for investing eventually led to a role as founding partner of Anchor Loans, a successful business that offers non-traditional real estate lending opportunities and expertise to developers and investors. As a result, over the years, he has dedicated a lot of time to those interests rather than playing poker full time.

In 1995 Dan won the WSOP Main Event, collecting a cool $1 million. He also earned another bracelet in the WSOP $2,500 No-Limit Hold'em event the same year. Because of his focus on business pursuits other than poker, Dan skipped a number of years at the WSOP, but has still managed to make the Main Event final table an impressive four times. In 2003, on the third of those occasions, there were 838 players in the field. Then, miraculously, in 2004 he did it again against a field of 2,575.

Let's hear what Dan has to say...

THE MAKINGS OF A POKER WIZARD

Understanding the Role of Luck in Poker

Often the best measure of how lucky you have been is how much bad luck you have managed to avoid. That's the true definition of having good luck—avoiding the bad luck. You actually have to read a book called *Fooled by Randomness* by Nassim Taleb to get a complete appreciation of the role that luck can play in one's success and how that can relate to games like poker or the stock market. For example, the stock market is just another game that involves a combination of skill and luck. As in poker, your problem is trying to separate the skill from the luck. Who are the lucky people and who are the skillful?

You cannot determine over a short duration of time if an individual is skillful. Most statisticians will tell you that it can take a lifetime to truly determine who is a good fund manager. By the time you can ascertain with a fair degree of certainty that a particular person is a skillful manager and you're ready to invest, he's retiring! It might take thirty or forty years to make that determination. You may ask how that can be possible when you look around and see so many supposedly skillful people.

Let's take a simple scam as an example using football sports betting. You select 5,000 people. You tell 2,500 that the Eagles are going to win and the other 2,500 that the Patriots are going to win. If the Eagles win you discard the 2,500 people that you told the Patriots were going to win and send a 50-50 prediction to the remaining 2,500. Finally, after doing this a few times, you'll have a group of people that have won five times in a row. These people believe that you are an absolute genius and will give you all their money because they've seen the proof that you are the smartest person in the world when it comes to sports betting.

To a lesser extent the same theory applies to the stock market or to poker. You have a race where there may be 10,000 fund managers who are all playing in a plus-expectation game. Poker players are actually operating in a much tougher environment because they're in a zero-sum game minus the rakes. Five years down the road in the stock market, you're going to see 30 or 40 people with a track record that seems to be far superior, but in reality you don't actually know. They may have been lucky. It's still too early to determine. It's very hard to separate skill from luck.

How do you equate that to poker? Very simple! Over a period of time a whole bunch of players have done well and are reasonably skillful. Out of that group there will be some that will perform above the norm and others that will perform below the norm. Some will also be right in the middle. If you happen to be in the fortuitous group that's above the norm, everyone thinks you're a genius. Given that the lifetime of a poker player isn't that long, and that the luck factor is greater there than it is in the stock market, it can take a long time to be really sure who the best players are.

The players that survive over the long term are toughened veterans. By the way, if you picked those people up and put them in the business world, I believe it would look like easy pickings to them. Big edges abound in the business world, but the same doesn't always apply to poker.

Understanding Equity

I think the cross-disciplines of the chess and backgammon tournaments that I used to play have had a strong influence on me as a poker player. In chess, I ended with a 2355 rating, which was considered to be that of a strong master, and also won the Massachusetts State Championship back in the early '70s. I then moved on to backgammon. I was fortunate because the co-author of my books, Bill Robertie, who was twice a World Backgammon Champion, was the person who taught me how to play. In backgammon, you learn how important equity is.

Positive equity in poker occurs when you put money into the pot and have a plus expectation of getting money back. If you put in $100 and think you'll extract an average of $120 at the end of the hand, that's a plus expectation. Having positive equity doesn't guarantee you'll win the hand; it just means that if you have enough trials, on average, that's what your outcome will be. In the investment world, having a 20 percent return on investment would be considered a pretty good expectation, but for some reason many poker players don't think it's such a good deal. Maybe in some cases it isn't, but overall, you should be taking advantage of opportunities with a positive expectation.

When Paul Magriel, who is a great backgammon theoretician and author, took up poker, he couldn't believe how many poker players didn't consider equity when they played. Lots of people will say things like, "I am only an 8 to 5 favorite; maybe I shouldn't play this hand, something better will probably come along." They don't understand that when you've got equity in front of you, you have to grab it.

It's a very simple concept that applies to both the investment world and the poker world. For every buck you put out, is only 90¢ coming back? Is $1 coming back or is $1.10 coming back? Let's look at an example. We will assume that the blinds are $50/$100 and someone in early position makes it $100 to go. Another person calls the $100 and you're on the button with 2-2. A pair of deuces is not a great hand. In fact, if you're in early position, I would recommend throwing deuces away because a number of people are yet to act and they may raise. Many times they will raise when they see all the callers in front of them. As a result, your expectations are a little bit hazy.

When you're on or next to the button, not many people are sitting behind you. You'll be one of the last to speak, so you can call. You know the deuces don't rate as the best hand after the flop and your odds against flopping a set are about 7.5 to 1 to make your hand profitable, but what odds are you actually getting? You have the two people who called in front of you, and also the big blind. The small blind is probably going to call as well, so it is likely that you'll have $400 out there ($500 if you call).

If you win, you'll be getting $400 back for the $100 you put out. Not quite the 7.5 to 1 that you need, but you also have to consider the implied expectation. Implied expectation is what happens if a deuce comes on the flop and you get some action. You could pick up twenty or thirty times the money that you put in if you flop your set. That raises the whole expectation to well over 7.5 to 1.

In this example, you are likely to be the last person to act after the flop, so you have position working for you as well. Sometimes the flop will be something like 3-3-4 and both players in front of you will check. Now you're pretty sure deuces are the best hand, so you should bet. You'll probably win the hand 50 percent or 60 percent of the time. Good position can really work for you.

Playing Cards versus Playing People

Some people think that the cards you hold are somewhat irrelevant in poker and you can just play your opponent instead. In my opinion, playing your cards is far more important than playing people in hold'em. I would be glad to be a lousy player versus a world-class player if you would give me A-A or K-K all the time. Let's see how well the world-class player does then!

You can win to a limited extent by just using your position and knowledge of the other players, but the problem is that everyone is on a pretty steep learning curve in poker and you can carry that too far. Your opponents don't have to be world class to eventually figure out what you're doing. After a while they're just going to say, "I've had it, that's it! I'm raising this guy no matter what he does." It is a bit like the movie *Network*, where a lead news anchor on national TV yells, "I'm mad as hell and I'm not going to take it anymore!" and all the viewers go to their windows and start yelling it as well.

If you are perceived as trying to win a lot of pots without actually having good cards, you won't be able to succeed. The reason that I can get away with it occasionally is that I'm perceived by others as a player who is not doing it. That's a tremendous edge. When your opponents suspect that you may be stealing, but are not sure, they will often let you get away with it and wait for a better opportunity to challenge you.

The Name "Action Dan"

The Nobel Prize for economics in 2002 was awarded to Daniel Kahneman for his work concerning human judgment and decision-making under uncertainty. One of his conclusions was that people like to latch onto adjectives during those times. They like to say things like, "This is a very tight, conservative player." The use of adjectives helps them reinforce their decision-making process. I decided to help those people by giving them something to latch onto.

I picked the name "Action Dan" because I wanted to reinforce in everyone's mind that I am not an action player. Someone said that among the active players, I am in the top third when it comes to aggression. I don't think that's necessarily true, but I do take reasonable chances when in position. I am certainly more aggressive than my reputation would indicate.*

TOURNAMENT STRATEGY

Doing Something Special to Win Tournaments

When you play in a tournament you have to go for the fences. You're going for an unusual result. Sitting there playing solid poker throughout the entire tournament just doesn't cut it. You have to do something special if you want to win. A famous mathematical work once postulated the following problem, which demonstrates the principle that I am talking about. You owe the Mafia $10,000 and have only $1,000 on you.

---

*Particularly with regard to online poker, when a player picks a name like "Action Sam," "All-In Bob," "Danger Man" or "The Rock," prudent opponents make the assumption that the player is trying to create an image which is opposite to that of his true nature. Hence, a good player would assume that an online name such as 'The Rock' is not always waiting for great cards before he plays, and "Aspen Bob" may not be an old road gambler—he just wants you to think he is. Harrington picked the name "Action Dan" because to many players it suggests that his style is more conservative than it actually is. —WD

Unfortunately you must pay the full amount back by tomorrow. What is the optimum way of getting the $10,000?

According to this particular theory, the optimum way to repay the debt within the allotted time is to bet the whole $1,000 on a 50-50 proposition. If you win, you've doubled up. You then bet those two units on a 50-50 proposition and win. Now you have four units. If you bet that $4,000 on a 50-50 proposition and win, you end up with eight units. Now, here comes an interesting problem: Your goal is to get to $10,000, not $16,000. The $16,000 would give you an overage of $6,000. The ideal strategy is to bet just two units. If you lose, you keep betting two units until you're knocked down to just two remaining units. Then you have to double up and try all over again!

This example seems a little far from the point, but is exactly what is happening in a poker tournament. You've got to go for an unusual result. That's why you often see good players at key points in the tournament willingly risk all of their money on a 50-50 proposition because they know it could enhance their overall chance of getting to the final table where the big money is.

This occurrence is what statisticians refer to as an "outlier effect." At one end of the curve you have the top three spots where all the money is, and at the other end are the first two or three people who get knocked out of the tournament. Everyone in between receives mediocre results.

Bluffing

There is a general perception among players that bluffing is everything in tournament poker. That just isn't true. Poker is a mixed package made up of many different factors. The one good thing about bluffing is that it fits into my concept of the outlier effect. When you bluff a lot, it is certain that you'll get larger swings in your results. The whole question is, do you get enough of the positive swings?

Some players such as Carlos Mortensen, who say that bluffing is the most important factor in poker, have proven that you can get more positive swings by bluffing a lot. He's been very successful at doing that, but it isn't easy.

I will point out, however, that the last time I played in a tournament with Carlos, he was playing very tight. He may talk bluff all the time, but even he doesn't always do it. Like many good players, he will bluff a lot in streaks when he think it's advantageous, but he is not doing it as much as he suggests.

Inflection Points

In *Harrington on Hold'em Volume II*, I speak about the importance of what I call inflection points. These are key times in a tournament where a significant change is occurring in the size of your chip stack in relation to the size of the blinds. At these points, taking a 50-50 chance is often the right way to go because it can earn you enough chips to do extra things in the tournament. Having a shortage of chips takes away a lot of your options and reduces your playing strength. If you're a superior player, you're capable of taking that chance at the appropriate time. Most people don't understand that point. They think that survival in the tournament is the only way to go—but it's not. You have another consideration, too. You have to end up in the first three spots in the tournament to make big money, and must do something unusual to achieve that. Most players hurt their chances of winning by not taking a chance when they should.

There are four separate zones based on the relative number of chips you have remaining. There is the **Green Zone** where you have 20 times the big blind or more. That's where you're safe and can execute a lot of different plays because you have a lot of chips. The **Yellow Zone** is when you get down to between ten and twenty times the big blind. Some of your opportunities become limited and you start to feel a little uneasy.

At ten times the big blind or lower, you are in the **Orange Zone.** That's where your options become severely limited. You have to look for opportunities where you think you're a favorite and can double up your chips. You definitely have to go for it. When you get down to five times the big blind or less, you are in the **Red Zone** and your situation has become really critical. You're just looking for any opportunity where you've got anything going at all. Even if you're an underdog, but there's a chance that you could have the best hand, you have to go for it right then and there.

When you have three units or less, you are in what I call the **Dead Zone**. That's where you're just floating, waiting for someone to pick you off. I advocate that you don't ever get to that zone.

Adjusting for the Different Stages of a Tournament

You're supposed to play very tight during the early stage of a tournament, but the truth is that many of the strong players, myself included, actually play looser than they should. They play okay in the middle stage of the tournament and too tight in the late stage when they should be loosening up.

Weak players are normally too loose at the beginning of the tournament. That's why a lot of them are eliminated very quickly. They play a little too loose in the middle stages, but when they get to the end of the tournament, they inadvertently end up playing at the right pace. That's why you see a lot of weak players win. You shouldn't be surprised they do. They're actually using the correct style for the later stage. What you should be surprised about is that they actually reached that stage of the tournament.

Even though the good players are playing too many hands early in the tournament, they differ from the bad players because they're able to save chips and get away from a hand when they're beaten.

There are two main opinions regarding whether good players should play looser in the early stages of the tournament. The one that I subscribe to is that they should play loose when they're at a weak table. Good players need to get involved with the weaker players because they require chips to make it through the tournament, and they have to get them somehow.

My philosophy is this: Get the chips from the bad players before your buddies do. If you don't, the players that win those chips are going to use them against you later on. The real question is: Would you rather try to take the money away from some unknown player or from Phil Ivey? As a consequence, if you're against weaker competition, you should play a little looser during the early stages of the tournament than is theoretically correct. You can get involved in a few inexpensive hands to see what's going on and look for opportunities to take the pot away from your opponents. In other words, you see what people are doing and try to exploit any edges that you can find.

If you are at a reasonably decent table with good players, you've got to play a lot tighter. Some players don't always make that adjustment.

If you're playing against people who just can't lay down a hand, don't try to take the pot away from them unless you have something. Those are the players I'm going to save my good hands for and use those hands to take all their money. If they can't lay down a hand, that's fine. I don't object to that; I just won't try to steal, that's all.

That's where some of my compatriots sometimes get carried away. They think that because a player is weak, he'll automatically lay down his hand and they'll have his chips. You should play with someone for an hour or two before you try to make any really strong moves against him. If he is an unknown, you just don't know what his behavior will be.

Final Table Play

"You dance with the girl that brung you" is how I feel about the style of play required for the final table. Many people wonder how they should change their style when they get to the final table, but they really should just continue to do what they did to get there. That's the style that has been most effective for them. You don't magically change your strategy because you're at the final table. However, you do have to make some technical adjustments as you become short-handed, and your starting hands change as a result of those adjustments.

When you consider the starting hands you should enter pots with, remember that they may be the recommended hands for a full table of nine people. If you are playing at a table with five other people (six total), you have basically eliminated positions one, two and three. In that situation, just ask yourself what your starting requirements would be for position four at a full table.

It means you play looser, but it is not a cut-and-dried formula. You're not changing your style. You are just making appropriate technical adjustments because your relative starting position has changed.

AGGRESSION

Selective Aggressive Opportunities

Players whom you perceive to be a little weak, or who exhibit certain systematic traits after the flop, often present opportunities that you can exploit. For example, they may

CARDOZA PUBLISHING ◆ WARWICK DUNNETT

be too tight after the flop and won't bet unless they have a made hand. That's easy: If you have position on them after the flop and they check, you just bet and take the money. Thank you! Or they may be the type of player who overbet the pot after the flop when they only have a mediocre hand, and thus tend to overcommit themselves. That's fine with me, too. I'll just wait until I have an above-average hand and take their money. Either way, the situation is exploitable. To be successful in poker, you have to be consistently looking for exploitable opportunities.

Whether you try to win the pot before the flop or at some later stage depends on a combination of things. Sometimes when you're getting into a rhythm and have very readable players behind you who are reasonably tight and not giving much action, you can pick up a lot of money before the flop by just raising. It really depends on the game. You could pick up chips after the flop or on the river. However, when I'm against weaker players I definitely prefer playing the flop.

How Much to Bet When Trying to Take a Pot
The correct amount to bet should be based on your powers of observation. What has caused your opponent to throw away hands in the past? Was it two times the opening bet? If so, that's your optimal investment because it's the least amount you can commit to obtain the desired result. Is it four times? If it is, then that is what you are probably going to have to bet, but you also have to consider that your risk profile has gone up enormously. Decisions such as whether you need to bet half the pot or the full value of the pot to win are always based on what you've seen your opponents do beforehand.

112   **POKER WIZARDS**

STARTING HAND CONCEPTS

> Unless stated otherwise, all of the situations discussed by the Wizards in the Starting Hand Concepts and Specific Hand Strategy sections are assumed to be at a full table, during the third level of a tournament. The blinds are $100/$200, and you have an average stack of around $11,000 in chips. It is also assumed that the players are displaying a moderate level of aggression and appear to be playing reasonably well.

These are approximate starting hands, and they vary depending on the types of players at the table. If I am up against very tough opponents, I am going to fold many of the marginal hands. If the table is weak, those marginal hands become more profitable. If first to act, I will raise about 70 to 80 percent of the time, but I will mix up my play and just call the other 20 to 30 percent of the time with the same hands.

Early Position
In the first couple of seats to the left of the big blind, A-Q suited and pairs down to around 6-6 would normally be my minimum come-in hands during the early stages of a tournament.

Middle Position
When I am three or four seats to the left of the big blind, I don't normally change my starting requirements that much. I may add A-J to the list of hands I'll play, but still only play pairs down to about 6-6.

To mix up my play, I will also occasionally come in and raise about 40 percent of the time, or call about 20 percent of the time with the better suited connectors such as 9-10, 10-J and

J-Q as well as playing the premium hands. The hands I play are determined largely by the type of table image I have at the time and the composition of the players to my left who are yet to act.

Late Position

From any of the last few seats, you should significantly adapt your play to suit the types of opponents who are sitting in the blinds. In the third seat from the button, I will start to play hands such as A-9 or better and pairs as low as 4-4. In the cutoff seat (the seat to the immediate right of the button), any ace becomes a reasonable come-in hand if you're still the first to act. On the button, hands such as J-9 or 10-8 and better usually are raising hands that can be included in your list of playable hands.

SPECIFIC HAND STRATEGY

It is important to mention that I play differently against different players at different stages of the tournament based on a lot of factors that are always changing. You have to consider the chips that you have and how many your opponent has, the mood of your opponent, your status in the tournament, your position, your opponent's idiosyncrasies and so on. All those factors combine to determine how you are going to play, so answers to hand-specific questions vary a lot from situation to situation.

A-A

I don't always raise when I have A-A in early position because I would prefer to try to trap somebody in the hope that he will raise me and I can then get all my money in as a 4.5 to 1 favorite. On the other hand, if the table is passive, I would be more likely to raise because I don't want to give anybody a free shot at my aces.

Aces often will win small or lose big. You have to be very careful with the hand and can't limp in too much. If you just call, you may get three or four callers behind you, but if you raise at a passive table, you may just get one caller. If you have an opponent beaten after the flop, there is a good chance you'll win a fair amount of money. Often you'll get involved in a big pot with A-A, suspect that you're beaten, and have to throw the aces away. That's all there is to it!

At a passive table where there is little chance that the players after me are going to raise, I want to make sure I don't get involved in a multiway pot with a high pair like A-A. However, in a normal tournament, there is no instance where I will throw my hand away when I'm a big favorite. You just have to accept the risk that the other person may outdraw you.

There are some popular tournaments today where it makes sense to throw your hand away, such as those where you have a flat prize distribution in a satellite for a seat to a main event. For example, suppose 100 people each put up $1,000 to try to win a $10,000 seat, which means that ten seats will be awarded. First place through tenth place all win the same value prize. If eleven players remain and you get dealt aces when you have an above-average stack, you have to throw your aces away if any smaller stacks have already moved all in. Your fold will allow one of the other players to get knocked out, thus assuring that you will win a seat into the main tournament.

But in a normal tournament, I would never throw away pocket aces before the flop. How often are you going to be a 4.5 to 1 favorite? That's a proposition that doesn't occur very often, so you have to take advantage of it when it comes along.

K-K

I play K-K in much the same way as all my premium hands earlier in a tournament. I raise with them around 70 to 80 percent of the time, and just call the rest of the time to mix up my game.

Getting Away from K-K Preflop

K-K is a very hard hand to lay down before the flop. Even if somebody puts in a third raise against me, I am probably going to end up getting a lot of money in the center of the table. If I have a substantial amount of prior information on my opponent and know that he is exceptionally tight and unlikely to reraise without holding A-A, then I can get away from the hand. Even though I do so occasionally, as a general rule I am very reluctant to lay down K-K preflop.

Q-Q

If I am first to act, I still make the same bet with Q-Q as my other premium hands, but I play them much more carefully than K-K. The trouble with risking a lot of chips with Q-Q is that you can often guess correctly, yet still find yourself up against A-K and only be a slight favorite. I am far more likely to fold the hand when I encounter strong opposition earlier in the tournament such as a raise and a reraise. If there is a raise and then I reraise, and the initial bettor comes back over the top of me, I just throw the hand away or slow down dramatically depending on the size of the bet.

A-K

A-K can be played a few different ways. You can raise with the hand or just call a raise and play the hand slowly. You can also play the hand very quickly by reraising, thus suggesting you have A-A. Good players play the hand all three ways.

Whether or not I call an all-in bet with A-K depends largely on how much money I have and how much money is in the pot. If I am heads-up and getting 2 to 1 odds or better, I'm definitely calling. Most likely, you are only an 11 to 10 underdog. You have to assess the position you are in. If you are fairly sure that your opponent has only an underpair and you are getting 2 to 1 on your money, you have to ask yourself how many times you are going to get good odds like that.

I am sure there are some strong players who would advocate throwing your hand away with those types of odds rather than risk their whole stack early in a tournament. I am just not one of those players. By the way, if you are, the other players will perceive it. I won't name any specific players, but there are a number of very good ones out there who are targets because other players know they won't risk their whole stack. Players take advantage of that and attack them. You can't do that and expect other good players not to notice. It is important to have the persona that, if it is a close decision, you are willing to fight and you're willing to go all in. That way, your opponents know they may have to gamble for all their money if they attack you.

Some people don't want 50-50 decisions early in the tournament. For example, I was involved in a well-known hand during the middle stages of the 1996 World Series Main Event against Howard Lederer in which I had A-K and he had Q-Q. We ended up getting all our money in before the flop and I won the hand. After it was over, Howard came up to me and asked how I could put my whole stack in as a slight underdog. I laughed and told him they were the best odds that I had seen all day. It was true.

J-J

A lot of people consider J-J a difficult hand to play from the first few seats, but it's a problem I would be happy to have every hand.

About 80 percent of the time I'll raise with J-J in just this situation. I don't like to play the jacks slowly because I don't want too many people to come in behind me, watch a couple of overcards come, and then feel sick with my jacks. The other 20 percent of the time I will just call with the hand to vary my play. You've got to just call with some of your good hands that you would normally raise with to stop people from getting a good read on what you are doing.

If you are one of the last to act and an earlier, fairly solid, player raises, my inclination would be to call rather than fold or reraise with J-J—assuming I'm in the earlier stages and we both have an average stack. I have a couple of things working for me: I have a good hand with position, and I can let that position work for me.

If I raise preflop and the initial raiser comes back over the top of me, my position has been taken away from me and I am faced with a difficult decision. So, against a solid player, I would normally just call the preflop raise.

10-10

I tend to play 10-10 in a similar way to J-J. The majority of the time, I still raise, but obviously, if I become involved in some heavy action, I'd be more inclined to fold with 10-10 than with J-J.

Small and Medium Pairs

I will play medium pairs like 9-9, 8-8, or 7-7 in the later positions; however, I tend to throw the small pairs away. The problem with small pairs is that you often start out with the best hand, but they can end up costing you a lot of money. Many pots are lost when you have a hand like 4-4, your opponent has two overcards like 10-J and, even if he doesn't end up making a pair, the cards come 7-7-8-8-2.

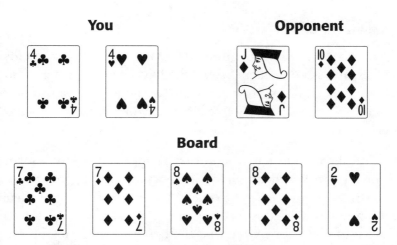

Your 4-4 ends up losing because your opponent shows the jack. He either ends up with a higher pair or with two pair and a higher kicker.

Many people like to play small pairs to try to make a set. However, unless you both have very large stacks, once somebody raises, you are generally not getting the correct odds to play. Also, by playing small pairs, you are making a number of assumptions that may not occur:

1. You are incorrectly assuming that you are guaranteed to see a cheap flop. Even if you are one player to the right of the button, you still have three people left to act behind you, and you really have no idea what they will do.

2. You are also assuming that you'll be in a heads–up situation, but it could easily be a multiway pot. In one sense, that helps you; in another, it hurts you. One of the reasons you called was the possibility that your 4-4 was the best hand. In a multiway pot that becomes substantially less likely, and you also have the increased probability of an opponent flopping a higher set.

PLAYING ONLINE

I actually prefer playing online to playing in live tournaments because it is so convenient. You don't have to go anywhere, you can stop and start anytime you want, and it is the best training ground to improve your game because you can focus on what you are doing.

The most frequent tells you get from opponents in any form of poker are based on their betting patterns. Forget about the twitches and stuff that other players say they base their million-dollar decisions; betting patterns give away at least 70 percent of the information that the better players pick up on. So when playing online, you're still getting 70 percent of the tells. When playing in a casino, you are also getting the other 30 percent. That extra 30 percent takes a lot of work. You have to use all your senses and a lot of observation to get that extra 30 percent. It can be very tiring.

MONEY MANAGEMENT

A Professional Gambler's Worst Sin

The worst sin that professional gamblers can commit is not being able to play because they don't have enough money. Lots of brilliant players have fallen by the wayside because they played outside the limits of their bankroll. When you start to run out of money and things don't go well, you start playing badly. It's human nature. That's just the way it is. Very few people can keep their mind in balance when they have to worry about their portfolio. By portfolio, I mean their *money*. The same concept also applies to investments.

A professional games player is supposed to take into account the volatility that is caused by luck and make sure he's always gambling within his bankroll. There are formulas to help with this, such as the Kelly Criteria in blackjack. If you can, you're supposed to determine what your edge is. If you assume in this example that your edge is 1 percent, you're supposed to bet 1 percent of your bankroll on the proposition. If you lose, then on the next bet you have 99 units. Now you bet 1 percent of 99 units and so on until you win. In fact, some advocate a more conservative policy of betting one-half percent. It means that you have a very high probability of surviving. To me, the whole nature of gambling is survival.

I have been very lucky in life's tournament, but I have always played so that I could survive and stay in the game. I have always kept my bankroll solid so I could afford to play. I am sure there have been numerous opponents over the years that were better than me, but just didn't get a chance to play because they ran out of money.

Bankroll for Cash Games

The correct bankroll required to survive depends on the game that you're playing. Mason Malmuth, whose background is that of a statistician, came out with some work on limit hold'em that is worth looking at if you want to try to understand what volatility is all about. Basically he determined that you can earn one unit an hour playing limit hold'em. Based on 2,000 hours of play, your chance of having a losing year is roughly 2 percent or 3 percent.

If you think about that, you realize that it is pretty scary. You're playing 2,000 hours, have a big win rate and still have a 2 percent chance of being a loser at the end of the year! By the way, very few people in the world have a win rate of one unit per hour in any kind of sizable game.

In a cash game, I believe a new player should start with the smallest bankroll he can play comfortably and beat the lowest game, then slowly work his way up. That's the safest way of doing it.

Bankroll for Tournaments

In the late 1990s, the main tournaments usually had about 200 entrants. At that time, David Sklansky postulated that a world-class player against an average field could expect to win only about one in every fifty tournaments. The volatility goes through the roof when you're talking about larger tournaments, because so many people are involved.

A smart young player with a bankroll of $20,000 should, in my opinion, only be playing in $200 events or less. He not only has to try to win, he also has to make sure that he makes it to the top couple of spots at least a few times just to cover his expenses between wins. That can be very hard in today's big tournaments. He is playing in a very volatile environment where his edge is not that great.

On the other hand, a competent player in smaller buy-in events has a slightly better edge because the competition is not always that good. He needs to exploit that advantage by making sure that his money doesn't run out if he has only a small bankroll.

Dealing With Losing Streaks

Like most players, I have gone through a few long periods where things weren't going that well and times were gloomy, but I have always managed to avoid a lot of stress because I was playing well within my bankroll. I didn't like the dry spells, but it never bothered me that much because I didn't need the money. I also knew that if I just kept plugging along and didn't overbet my bankroll, things would eventually straighten out. And that is what always happened.

Back when I was playing poker on a more regular basis, I had times when I went seven months without a significant win. During the harder times, when you're not going well, it can be smart to play smaller. That can help you win, which helps you get your confidence back.

It doesn't matter who you are, your confidence gets shattered when you go on a long losing streak. I have seen it happen to the best players in the world. You just have to do something about it. Otherwise, you can't go out there and play against the best players in the world because they will be playing a lot better than you are and your chances of winning will be greatly diminished.

I always maintain that you score your biggest gains in poker during your losing streaks. The reason is that if you can consistently keep your losses down during those losing streaks, and play reasonably well when you are winning, you'll end up being a big winner overall in the game. How you manage your losses is a very important part of poker. When people are going through a good period they tend to play pretty well. It is when they start losing that you see the big differences between players.

If a player takes a couple of bad beats and then starts to play badly, the good players are like a pack of sharks that smell blood in the water. They will circle that individual just waiting to take a big bite out of him.

FINAL WORDS OF WIZDOM

One saying I like is this: "Try to live well until you die because that's all there is." I don't believe in an afterlife and think you should do your best to enjoy life while you are here. In my opinion, you're not going to enjoy any other higher spiritual reward after you're gone. Another of my favorite quotes is by Woody Allen: "I don't want to achieve immortality through my work. I want to achieve it through not dying."

It is important to live your life in a way that provides enjoyment. Do a lot of hard work, but also try to avoid a lot of stress because being overstressed definitely shortens your life span.

I was probably most serious about chess, but I believe it is important to not let games take over your life. One of the things that I am proud of is that, in all the games I have been associated with throughout my life, I have tried not to take them too seriously.

Too many people want to use poker as a metaphor for life. It is just a game—a way to make money and have fun.

> **WD:** Dan Harrington's series on tournament play, written with long-time friend and backgammon champion Bill Robertie, has significantly influenced the way many players approach tournament poker. When competing in tournaments today, it is impossible not to notice the substantial number of players who are clearly aware of what Dan terms "inflection points." Many competitors who once would have waited far too long for elusive premium cards are now more proactive in making aggressive moves before their stack dwindles to a point of no return. This increased player awareness of the need to take on additional risk at appropriate times in a tournament—due to one's relative stack size as compared to the blinds and those of the other players—has substantially contributed to the rise of a better informed group of players.

MARCEL LUSKE

The Flying Dutchman

Career Tournament Earnings Exceeding $3,300,000
Winner, Five Star World Poker Classic Limit Omaha, 2003
Winner, Barcelona Open €1,000 No-Limit Hold'em, 2003
Winner, European Poker Classic €1,500 No-Limit Hold'em, London, 2003
Second place, WSOP Seven-Card Stud, 2004
Tenth place, WSOP Championship Event, 2004
Winner, Crown Australian Pot-Limit Omaha Championship, 2005
Winner, Five Star World Poker Classic, $2,000 Limit Hold'em, 2005
Winner, €10,000 No-Limit Hold'em Hall of Fame Poker Classic, Paris, 2005
Second place, WSOP H.O.S.E Circuit event, Caesars Las Vegas, 2006
Winner, Five Star World Poker Classic, $3,000 No-Limit Hold'em, 2006
Winner, World Poker Showdown, Nassau, Bahamas, 2008
First, Netherlands All-time Money List

Sitting Down With Marcel

When you first spot Marcel Luske engaging those around him in conversation, his demeanor, stature and dress remind you of a sophisticated royal from a European principality who has just stepped out of the Club Privé at the Casino in Monte Carlo to sign autographs and engage admirers in friendly chit-chat. You can always recognize him at the table, not simply because of his height or handsome features but because he will be the best-dressed man in the room—and certainly the only one wearing black sun glasses upside down while singing for the crowd.

With great anticipation, I walked toward the Bellagio Hotel Café where I was to meet the tall proud Dutchman who had knocked me out of the no-limit warm-up to the main event in Australia in 2005. My ruin had been implemented in such a gracious, unassuming way that I found it to be a practically painless experience, yet the recollection of some hands stuck with me for years. I still wanted to fully understand how this icon of the European poker scene could dispatch players such as myself to the bleachers so easily and with such style and grace. Even when Marcel is the one walking to the rail, cameras poised to catch any negative emotion, his composure and positive attitude are always impressive. He is a true ambassador of the game, kind and respectful to other players and, above all, entertaining. A private discussion about poker strategy with Marcel Luske was certainly going to be a privilege.

An impressive track record in tournament play has not only confirmed Marcel as one of Europe's top hold'em players, he is also regarded as one of the best and most charismatic Omaha players in the world. Marcel is also passionately involved in many facets of the poker industry including the development of FIDPA (Federation Internationale de Poker Association), whose goal is to represent, preserve and increase the level of fairness and integrity of the sport. Further, Marcel has developed an instructional poker game and DVD called TOCK Poker—Tactics, Observation, Concentration and Knowledge—designed to teach people learn how to play poker at home. The game reinforces these four principles by letting players see the likely outcome of a particular hand, and how that projected outcome changes based on the composition of the flop, turn and river.

Let's hear what Marcel has to say…

MARCEL LUSKE

THE MAKINGS OF A POKER WIZARD

You need five important qualities as a foundation for being a successful poker player. Let's look at them.

1. Be Physically and Mentally Prepared

The ability to become a top player is not only based on a player's card-playing skill, but starts with his desire to prepare for battle. If you want to get the most benefit out of your knowledge, you have to be prepared both physically and mentally. If your body and mind are not one, you may win a tournament occasionally by accident, but you'll not be able to consistently succeed in the large competitions that we see today.

Poker is a mind game. Your mind has to carry the pressure, but your body has to carry the load. For my preparation, I go to the gym to work out. I studied karate for twelve years, and also use zen to meditate because it helps clear my mind. It is harder to do these things now, because as I became more popular and started winning tournaments, the media's demands added to my everyday obligations. Some days I lose my voice from talking on the phone, doing interviews, being busy all the time. These are things that I never had to think about before.

2. Play Within Your Bankroll

You can help affect the amount of mental pressure that you face by selecting the correct limits to play. If you're in a game that puts a lot of financial pressure on you, you're under stress from the start. Let's say a player has $1,000 in his pocket and sits in a $1,000 tournament. He knows that when he loses, that's it! No more money. On the other hand, if he has $10,000 in his pocket and sits in a $500 tournament, he has no financial pressure at all. That makes a huge difference.

3. Be Patient

Often, the cards are just not coming in your favor. It is important to be patient during those periods and not become too aggressive or change your style of play significantly.

4. Use All Your Senses

The feeling you get when you're focused is the most important thing in the game of poker. When you're focused on your A-game and tuned in to the table, that's the moment you start to feel the cards. The voices you hear from the other players, and the moves they make, create a small movie for you. From the way they make their moves and bets, you can smell and feel if they're bluffing or actually have big hands.

You have to know what is going on around you. In a world where there is so much noise, we don't use all of our senses fully. To understand this, try turning off the lights and make the room you're in very dark. Just breath deeply, relax and feel what is around you. Imagine a picture of your surroundings; suddenly you'll start to imagine that you can touch things with your mind. This is a difficult concept to explain, but what I'm trying to say is that you have to use all the senses that are available to you at the poker table if you want to be successful. Some people refer to this type of awareness as intuition or gut feeling. It's very important.

5. Develop Your Own Style

Any style can win in poker—you don't have to stick to any one way. For example, if you put Phil Hellmuth, Howard Lederer, Chris Ferguson and T.J. Cloutier next to each other, you would find that they were all very different types of players. Each one has his own set of distinctive qualities.

Characteristics of a World-Class Player

Most of the top names are outplaying their competitors by using position, getting a good read on them and, of course, using superior knowledge. The top thirty or forty players in the world generally have a lot of experience and are like fish in water. They move, they make bets correctly, they move again; they adjust and create situations where they can read the other players. Once they do that, it's only a question of time before they take advantage of the information they have gathered. The way they play gives them more knowledge. And at the poker table, knowledge is power!

They read what you have and how you play. They know whether you have a weak ace or a small pair. If the flop comes down K-Q-2 and you have 8-8, the best players are going to make you very unhappy. They will see the expression on your face and how your body reacts when the flop comes out. People react differently when they're under pressure and when they're relaxed. The great players pick up on that.

Take a look at Sam Farha. He will often play back at you even though he missed his hand just because he thinks you missed yours as well. Let's say you have an A-Q, the flop comes down K-Q-2, and he moves against you.

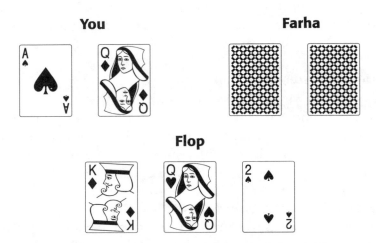

You   **Farha**

Flop

Do you think you're going to call? Not many people are going to risk most of their chips with the second-best pair. When people are attacked, they look at what can kill them, and the king in that flop doesn't look good for them. It creates fear, and a player such as Sam will take advantage of that fear.

The Luske Style

The style I play is fair, open, aggressive and based on adjusting to the people that I am up against. When I say I am a *fair* player, I am talking about the way in which I play. In the old days, players could make bets in a deceptive way to gauge an opponent's interest more easily. Some players would gain information by making a bet with their hand covering a stack, or moving their chips forward, cutting them and changing the amount of the bet. By watching players and their reactions they could better understand their level of interest. I don't like to play that way. That is why a "betting" line is now painted on modern poker tables, and why a lot more rules are in force. Your movements are better regulated and all players have to play to the same standard. It is much better for the game.

By *open*, I mean that I can play any two cards in any spot, at any place on the table. It doesn't matter if I am under the gun, on the button, or in the big blind, I can come over the top at any moment with a big bluff or may have the stone cold nuts. It's very hard to estimate what I have. I'm a very unpredictable player, which makes me dangerous to the other players and creates frustration among the non-professionals who play against me and don't know what to do.

TOURNAMENT STRATEGY

I am normally either knocked out of tournaments very quickly or get a lot of chips fast because of the way I play. The days when I get knocked out early are the days that I can work on other projects. And the days that I really get through and accumulate chips, I'm one of the dangerous players in the tournament with a good chance to win. Once you have a large stack, you can lose a hand without getting knocked out by a normal stack; only one of the chip leaders can get you.

I will adjust my strategy based on who my opponents are, how they play, and what I think is going on in their minds. I'm always changing gears and can go from playing aggressively every hand to a stage where I go stone cold and play conservatively—just relaxing, watching and observing.

When I have an edge on somebody, I want to get as many chips in the pot as possible. In these large tournaments, where it takes a long time to get to the final table, it is especially important to get a lot of chips. When you do, you feel comfortable and enjoy the game much more. Playing just to survive is a tough way to play tournament poker. When you're on a short stack you're under pressure all the time, waiting to make that one single, all-in move. With a short stack you eventually end up committing yourself to a single pot. Not many players survive with a very conservative style of play.

Adapting to Different Stages of a Tournament

You must be able to change gears at the different stages of the tournament, but let me re-emphasize that you also have to adapt to different kinds of players. You have to watch your opponents, frame them in your mind. A top pro will reraise you if your bet is not big enough.

You have to adjust your style based on the amount of chips you have and the chip count of the other players because it is important to understand where and when you can put your opponents on the edge. In the beginning of a tournament, if you're up against a tight player, even a small ace will be enough of a hand to put pressure on him and find out what kind of hand he has. A good, tight player will not go all in with his A-K; he wants to see the flop. In the earlier stages, I normally play more aggressively trying to accumulate chips, which will make it easier to survive for a long time in the middle stage of the game.

If a dealer gives you forty hands an hour, you have roughly a one in five chance of getting a pair of aces during that time and the same with kings or queens; therefore you'll probably get a few premium hands during each level. You won't know which position you'll be in when those hands come and you won't know when, but if I create a chip lead early in the tournament, I can afford to change gears and be more patient during the middle stages. With enough chips, I can start playing big cards and my game changes; I don't have to play 9-7 or 6-8. With my larger stack I can afford to wait for premium hands, but if I want to, I also have enough chips to clash with a larger than average stack and survive. The chip leader cannot bully me because I will play aggressively and let him know I'm there, unless I think he has the best hand.

On a recent occasion, Barry Shulman was the big stack and held the A♦ K♦. I was in position with 7-6 suited and called his raise. I had another $50,000 in chips in my stack and he had $80,000. The flop came Q-7-6 with two diamonds.

Shulman   **Luske**

Flop

Barry Shulman moved all in with his two overcards and the nut-flush draw. I called with my two pair. He was about a 2 to 1 underdog when he went all in, although he thought he was further ahead at the time. He won the hand by making his flush.

This is the type of hand where you can take a lot of chips from somebody when they don't expect it. He could have easily lost $60,000. He probably thought that I had A-Q or a hand like 10-10 and he could hit his ace or king or any diamond to win the hand. He also had the benefit of being the aggressor. If I had J-J or 10-10, I would easily have laid down the hand because the queen was out.

> ## A Flush Draw and Two Overcards
>
> A flush draw and two overcards is a 53 to 47 percent favorite over a hand with top pair. When Schulman went all in, he was probably assuming that even if Luske had a queen in his hand, he might not be willing to call for all his chips, and if Marcel did decide to call with just top pair, he still had around a 50-50 chance of winning the hand. Unknown to Schulman, after the flop Marcel was actually a 64 to 36 percent favorite to win with his two pair. —WD

Playing People versus Playing Cards

It's more important to play people that your cards. If you play people, you can push them to the edge, forcing them to make really tough decisions. Let's say I know that a person only plays good cards. If you give me an unpredictable hand and position with enough chips, that player will not make it, no matter how good he is because he will always be playing with predictable starting hands. Sooner or later he is going to walk into a big hand, which is not predictable. For example, if I play 8-6, J-9, 10-8, or smaller cards like 6-5, people don't expect it.

> ## Playing People versus Playing Cards
>
> Playing people refers to a type of strategy that primarily uses tells, an opponent's betting actions, his style and your general read on your opponent as the principal factors in your decision-making process. Playing the cards uses the strength of your holding as the primary determinant of your actions, not your read on the other players. —WD

In one hand I played, I limped with 5-4 under the gun and somebody raised it from $400 to $2,000 all in. By the time it got back to me, another player had called and I also called because the pot represented good value. After the hand was over, the initial raiser could not understand how I could play a 5-4 for $2,000. What he didn't realize is that I had $15,000 in chips in front of me and could afford to do it. If I hit my hand, I would win a lot of chips from the third player and had to put in only $1,600.

Good players know that if you pit an A-K against two random cards, the A-K is only about a 60/40 favorite. If you play two random cards against somebody who has an A-K, A-Q, A-J or even Q-Q, you have to also consider the value that comes when you surprise them and they lose their whole stack when they least expect it. In my mind, that's much better than waiting for A-A or K-K. You'll get a pair of aces on average once in every 221 hands, but everyone has that same chance. That's why, when I have enough chips, I sometimes like to play unusual hands.

AGGRESSION

Aggression will eventually fail without good hand selection. You can't simply be aggressive with no other moves because there is no way you'll survive in the long run. However, aggression can be very effective at the appropriate time. If you want to give yourself a chance, it's important to think about the field. For example, if you have a small pocket pair, and you're up against a single opponent with a hand like A-K, you're a favorite. If you're up against three opponents, then you're no longer a favorite to win the hand. However, there may be a lot more money in the pot. You now have to decide the best way to play the hand. If you play aggressively, you can walk into a big hand, but if you play very aggressively, people aren't really going to call you with a hand like 7-7, A-10, or A-J. They will fold most of the time.

By being aggressive, you create favorable situations for yourself when you're in position and put pressure on people in order to get a read on what they have—or you can take the pot then and there. The person who is not aggressive enough and just waits for a big hand has already given you a read. By the time he decides to play a hand, at least you know where you're at. If he knows you're aggressive and suddenly raises you, he's not going to be doing it with a poor hand. So you already have a read and don't have to play. But the nice thing is that when you find a playable hand in position you can just call, knowing that opponents will usually pay you off all the way if you hit your hand.

Of course, it depends on your opponents, but while there are many shrewd players out there, there are only a small percentage of them that are really good. Those very good players will know what you are doing and may come back over the top of you. Even then, not many people will come back over a reraise unless they have A-A or K-K.

Opportune Times to Be Aggressive

The best time to be aggressive is when you're just starting the tournament because people are overly cautious and more willing to muck quality hands. Even if your opponent has Q-Q, an ace or a king on the flop will scare them if somebody comes back over the top of them after the flop. You can take advantage of that fear.

I recently played a tournament at the Bellagio in Las Vegas in which the player in front of me moved all in for the rest of his chips, around $16,000. I looked down at my cards and found J-J, but also noticed that the woman behind me seemed to be excited when she looked at her hand. I raised it another

$15,000, trying to push her A-K or A-Q out of the hand. She had about $60,000 in chips and thought for a very long time. I knew that if she had a great hand like A-A or K-K, she would come back over the top of me. In that case, I would be able to fold and still have $30,000 of chips in my stack. Also, if she did have a hand like A-K or A-Q or even Q-Q, I may be able to get her to fold. She finally just called after a long two minute wait. I then knew she was probably thinking, or at least hoping, that I had A-K and wanted to see the flop with a high pair other than A-A or K-K. She was afraid that if she moved all in, I would call her.

The flop came down A-7-2, and I moved in for the rest of my chips, representing top pair. She showed everybody Q-Q and folded. I had to show everyone the J-J because I was also all in against the first player, who held 8-8.

I didn't think she had a hand like A-K because she was a tight player, and she had to put in half of her stack after a couple of players had made a big move before the flop. She was very scared that I might have a big hand such as kings or aces. It was clear to me that she had a big hand, but she wanted to see the flop first. On that occasion I made a perfect read.

Being Aggressive Near the Bubble

When you're close to the money where twenty-seven people get paid and twenty-eight or twenty-nine players are left, you have a fantastic opportunity to accumulate chips by being aggressive. If you're unlucky, you could walk into a big hand; but even if you win just a few pots, you can build your chip stack very quickly.

Even though good players know what I'm doing, and could come back over the top of me, the reality is that most of the time, players don't want to give up their chip position that close to the big money. If the average stack is around $10,000 or

$12,000 in chips, a better player with $40,000 in chips in front of him, knows that one of those smaller stacks can really hurt him. If he loses an all in bet to that smaller stack, suddenly the small stack has $22,000 in chips and now he has only $30,000. He has created a second chip leader at the table and is no longer the dominant stack. The large stack is often not willing to take that risk just to stop you from picking up a $3,000 pot.

Preflop versus Post-Flop Aggression
If you are too aggressive preflop you actually give away some of your edge, because people will make their decisions with the knowledge that you are always aggressive. On the other hand, you can be more aggressive against a top player who likes to see a lot of flops. If you play him aggressively before the flop, you take away his game. If he does get to see the flop, you have to be very careful if it comes with small to medium cards because top players often play connectors.

Small-Bet Poker
When possible, I also advocate what some people call "small bet poker" to get information. It is not always necessary to make a huge bet. Let me give you an example.

Kirill Gerasimov was playing Alan Goehring three years ago in a WPT event. At the time, I had coached Kirill about the best way to play Goehring. When they first started playing heads-up, Kirill had around $1.8 million in chips and Alan had around $3.6 million. They played a hand where the flop came Q-7-5. There was no movement for a while, then Alan checked and Kirill also checked.

The next card was another 5. Alan made a bet and Kirill came back over the top all in, with no hand and no outs, as though he had hit something. Alan called, of course, because he had Q-Q in his hand, giving him a set on the flop.

It obviously was a big mistake for Kirill to move all in. If he had raised $400,000, for example, he would have gained the same information without risking all his chips. If Alan Goehring didn't have a good hand, he would probably be willing to throw it away. It wouldn't have mattered if Kirill had bet $400,000 or $2 million, he would have obtained the same information— and still be in the tournament.

STARTING HAND CONCEPTS

Unless stated otherwise, all of the situations discussed by the Wizards in the Starting Hand Concepts and Specific Hand Strategy sections are assumed to be at a full table, during the third level of a tournament. The blinds are $100/$200, and you have an average stack of around $11,000 in chips. It is also assumed that the players are displaying a moderate level of aggression and appear to be playing reasonably well.

My recommendations for the hand discussions that follow also assume that we are talking about a four day tournament and I am at a table of relatively unknown players.

Early in a tournament you want to see a reasonable number of flops, but unless you have a dominant hand, you want to see them when in a strong position. If you continuously play marginal hands from up front, they will finish you off over the long term. For example, if you always limp in with the smaller pairs from the earlier seats, you are not going to hit a set that often. And in many cases, somebody from behind you will raise, so it becomes too expensive to continually call those raises and be profitable. The same hand in late position are much stronger because you have an opportunity to see what happens before it is your turn to act, and the chances of a reraise are also substantially reduced.

My general philosophy in the earlier stages of a major tournament is to play only very good hands unless I have a positional advantage over my opponents. Even when in position with the marginal hands, I generally tend not to attack the pot preflop, preferring instead to keep the pot small until I am fairly sure that I am ahead in the hand. With a substantial stack, you run the risk of losing a lot of chips with a marginal hand in a confrontation for a large pot, particularly when out of position.

Early Position
My preferred starting hands are A-K or better and pairs 7-7 or better. I will also play A-Q on most occasions but it is a hand that you really have to be able to get away from after the flop. That can be tough for many people if the ace comes.

If you don't feel comfortable calling a raise with a hand, you should not be playing it from one of the early seats. I recommend staying away from all the trouble hands such as the small pairs, A-J, A-10, K-Q, and so on.

Middle Position
In one of the middle seats you have a little bit more air to breathe and can be somewhat more flexible with your starting hands because one-third of the field is gone and you now have less people behind you. However, you shouldn't overdo it and loosen up too much. You still need to be in there with good cards.

In middle position at such an early stage of the tournament, my starting hands are very similar to the my early position hands, but I feel more comfortable playing A-Q and pairs down to 5-5 and 6-6. If I am getting a lot of respect and can limp in without expecting a raise behind me, I will also play some of the higher suited connectors such as K-Q, 10-J and J-Q. However, these are cards that one really shouldn't call a raise with.

Late Position

When in late position, most of the time I actually prefer playing from the cutoff (the seat directly to the right of the button), because the other players often give you more credit for having a good hand. If you have raised from the cutoff, you have come out betting and have taken over the button. Further, you have made a bet knowing that the button could come back over the top of you. That gives you a lot of credibility. As a result, I would rather have a hand like A-J in the cutoff than A-Q on the button. In many cases, when you raise from the button, somebody with a hand like A-9 in the big blind will be far more likely to take you on than if you raise from the cutoff seat, because he is more likely to think that you are trying to steal.

From the last three seats at this stage of the tournament, I am looking for cards like A-10 or better and pairs 4-4 and above. In most cases, I will be raising if I am the first to come into the pot. I will also smooth call with suited connectors 7-6 or better if it will cost me no more than 2 to 3 percent of my stack.

I treat the suited connectors much like any draw. I don't want to build a pot and make people with better hands commit themselves to it until I am ahead. Therefore, initially, I would much rather just smooth call than attack the pot with them.

SPECIFIC HAND STRATEGY

A-A
If I'm first to act, I would normally make a small raise with pocket aces. If the blinds are $200/$400, my initial raise would be somewhere in the range of $900 to $1,000. That may vary depending on the players I'm up against and the money that is on the table. I think if you have a big hand you have to make money with it. I hate to wake up with aces and just win the blinds.

A-K
I'll often flat call with A-K. If somebody comes over the top of me I still have an option to call the raise or reraise him. If it's a player that will play any two cards and likes to come over the top, bluffing and playing a lot of hands, I'll be more likely to call a big bet. Even if you're up against an A-K, any two random cards have a 35 to 40 percent chance preflop.

Many players fall in love with A-K. They think it's a huge hand. The shrewd player is playing his A-K to see a flop before he invests too much money. In poker, you want to have a draw costing a small amount of money that will pay off for a lot of money when you hit your cards. When you go fishing, you don't throw in big fish to catch small ones.

I would be more likely to make a preflop raise in a cash game. In a tournament I see more value in playing A-K less aggressively from an early position. That way, it is easier to get away from the hand when faced with a big reraise or a terrible flop. Getting knocked out is less of a concern in cash games.

Medium Pairs: J-J, 10-10, 9-9
I normally make a small raise with a medium pair like J-J. After my initial raise, my next action depends on the person who calls or plays against me. I try to make a small raise to

indicate I have a big hand to get people out of there who have A-Q. It's not very likely that somebody will come back over the top with that hand, but if someone does, you have to make an adjustment.

Jacks, tens and nines are all hands that represent a grey area. Here's an example. In one hand, I had 9-9 and called a raise from the button. The flop came 4-5-9 with two diamonds.

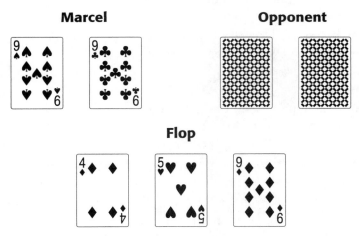

Marcel **Opponent**

Flop

My opponent had a diamond flush draw, and we ended up getting all our money in the middle. I won that particular hand, but the next day I lost all my money in a similar situation.

If your opponent hits his draw, it is irrelevant whether you have trips or two pair. Either way, you're out. Your winning percentages are better with trips of course. The best way to play those medium pairs in a heads-up situation is based largely on your read of the other player. Here are a couple of examples of how I played J-J differently.

Example 1

In this hand, a player raised $3,600 under the gun. I had $9,800 in chips and looked down to find J-J. I thought about it for a while and then, because of my positional advantage, just called, wanting to see the flop. The guy behind me in the small blind raised and then the first player moved all in. After some thought and observation, I said, "I'll put my money in." I thought these two players had a 10-10 and an A-Q or A-K. I moved all in and my hand held up. It's a beautiful thing when you're correct and your hand holds up. In poker, you can often be correct, but lose anyway when the wrong cards come out. Nevertheless, making the correct choice with a hand like J-J is often based on your feel for the situation.

Example 2

In another hand when I had J-J, there was a raise and a reraise in front of me, and I mucked my jacks. I knew that one of the players was tight. The two players showed 10-10 and A-A. It is really the same situation; however, it demonstrates why feel is so important. If the person is a solid player, why would you call a reraise or come over the top? You're probably going to need a better hand than J-J to get the chips.

Medium Pairs in Middle and Late Position

You don't want to hang yourself with middle pairs in situations where it is a crapshoot. The middle pairs are okay if you're a favorite and you know where you stand against a person who you think you can outplay. In important tournaments you want to avoid all-in bets that are close to even money. I don't want to be just a 10 percent favorite, or worse, a 10 percent dog. Why go all in with your A-K suited against a player that you think has 9-9 or 10-10, especially if you know you can outplay him later and accumulate chips without even seeing flops?

The same applies if you're the one with the low pair. It doesn't always make sense to call if you're going to get knocked out of the tournament, even though you may be getting correct pot odds. If I have a big edge over the players I am up against, why should I take part in a crapshoot that can knock me out?

If I play pocket tens in early position, I will often just call to see the flop, to find out what's happening. If I have position over a player to my right who bets, I may come over the top with a reraise. It depends on the chip count.

I play the later positions more aggressively and normally raise about three times the big blind in the last two or three seats. If I play a hand like 10-10 on the button, I just make a small raise so it doesn't look like I'm stealing. Here again, it depends on who's sitting there. Is it somebody who's aggressive or taking it personally? If so, you have to try to get into their head via the betting. When you make a bet, you're telling the other people a story. That is why it is so important to be focused on the game and the other players. You have to know how they're likely to react to the story you are telling.

Small Pairs: 7-7, 6-6, 5-5
Small pairs are a headache wherever you are sitting. In particular, I try to avoid playing small pairs like 3-3 or 4-4 unless I get really great value. Those hands are bad because the flop may come down with cards like J-7-4. You now have bottom set, but could easily be drawing to just one card if somebody has a higher set. It can also be a disaster when the flop comes J-10-4. You have to play the hand and you're going to get people who will call you, but you don't really know where you stand. They may have two pair or a hand like K-Q, but if they have J-J or 10-10 then you're nearly dead.

How and when I play small pairs has a lot to do with the size of my stack. If I have a small pair, I prefer not to invest much more than 5 to 7 percent of my stack trying to hit a set.

HAND MATCHUPS

The hand matchups below show the probability of success if played to the river. Percentages are rounded to the nearest whole percent. Unless stated otherwise, assume that all four cards are of different suits. In some cases the total percentage may not equal 100 percent because of a possible tie.

Given an Uncoordinated Flop of J-10-4

4-4 versus K-Q   74%   26%
(Three of a kind vs. open-ended straight draw)

4-4 versus J-10   83%   17%
(Three of a kind vs. two pair)

4-4 versus J-J   4%   96%
(Three of a kind vs. higher three of a kind)

Suited Connectors

Suited connectors are good hands to accumulate chips with. Let's say somebody in the first few positions makes a small raise. If the players behind me are solid players who are not overly aggressive without a good hand, I will normally call with suited connectors. However, if the people behind me are loose-aggressive players, I can't call because they're probably going to reraise with hands such as A-Q or A-J. Then I will have to call a reraise. Suddenly it isn't costing me 5 percent of my stack, but 25 percent. That's not what I want to invest with a 9-high hand. With suited connectors you want to invest as little as possible to see the flop, or have good pot odds and a lot of chips in front of you.

However, if a couple of players call a raise, you call, and then the big blind makes a raise that everybody calls, a lot of money is in the middle by the time it gets back around to you. If I have a lot of chips in front of me, I will definitely call, particularly since I figure the raiser has a big hand. Why not?

This type of situation happened to me recently when I had a 9-8 in my hand. Early in a tournament the pot was built to just over $1,000 in chips prior to the flop, which came 5-8-9.

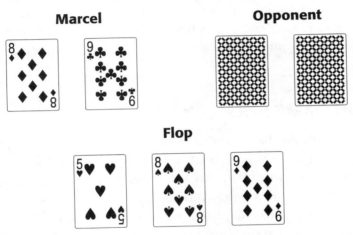

I bet $1,500 with top two pair. My opponent called my $1,500 and raised another $3,000. I then reraised all in for another $8,500. He called my all-in bet and turned over A-A.

If I had been the player with A-A, I would have been very suspicious of a 5-8-9 flop. I would not have raised $3,000; I would have either moved all in or folded because I couldn't control the hand. Why raise another $3,000 after my opponent had bet $1,500?

If I had totally bluffed into the A-A, I would have thrown the hand away, but if I had 7-6 for a straight—or 5-5, 8-8, 9-9, 9-5, or 9-8—I would push all my money into the middle. It is very clear. Also, the fact that I pushed all in made it extremely unlikely that I was on a straight draw with a J-10.

Another mistake that the player with the A-A made preflop was not raising enough. If you make a bigger raise, your opponent needs a bigger hand to call, and you know what you're up against. If you only make a small raise preflop, any number of hands may call and you still don't know where you stand.

Unfortunately, another ace came on the river and he knocked me out of the tournament. Otherwise I would have been the early stage chip leader and he would have been sitting on a small stack trying to play tight poker as the blinds and antes went up.

CASH GAME STRATEGY

Your best profits lie in games where people are being sociable and having a good time. Players tend to play a bit looser in that type of environment and are definitely less focused. If you are trying to make money, you are far better off playing with people who are just there to have fun. If they're recreational players who only have a few hours to play after work or before a show, they will be far less likely to wait two hours for aces and will be mixing it up more to get some action. Meanwhile, the guy who is making a living out of it is going to wait for better hands.

If you find a table you like and expect to be playing there for a few hours, it is best to create a pleasant ambiance. You can play a little bit loose and go after small pots at first, and perhaps end up losing some money. But eventually, you can change gears and create a big edge. Just because you are being friendly and having fun doesn't mean you can't play to win. Often, people prefer to be social rather than cautious and will play a lot of hands so they can be a part of the camaraderie you have helped create.

It is similar to a group of people going for a coffee. You may rather have a nice glass of orange juice, but you actually have a coffee because that is what your friends are doing. The same will occur in a cash game if people are enjoying themselves; they will play hands that they shouldn't. Being aware of that phenomenon is one of the best ways to make money in cash games. The big difference between you and the other players is that you are going to make sure that the percentages are in your favor when the big money goes in.

TELLS

In poker your read on other people is very important. You must be aware of how they play in different situations, how much money they have in front of them, how they behave, and what kinds of decisions they have made in the past. As Mike Caro says in his book on tells, you have to be aware of the player who is shaking his head like he's having a hard time after seeing his cards and then makes a big bet. You won't pick up that type of information unless you are watching the other players.

You only need a few hands to know how a person plays and what type of cards he is likely to have in certain situations. If you have just come to the table and don't know how anybody plays, it's a crapshoot anyway because a better player can have any cards when he bets. Once you play with opponents for two or three hours, you have a read on them. You know what they're thinking. You know what type of cards they're playing and how they act.

On the other hand, people have a hard time getting information from me because I can sing, dance or act like I'm happy when

I'm making a bluff. Maybe I'm bluffing, maybe I'm not. I keep changing. I can sing when I have it and sing when I don't have it. People get frustrated watching me, trying to observe if I have a tell or a particular play in mind. Sometimes I don't even look at my cards. How could anybody possibly get a read on me in that situation?

Here is an unusual tell that I noticed in a tournament. A player in the first few seats made a substantial raise and then I made a reraise from the button that would put him all in. While the two players in the small and big blind were deciding what to do, the original bettor ordered a mixed-fruit cocktail from the waitress that was clearly going to take a while to make. If he called my bet, there was no real way of knowing if he was going to be around 15 minutes from then as he would be all in and could have been knocked out of the tournament. What he effectively did was tell the two players yet to act that he was not going to call my bet. That' was a clear tell.

Physical Tells

You'll see many of the traditional tells that Mike Caro talks about in his excellent book, *Caro's Book of Poker Tells*. Many people will look away, but keep a hand on their cards when they're strong. They want to act like they're not interested in playing, but at the same time are worried that the dealer may take their cards. Another tell you often see is people looking at their hands and suddenly straightening up in their chair and becoming more interested in the game. They're clearly indicating that they want to play.

In the big tournaments, when people start to cut their chips over and over while they're thinking, they want to be in the spotlight and get lots of attention. That is the moment you know they have a big hand and are putting on a show. Everybody likes to have a lot of attention at the moment when they're going well. They particularly like to be filmed raking in a big pot.

MONEY MANAGEMENT

Recommended Bankroll

I recommend that a person trying to play tournaments for a living should have 100 times the size of the entry fee as his bankroll. For example, if he is playing $1,000 events, he should have at least a $100,000 bankroll. When playing tournaments you have a lot of big swings.

If you want to be a professional player you have to be aware that you have costs you can predict and also those that come up unexpectedly. People who don't play poker have to be prepared financially for expenses caused by, say, a car accident or bad health. The same theory applies to poker. You must have enough money to cover both your regular expenses such as tournament entries and also enough to cover the long periods of losses that sometimes occur.

If you consider yourself to be one of the top hundred players in a typical five-hundred-player event, statistically you are only going to win less than one out of every one hundred events. It may take an even longer time to win! Even the very top players can easily go for a whole year without a significant win. A lot of money will be going out over that period, and you have to be financially prepared. One way to cushion the impact is to play cash games to subsidize your weekly tournament expenses.

Many people think that $100,000 is enough to play $5,000 or $10,000 events, but it just isn't. Nobody can consistently beat a field of 500 players. Even the best of us will have periods where our costs are significantly higher than our winnings. My personal expectation is to win about one out of every twenty tournaments that I enter and, on average, be in the money three to five times out of every twenty. But like I said, there will often be long dry spells.

FINAL WORDS OF WIZDOM

Advice For Players Trying to Become Semi-Professionals

Avoid playing hands that you personally have the most trouble with until you feel comfortable playing them with force. Lots of players have trouble playing hands like A-J, A-10, K-9 and small to medium pairs. They often lose a lot of money with them because they're not comfortable playing them hard enough. Put another way: If you can't go to war, don't start one.

For example, if you hold 7-7 in early position, you are generally not very happy because it is a tough hand to play. If you make a small raise and are reraised, you have a difficult decision to make. If you call the reraise you'll be out of position for the rest of the hand. You are often better off making a solid preflop raise. In doing so you are also taking a lot more risk. If you are not comfortable dealing with the increased risk, you may be better off not playing the hand. My advice is to avoid playing hands out of position that you are not comfortable playing strongly. An alternative is to just call preflop rather than make a half-hearted raise.

The biggest trouble hand for average players is A-K because it looks so strong. Big Slick is definitely the most overplayed hand in poker so if you are a new player trying to get better, I urge you not to go crazy with it. This advice may save a lot of chips.

A lot of times when you hold A-K and people call or come over the top of you, you'll be up against a pair such as 9-9 where you are at least 10 percent behind. You're hoping your opponent has A-Q or A-J. Often, somebody will make a stand in a tournament with a hand such as 10-10 or 9-9. They will come back over you with an all-in bet, leaving you with nothing but a draw.

On the other side of the coin, in Monte Carlo I recently saw a professional play a 5-4 incredibly well. He won a huge hand from me when I was the one with A-K. Who am I to say what a trouble hand is! Each individual has to decide which hands he has the most trouble with and learn how to play them the best way. He must also be cautious of hands such as Q-8 that will give him something other than the nuts when he hits the flop. It is easy to be thrilled when the flop comes 9-10-J and you make your straight, only to lose everything when your opponent has the higher straight. Sooner or later you do walk into those types of situations.

In summary, if you're trying to improve your game, I would recommend focusing on hand selection, and above all, only playing cards that you feel comfortable with.

> **WD:** The memory in my recorder was low and the chatter from the morning crowd at the café was growing to an uncomfortable pitch so we finally concluded our discussion. I bid Marcel goodbye as he went off to prepare for the upcoming main event. As he left, a young boy ran up to him and asked for an autograph. Then another admirer approached who wanted to shake his hand. I couldn't help thinking at the time how some people are just born to stardom. Marcel Luske is definitely one of those people.

KATHY LIEBERT

"Poker Kat"

Career Tournament Earnings Exceeding $4,200,000
Winner, Party Poker Million Limit Hold'em, 2002
Second place, WSOP $1,500 Limit Hold'em, 2003
Winner, WSOP $1,500 Limit Hold'em Shootout, 2004
Third place, WPT Borgata Poker Open, Atlantic City, 2005
Winner, Poker Royal Battle of the Sexes, Las Vegas, 2005
Second place, WPT Foxwoods Poker Classic $5,000
No-Limit Hold'em, 2006
Third place, WSOP Circuit event, Harrah's San Diego 2006
Winner, Las Vegas Open $2,500 No-Limit Hold'em, 2007
Winner, Las Vegas Open-NPL, The Venetian, Las Vegas, 2007
Number One on the Women's All-time Tournament Money List

KATHY LIEBERT

Sitting Down With Kathy

On March 4, 2005, the stage was set for a classic poker battle of wit and strategy between some of the world's best poker pros. The Poker Royal Battle of the Sexes was about to start and the event would be filmed and broadcast on the GSN cable network. According to some, the sides were unevenly matched. The three top point scorers from each of the female and male teams over the previous episodes would now face off at the final table of six players to compete for a $130,000 prize pool. During the previous games, the men had dominated play, but it appeared that they had become overconfident.

When the battle was over, Amir Vahedi, Antonio Esfandiari and Layne Flack all stood at the rail wondering how they had been dispatched so easily. Kathy Liebert had been able to capitalize on her opponents' aggression, coming from behind to take first place in yet another tournament, her prediction realized. She said, "I let them think I had a poor hand. I knew if they smelled weakness, they would try to bluff me. I had the nuts! The guys put all their chips in when I had the superior hand. Their egos got the best of them."

"Poker Kat" was born in Tennessee, grew up on Long Island, and these days, when not on the road playing tournaments, spends most of her time in Las Vegas. When Kathy graduated from college with a degree in business and finance and applied to Dun & Bradstreet for a job as an analyst, she never imagined that life's journey would eventually follow a distinctly different path.

Unhappy in the 8-to-6 investment world and tired of staring at a desk crammed with company reports, Kathy decided to take her mother's advice and find a vocation that she truly enjoyed. "The money will follow," her mother told her, and it certainly did! Combining her cool confidence and business acumen with a highly competitive nature, patience and quick-witted math skills, she would go on to become a world-renowned poker player, WSOP gold bracelet winner, and the first female player to win a tournament with a $1 million first place payout.

After leaving Dun & Bradstreet, Kathy ended up in Colorado in 1991 where she sold automatic teller machines for a while before finally discovering her talent for poker at the $5 limit tables in the Rocky Mountain towns of Blackhawk and Central City. In 1994, on a trip to Las Vegas, she entered her first tournament and was immediately successful, finishing second in an Omaha high-low event and then duplicating that success a week later in a Texas hold'em tournament, bringing home a total of $34,000 for seven days' work. It didn't take long to realize that poker offered a new and exceptionally bright future. She moved to Las Vegas soon thereafter to play as a full-time professional and is one of only a handful of women to be consistently successful at a high level.

Let's hear what Kathy has to say…

THE MAKINGS OF A POKER WIZARD

Being focused, having a lot of discipline, and possessing a good understanding of hand values are probably the most important characteristics that a player needs to be successful, but there are additional elements that are important as well.

Focus

Focus means watching how your opponents play and getting to know them so you can make the appropriate adjustments to your game. Knowing when to be aggressive, when to be patient, when to be solid and when to grab the chips are all a part of observation. It is what people call feel, but feel is what you get from paying attention. They're both combined.

When you focus, you also start to pick up physical tells. If you are paying attention you'll notice when players show signs of weakness or strength. Sometimes it is with their hands, sometimes it is with their eyes. Often, it is easy to see when somebody is giving up just by the way he looks. At other times, it becomes obvious when a player is very interested in the pot. If you see somebody that does not like his hand, obviously you are more likely to attack that person than if you were not paying attention. Through focus and observation you also see the types of hands your opponents play and what they do with them. Knowing whether your opponents can fold to a reraise or will almost always call when someone reraises is valuable information.

Watching how your opponents play provides the information you need to beat them. If they're overly aggressive, or are playing a lot of weak hands, you are going to play differently than if they only see a flop every two hours. You understand what kind of cards they're more likely to hold, how they're playing them, and can adjust your strategy accordingly. Against very tight players, you may be more likely to try to get them to lay down a hand or rob their blinds. If another person is playing very loose, you can change your starting requirements. To be successful, it is important to make adjustments based not only on your cards but on your opponents as well.

Gut Feeling
All the best players have a gut feeling for when it is appropriate to make a play and when not to. Gut feeling is based on focus. It is not just a sixth sense. People with a good feel have watched and carefully observed the game. They know how the other people are playing. The best poker players are picking up a lot of information all the time, which is where the *feel* comes from. They are disciplined enough to wait for the right opportunities and the correct hands.

Understanding Hand Values
Knowing the value of specific hands and the odds of being dealt those hands is also important, especially in limit games.

A good understanding of the pot odds you're getting to make a particular play and your likelihood of success are key factors in many of your decisions. For example, you would not want to draw to a straight if it will cost you the size of the pot, unless you were expecting a big payoff.

Draws and Implied Odds

If you have an open-ended straight draw or four cards to a flush on the flop, your chances of making your hand by the river are about one in three. If you are heads-up and your opponent makes a pot-size bet on the flop, you are not getting the correct pot odds you need to make the call unless it is possible to extract a substantially larger amount from your opponent if your card comes. High implied odds sometimes make calling or raising a more interesting proposition. In no-limit, you can probably expect another large bet from your opponent on the turn if you flat call on the flop. Thus, in heads-up play without a big pot, playing a drawing hand is generally unprofitable unless you expect to get paid off in a big way on the river. —WD

An Ability to Read Your Opponents' Strength

I don't believe it is necessary to exactly pinpoint my opponents' hands. Often it is more of a sense that they're strong or weak. If you narrow it down too much and put them on A-A or K-K or whatever, and you are wrong, it can be a costly mistake. From time to time you can be specific, but it is not essential.

For example, suppose your opponent raises preflop and an ace comes on the flop. If I pick up some sort of verbal or non-verbal indication that he hated that ace, I may bet into him. If he just calls, I can narrow down his hand. He had a hand before the flop that he liked when he raised, and just called my bet when the ace hit. Does he have a big ace? I wouldn't think so. He is more likely to have K-K or Q-Q. That is the type of reasoning that I use.

In general, you should develop a sense of the range of hands that your opponents likely hold, and the reactions you can expect from them if you are correct. Let's say a solid player looks at his cards and I surmise that he doesn't love his hand. I may just see something in his eyes. Now he raises from an early position. What does that mean? Well, he has some sort of hand that he thought was worth raising with, but he does not love it. Because I know this player, I may come to the conclusion that he has a hand such as A-J. People are amazed sometimes when you call their raises.

Play People, Not Just Your Cards
In no-limit, playing people is often more important than just playing the cards you hold. I certainly do both, regularly waiting for good hands, but if a situation arises where I can play the people rather than the cards I will do that as well.

In order to play people you must have a good sense of how they play. If you don't have a lot of experience or a good understanding of what the others at your table are thinking, a solid approach of just playing cards makes a lot of sense. On the other hand, if you have a good feel for how people play and can sense weakness, you can play more hands and play the people more. However, for average players or beginners, waiting for good cards is more important then trying to read opponents. Trying to get too creative can get beginners into a lot of trouble.

TOURNAMENT STRATEGY

I describe my playing style as solid-aggressive, which is another way of saying that I am selectively aggressive. It is the style that most poker professionals use. Certainly, there are some players that are more aggressive than others, or more solid than others. In general, I don't play very many hands and when I do play I usually play them aggressively. I do occasionally mix it up and vary my play. That's a necessity so that you're not completely predictable. Most top players pick their spots to be aggressive, they don't play a lot of hands, but when they do play, they try to pick the *right* person to play against.

I am more selective and patient than some of the top players. I am not super-aggressive, always trying to pick up every pot or being ultra-creative. I wait for my spots and make my moves when the timing is right.

My style during a tournament varies depending on the other players at the table, how many chips each player has, and my image. I tend to play more solid, patient poker early on. I play more like I am in a cash game during the first few levels of a tournament. Sometimes I will limp in with some hands that are speculative, but for the most part I am not trying to steal the blinds. I am just watching how the other people play and waiting for optimal situations. Later on, as the blinds get bigger, I am looking for places to pick up some blinds. Occasionally, I will also be going after the chips of players that I think are overly aggressive.

There are no absolutes in poker. How you play during different stages of a tournament will be influenced by many factors. The cards you get is simply one of those factors. Sometimes it just depends on how you view the other players and how they view you.

Common Tournament Mistakes

The weaker players generally call too often. If they have a good hand, they usually call instead of betting or raising. Another common mistake is not being able to fold hands. For example, it is often necessary to fold top pair with a weak kicker, but weak opponents play those types of hands too often and then lose a lot more than they should if they hit the flop.

Frequent Preflop Errors

The biggest mistake I see people make before the flop is calling with weak hands, especially the trap hands such as an ace with no kicker; or hands such as Q-J that are often dominated if they hit. Limping or just calling preflop can sometimes be a good play, but for inexperienced players it is usually a big mistake. Playing weak hands out of position will usually end up costing you chips. Occasionally, there is nothing wrong with limping in and mixing it up, but you shouldn't be doing it with weak hands out of position.

AGGRESSION

A lot of the top tournament players play an aggressive game, but it is not the only characteristic you need to be a good player. Sometimes, if I am playing against somebody that is overly aggressive, a passive style works better. When I get a big hand, I can check to them and let them be aggressive. Often, they will hang themselves. However, checking and calling is not usually the best strategy. If you are not raising a fair number of times trying to pick up those pots, you are probably not going to be a big winner in the long run.

Specific Aggressive Opportunities

If a loose-aggressive player bets into a flop that was unlikely to have helped him, I would not necessarily reraise to try to take away the pot in a no-limit tournament. Don't forget that just because a person makes a continuation bet it doesn't mean that he has nothing. However, if I think he has nothing and I also have nothing, raising is probably the right play.

If I have a big hand that is not vulnerable to a card coming off, such as a straight or trips, calling might be a better option because I don't mind facing another bet. If I think that the flop did not hit my opponent, I may just call hoping that my opponent makes a pair on the turn or keeps bluffing.

However, if I have a hand that is vulnerable or weak and/or I think my opponent is weak, raising on the flop is usually a better play than just calling. I don't want to give my opponent a free chance to improve. If I wait until the turn to raise, it may cost a lot more because I have then called the bet on the flop and my opponent may bet again on the turn. At that stage, a much larger investment will be required to come back over the top of him.

The Abandoned Pot

Sometimes you can just tell when the pot has been abandoned. When you sense that everyone is weak, try to benefit from the situation. The more people involved in the pot, the less likely it is that a bet is going to work. But sometimes, even when four or five people check ahead of you, a bet can take the pot if you sense they're all very weak.

How much you have to bet to pick up a pot when the other players are clearly disinterested varies from hand to hand and, to a large degree, is also dependent on the size of the pot. If you decide to bluff, you want to bet as little as possible to pick up the pot. That way, if you are wrong and someone has a hand, it is not going to cost you too much. In general, as long as neither you nor any of your opponents have a short stack, I would say about half the pot is the right bet, but sometimes it can be less.

Some weak players will call a big bet before the flop and fold for a relatively small bet after the flop. Those players are giving up a lot. If I don't think they hit their hand, I will make a smaller bet because I don't have to risk as much. If your opponents don't have anything, they're going to fold; and if they do have something, you're not going to lose too much.

Your bet should also be based on how many opponents you are up against, your hand, and what you think they have. If I know that my opponent is likely to have a straight draw or flush draw, I will normally bet the amount that makes it incorrect for him to call. Some players still call because they don't realize they're getting incorrect odds, so you have to bet the whole pot if you want them to throw their hands away. At other times, you can bet half the pot and they're still getting the wrong odds, but it looks more enticing for them to call.

Position Plays

Early in a tournament, let's say that a reasonably tight player makes a standard raise of three times the big blind from an early position and I call. The flop comes 5-5-9, with two cards of the same suit. The raiser bets half the pot. How I play here depends on my opponent.

If a solid player is raising from under the gun, I will usually fold my hand unless I am very strong. If it is a really tight player who makes the initial bet and I then raise, he may put me on an overpair and I can get him to fold. But in general, if I am going to make a position play, I'll pick an aggressive player who is less likely to have a hand than a fairly solid player. In addition, if I'm going to bluff, it is much better to reraise somebody who is coming in from a later position, not an early position. The early position aggressor will be far more likely to have a good hand, especially if he's a solid player.

KATHY LIEBERT

Many pros are very aggressive and creative, but I don't particularly want to make outrageous bluffs and just hope for the best. If you have J-J against A-K and make that type of play, at best your odds are around 50-50. If you are right, and he has A-K, A-Q or A-J, then maybe you can get him to lay down the hand. But if your opponent actually holds Q-Q, K-K, or A-A, then you're in a lot of trouble. On the other hand, if you're up against somebody who is a habitual raiser in late position, then you can reraise before the flop and probably take it away from him a lot of the time. I will certainly make that kind of play on occasion.

Some players will call a bet after the flop with virtually nothing, just to see what the preflop raiser does on the turn. If they know that the original bettor may put in a continuation bet and then shut down on the turn if he doesn't have a hand, it is sometimes possible to make a call with nothing and then bet the turn if your opponent checks. However, I try not to get involved in lots of situations just so I can bluff—they can turn into expensive mistakes. Usually I bluff because I have some sort of hand that I have missed, or because I can tell that my opponents are weak.

Taking a Pot Away When You Sense Weakness

In a recent tournament, I called preflop with two sixes, and a player behind me raised. I called the raise and the flop came down king high. I wasn't sure whether I had the best hand, and I checked. My opponent checked behind me. After a non-threatening turn card, I checked again and she bet. I am now saying to myself, "Okay, if this person really has the king, I think she would have bet the flop. Now she is betting even though she has shown weakness twice." So, I check-raised. It looked to her as though I was slowplaying a big hand and she folded. I just sensed that my opponent did not have the hand she was representing and I made a play. Some people might check three kings in this spot, but again it's a matter of focusing and watching the other players. You must have a sense of how your opponents play if you want to be good at poker.

STARTING HAND CONCEPTS

> Unless stated otherwise, all of the situations discussed by the Wizards in the Starting Hand Concepts and Specific Hand Strategy sections are assumed to be at a full table, during the third level of a tournament. The blinds are $100/$200, and you have an average stack of around $11,000 in chips. It is also assumed that the players are displaying a moderate level of aggression and appear to be playing reasonably well.

When I am first to enter a pot, I come in with a raise almost 80 percent of the time. My starting requirements are primarily based on a read of the people behind me rather than a formula that is set in stone. The following is a rough outline of my starting hands, but they will vary a lot based on who I am up against and how many chips I have.

Early Position
I want to have a pretty big hand when I come in from one of the early positions, usually A-Q or better. While hands such as A-10 and K-Q look like good hands, they are often trap hands; that is, hands that are likely to be dominated when you get action.

With regard to pairs, it depends partially on the number of chips I have and the other players at the table. Small pairs should often be folded in early position if you're somewhat low on chips. If I have a larger stack, I lower my starting requirements. I obviously play all the high pairs, A-A, K-K and Q-Q, but with a large stack I can also play medium pairs 7-7 through J-J. When I play a small or medium pair, or hands such as A-J or weaker, I'll normally fold if I get raised.

If you don't have enough chips to fold your hand and still be left with enough chips to be competitive if someone either raises or reraises, you are better off either folding or moving in with those hands before the flop. That decision depends largely on your stack size. If I have less than ten times the big blind, I will be moving in with medium pairs, big pairs, A-Q and A-K.

Middle Position
In one of the middle seats I may reduce my requirements to include A-J, A-10, K-Q, and small pairs.

Late Position
In the later positions, the hands I play are very dependent on who is in the blinds and how likely they are to defend. If the players to act after me are really tight, I am going to come in with a much larger range of hands. If they're loose-aggressive and are reraising a lot, my requirements will be higher, similar to the starting hands that I want from one of the early positions.

SPECIFIC HAND STRATEGY

A-A
Assuming I am the first person to bet and I am going to play a hand, regardless if it is A-A or not, I generally start by making a standard raise, about three times the big blind. I will occasionally slowplay aces from one of the early positions if I have very aggressive players behind me, but it usually is not the best way to play the hand.

Normally with A-A, you are better off raising and being able to reraise if your opponent actually has a hand. If he is aggressive, he may reraise you even without a premium hand. On the other hand, if you slowplay A-A, get raised, and then you reraise, your opponent will be more likely to fold the hand. Sometimes you make less when you slowplay even though you get the raise you are looking for. In my opinion, it is better to come into the hand with a standard raise from the very beginning.

K-K
Preflop, I play K-K the same way as A-A. I don't think I have ever folded K-K before the flop. There might be a situation where I could, but it would not be because I was afraid of getting knocked out by a bad beat. It would only be because I thought that particular player would not move in with less than K-K. Then I may fold, but generally with A-A and K-K, you are not going to get me off that hand. If you have me beaten, so be it.

Q-Q
Pocket queens are trickier to play than aces and kings because your hand is more vulnerable. It is also a difficult hand to fold preflop as it is the third-best starting hand, but in the face of a reraise, you may be up against A-A, K-K, or A-K.

I usually play Q-Q strongly, but if I face a strong reraise, I can get away from it when the chips are deep. Against aggressive opponents, I'm probably willing to go all in with the hand, but against a tight player who moves all in, it is normally prudent to fold when you have enough chips to wait for a better situation.

A-K
When I have a playable hand, whether it is up front, middle or late, I raise about three times the big blind. Certainly, I will

sometimes mix it up and just call with A-K as well. I don't think just calling is a terrible play because somebody behind you might raise with A-Q or A-J. They might not be as likely to play them if you have raised, but in general, I don't like limping in. I will normally come in for a raise.

If a player to my left with an average stack makes a small reraise, I might call with A-K to see a flop. If he makes a big raise, more likely than not, I will either move all in or fold. On the whole I don't like calling a substantial raise with Big Slick because I will end up hitting my cards on the flop only about a third of the time. Continually calling big preflop raises just to see if you can hit your cards on the flop is not a great way to play no-limit poker.

If I make a bet and am reraised by a loose player that I think is probably not going to call, or if I think I have the best hand, I may move all in with A-K. Alternatively, in a tournament where I have a lot of chips compared to the blinds, I might be more likely to think, "Okay, you know what? I can wait for a better spot." Later, when the blinds are often large relative to my stack, I may not have the luxury of waiting for something better to come along. In other words, as the blinds increase in size relative to stack size, A-K becomes more valuable. I have gone broke with A-K many times, but the hand is good enough to gamble with at the right time.

A-Q

I don't like A-Q as much as A-K, but you play it almost the same way as Big Slick. If I am up front and first to act, I make the same standard raise with A-Q that I do with A-K. If there is a raise and I think the player is out of line or I don't think he has a big hand, moving in with A-Q can be a good play late in a tournament if I have a short stack. Moving all in would be questionable if we both had a lot of chips.

J-J

Pocket jacks is a tough hand to play. Depending on the circumstances, just limping in with J-J is not a bad way to play. If a player subsequently raises, you can make a decision whether to call, reraise or fold. It is a tricky situation. There are times when I have raised and then folded when I was reraised. There are times when I have moved all in, and other times when I have called and seen the flop. A lot depends on your chip situation and your read on the player or players you are up against. If the blinds are $100/$200 and I have $2,000 in chips, I am not getting away from J-J. However, if I have $10,000 in chips and the blinds are $100/$200, it is a lot easier to get away from the hand.

If a solid player to my right makes a preflop raise, often I will just call with J-J. As usual, it depends on the situation and how much it costs to play. If the blinds are $50/$100 and somebody makes it $300, it is an easy call with $10,000 in my stack. I'll see the flop. If my opponent checks on the flop, I am probably going to bet. If he bets, I'll usually raise. A lot of poker is feeling out the situation and getting a read on the other players, but in general J-J is a hand that is playable. You are not usually going to throw it away before the flop, but if you raise and get reraised, you can fold.

9-9, 8-8, 7-7

Suppose an opponent to my right is playing a lot of hands and makes a standard raise from up front. I have sevens, eights or nines in late position. How I play depends on the player and the chips. If I have a lot of chips compared to the blinds—for example, $10,000 when the blinds are $50/$100—a call is reasonable to see if I can hit a set on the flop.

If a solid player that I respect raises in early position, and I have a small stack or an average stack that is ten to twenty times the size of the blinds, I am going to fold my hand. If my stack is much larger in relationship to the blinds, I have a lot more flexibility and can consider other options.

As I said before, calling a big preflop raise to try to hit the flop is normally not good poker strategy. You have to determine whether your pair is big enough preflop to gamble with it. If the raise is small, you can call, of course; and if you hit your set, that's great. If you don't improve on the flop, you can get away from it. If you are calling a big raise, it is very important to know what you are going to do with your hand after the flop if you don't improve.

Now suppose you are facing a raise to your right, you reraise with your small pair, and your opponent reraises. Forget about getting a chance to hit your set—you have to dump it. If your opponent is raising from late position, you can reraise with the smaller pairs when you think he is weak. But if someone raises from an early or middle position and you have no reason to believe that he's weak, calling is a better play when you have a big stack.

Suited Connectors: 5-6, 6-7, 8-9

I won't play small suited connectors unless I have decent chips compared to the blinds, though I'll sometimes limp in or raise as a deceptive play. If I have not been playing many hands, I'm perceived as a tight player, and if the players in the blinds don't call a lot, I might make a standard raise with suited connectors just like I would with A-A or K-K. If somebody has come in raising, or if I don't have a lot of chips compared to the blinds, I won't normally play suited connectors. You can't afford to make speculative moves like that when losing those chips would put a serious hurt on your stack.

CASH GAMES

Tournament players don't generally do as well in live cash games because they play too loose. In a cash game you are not under the pressure of huge blinds; therefore you can wait for good hands and play a solid, patient game. In tournaments you are often under more pressure and have to steal the blinds or make more aggressive plays because if you don't, the blinds will eat you up.

Making Money Consistently in Cash Games

The best way to make money in cash games is to fold weak or moderately weak hands in early position. Play the above-average hands and play them strongly. If you get K-J or something like that under the gun, you don't have to play it, you can just throw it away. You don't want to call too much and play as many marginal hands as most players do. If you want to be a winning player, you need to play selectively so that when you do play, you have the best of it. If opponents want to try and outdraw you, make them pay for the privilege. If you are in there with marginal hands all the time, you'll be in too many situations where you wind up giving away your money.

Playing Live Sit-and-Go Satellites

A live single-table satellite for a main event is a winner-take-all event. It is best to play fairly solid poker early on and wait for a good hand. Later, you have to play more aggressively, but you must adjust to the fact that there is only *one* winner. As the field gets smaller, you'll have to play more hands. You are there to get all the chips, so you are looking for hands that you can commit all your chips to.

At the final table of a large tournament you get paid substantially more for every spot that you advance, so you might play a more solid style and pick your spots to be aggressive since survival becomes more important. In a winner-take-all-tourney, just moving up the ladder is not going to do you any good. You have to be willing to risk your chips more often to be the last player standing.

TELLS

Physical Tells

Amateurs often display significant tells. When they look at their cards, sometimes you immediately know if they like them or not. A common tell you see is people betting aggressively or forcefully when they're weak, trying to show extra strength. And if they bet lightly or softly, they're strong, trying to look scared to lure you into the pot.

When people shrug their shoulders and act like they don't like their hand, but still raise, they're giving off another common tell. They're trying to act weak, but are actually strong. In general, when they are acting weak, they're strong.

Some tells are very subtle. Something as simple as an eye movement can let you know that a person likes or dislikes his cards. Maybe he rolls his eyes and shows disinterest, gives a little bit of a frown, or moves his mouth in a way that says he's disappointed.

Some players bet their chips differently or sit up and look around more when they have a hand. When they don't have a hand, they're clearly disinterested, as though they're just getting ready to fold—which they often do. Everyone has different types of tells and the more you pay attention and watch them, the more you'll work out what they mean.

Betting Patterns

There are two types of betting patterns to look for. One is the way your opponents physically bet their chips; the other is how much they bet and when. Do they tend to underbet the pot when they have a big hand and overbet when they have a weak hand? Will they always raise? Some people who raise before the flop always bet after the flop. If you pick up on that pattern, you are less likely to give them credit for a good hand the next time they bet after the flop. On the other hand, many players will reliably check when they don't have anything. If they have a good hand, they bet in a particular way. A lot of people develop a strategy where they're making the same types of bets all the time. Some people are trying to rope you in with small bets. Other people are trying to get you out with big bets. If you are observant of your opponents' betting patterns, you can adjust your strategy accordingly and make the right plays.

PLAYING ONLINE

There are a lot of attractive tournaments online. Many get over 1,000 entrants, pay 200 or more places, and represent great value. It is also worth playing some sit-and-gos because they're a good way to reduce your risk and expenses while you practice playing final tables.

Single-Table Online Tournaments

One-table tournaments online usually pay three places, so it makes sense to play more conservatively and cautiously early on. Normally, a lot of players will bust out early. Therefore, all you have to do is sit back and play solid poker during the early rounds. If you get a hand, play it, but you don't need to take undue risk. Before you know it, four or five people will be out. If you can then win one or two big hands, you can make the top three fairly often. As a pro, if I play ten single-table tournaments online, I would expect to make the top three places five or six times and win three out of ten times.

Online Strategy

I play selectively aggressive online and bluff less than I would in live games. Many Internet players are not experienced, so making a lot of fancy plays, bluffing a lot and being super creative is not the best way to be successful. Playing solid poker and waiting for the best hand is a better online strategy.

A lot of players are looser online; this means they play more marginal hands. It's easier for a person to make a bet against you when they can't see you across a table than it is in person. It is usually correct to call more often online and, in general, many players do tend to call more online because they don't know who they're up against.

STATE OF MIND

Dealing With a String of Losses

When you are trying to deal with a string of losses, it is usually best to take time off, play less, or compete in smaller buy-in satellites to get a win or two under your belt. If you can't seem to get results, you should change your game slightly, reevaluate what you are doing, and talk about poker with other players to figure out if you're doing something wrong. Maybe you're giving away tells or you have an obvious weakness in your game. If your friends are knowledgeable and are watching you, sometimes they'll pick up on something that you are unaware of.

If you are running bad but feel like you are playing well, keep playing—your luck will change. Remember that unlucky streaks are as much a part of the game as are lucky streaks. You just have to wait it out.

The Closer You Get, the More Frustrating It Is!

You can go for a long time without winning a tournament. It is very frustrating to go for a while without winning, getting very close to the major payouts, knowing that had you played just a little better you would have made a lot of money. For example, in 2004, I had a sixth - and an eighth-place finish in large tournaments and came between tenth and thirteenth a number of times. Even though I had a couple of wins, I did not have a great year overall. There is a huge difference between the payout for eighth place and first place, especially in a big tournament where $1 million is achievable.

Remember, You're Not Invincible

When you win, it is easy to get a bit of a high feeling and believe you're invincible. But the danger is that you can lose focus for the next couple of tournaments. You don't want to be in a situation where you're gambling more, talking more and having a good time; in other words, not really focusing on the game. Certainly, if I try to play a tournament the day after a big win, I might not be 100 percent. Feeling the high from a big finish the day before can be an advantage as well—going in there with no fear and feeling good—but you can also feel tired and be less focused on the game. I believe I'm at a slight disadvantage if I too play soon after a big win.

Think Before Making an Important Decision

I keep reminding myself is that, although it is okay to act on first instinct, it is always a good idea to take sufficient time before making an important decision on a hand.

When big decisions come up, I find that some players go on pure instinct and act too quickly. When they do that, it's often a mistake. Stay focused and take your time on every decision. Maintaining focus all the way through the tournament and not acting rashly or impulsively is one of the most important things that I have learned. Even if your gut tells you that you are making the correct play, take twenty or thirty seconds before you act. You may come up with a valuable alternative play that ends up saving your tournament.

Be Positive When You Play

You must be ready to play your best game when you enter an event. If you don't feel confident you should just wait for another tournament. You have to be willing to play the game knowing that you may lose, but trying to do your best. Thinking you can win gives you an edge, but feeling defeated before you sit down puts you at a big disadvantage.

Maintain Focus and Control

If you have to lay down a series of great hands or take a couple of bad beats, you have to maintain your composure and play your normal game. It is very easy to play recklessly or differently out of frustration. It has happened to me and it has happened to a lot of great players; in fact, just about all of them. You have to put the mental stress of bad beats and big losses behind you as quickly as you can.

One option is to say, "Okay, I know people might think I am going to go on tilt," then wait for a big hand and try to act as if you really are steaming so that you get action.

It is not a bad idea to just walk away from the table for a while and take a breather to get some fresh air. If you are really steaming, it is better to miss a couple of hands than to make a mistake because you are on tilt. You may lose a blind or two, but if you don't take a break, you may lose more than that— your stack could get crippled or you might even get eliminated. The best players control their emotions, put bad hands behind them, and wait for good cards.

MONEY MANAGEMENT

Bankroll Requirements

To play tournaments on a regular basis, you need a big bankroll. More often than not you are going to lose. How much a bankroll you need varies a lot because the fields are so big these days, meaning the volatility has increased substantially. In a field of 1,000 or 2,000 players, you'll have a lot more misses than hits. In the smaller fields, your odds of getting there are higher.

There are a lot of factors involved, but if you only have a $20,000 bankroll, you don't have enough money to be playing $500 or $1,000 tournaments. Tournament poker involves a lot of risk and is much too volatile for a small bankroll.

I am probably more conservative than most, but I would not play $1,000 buy-in tournaments on a regular basis unless I had at least $40,000 in my bankroll. As an alternative, you can get investors to put up some of the money in exchange for a piece of your action. Most poker players take much more risk than their bankroll would allow by playing big buy-in tournaments without sufficient funds. If you don't have a big enough bankroll, you should be playing satellites, cash games, or smaller buy-in tournaments.

Pro Expectation: Making the Money

Tournament results can be streaky. Sometimes I'll run well and make more than five final tables in a short period. At other times I run poorly and can play 20 times without even making the money. Even the best players out there do not win first place very often.

The bigger buy-in events involve more skill because you have more chips and the levels are longer. Out of 40 big buy-in tournaments, I would think that if I am not running badly, I should probably make the final table four or five times. That is a high number. You'd probably make fewer final tables than that, particularly if you are playing tournaments with large fields. Technically, if there are 700 people, your odds of making the final table are only one out of seventy. If you make one out of twenty final tables, that is very good. If you win one tournament out of forty, that is a great result.

FINAL WORDS OF WIZDOM

Advice to Improve Your Game

If you want to play better, observe how other people play, especially players you respect. If you know good players, ask them questions. Learn from them, watch them, study the game and try to improve. After you leave a game, think about how you played. Even if you won that session, think about how you might have played better, how you might have maximized a particular hand. Some players who win always walk away thinking they have played great poker. On the other hand, when they lose they think they have been unlucky. But it is not necessarily your results that are indicative of your session. By evaluating your play and considering how you might have done things differently, you can become a much better player.

WD: As I drove away through the winding roads of the exclusive gated community where Kathy was living in Las Vegas, I wondered how many of the other residents in this palm-fringed oasis could make grown boys cry while playing cards, gathering millions of dollars in the process, yet still be one of the most relaxed people you could ever meet!

Some of Kathy's female counterparts in the world of professional poker rely on flashy media coverage rather than skill to obtain notoriety. With a less assuming image and understated confidence, Kathy often slides under the media radar. However, don't be fooled by her friendly and casual demeanor. She is one of the most consistent players on the tournament circuit today and a substantial force to be reckoned with among professional poker players everywhere. If you want to take a closer look at Kathy Liebert, check out her web site at www.PokerKat.com

T.J. CLOUTIER
"TJ the Magnificent"

Career Tournament Earnings Exceeding $9,000,000
Inducted into the Poker Hall of Fame in 2006
Second place, World Series of Poker No-Limit
Hold'em Championship, 1985
Winner, WSOP $1,000 Limit Omaha, 1987
Winner, Diamond Jim Brady $10,000 No-Limit Hold'em Championship,
1990-1991-1992
Winner, WSOP $1,500 Omaha High-Low, 1994
Winner, WSOP $2,500 Pot-Limit Hold'em, 1994
Winner, WSOP $2,500 Pot-Limit Omaha, 1998
Third place, WSOP No-Limit Hold'em Championship event, 1998
Second place, WSOP No-Limit Hold'em Championship event, 2000
Winner, WSOP $1,500 Razz, 2004
Winner, WSOP $5,000 No-Limit Hold'em, 2005
Winner, No-Limit Hold'em Main Event, Scotty Nguyen Challenge IV,
Tulsa 2007
Player of the Year (*Card Player* Magazine) 1998 and 2002

Author
How to Win the Championship: Strategies for the Final Table
Co-Author (with Tom McEvoy):
Championship Hold'em Tournament Hands
Championship Hold'em
Championship Omaha
Championship No-Limit and Pot-Limit Hold'em

T.J. CLOUTIER

Sitting Down With T.J.

When you first meet him, you realize immediately why T.J. Cloutier was a successful football player during his youth. Even in his late sixties, T.J. is indisputably a big man. Solid as a rock and standing 6'3," like a big grizzly, he looks you in the eye with a fearless, probing gaze. When he decides that you're friend not foe, he reveals his well-known jovial personality, and can teach you more about poker in a couple of minutes than most people would learn in a year.

His smile and laugh are contagious, but when he becomes serious and looks at you with cold, deep eyes that seem to bore into your soul, it is hard not to involuntarily wriggle in your seat and turn your gaze toward the nearest exit sign. When we met, I was glad that the table between us was covered with coffee cups not cards. If I had been facing him across a poker table, I'm sure my learning experience would have been more expensive!

It was truly a privilege to be sitting with T.J. Cloutier. One of the very first poker books I read when I became serious about poker was *Championship No-Limit & Pot-Limit Hold'em*, by T.J. and Tom McEvoy. This easy-to-read yet astute book provides an excellent introduction to the minds and strategies of two world-class players. Even today, it provides a cornerstone of the rationale that I use to help maintain the strategies that first allowed me to become a profitable player.

As a winner of over 60 major tournaments, six WSOP bracelets, and more than $9,000,000, T.J. is one of the best poker tournament players in the world. He has authored or co-authored five poker books, all of which are an exceptional resource for serious players who wish to further their skills and duplicate some of his winning strategies. His acumen for the game is born of an amazing ability to recall how his opponents have played in the past, an uncanny power of observation, and more than four decades of experience as a professional poker player.

Most of his early years as a poker pro were spent fading the long white line as a road gambler. While haunting the smoky back-room games of Texas and Louisiana with his imposing stature and fearsome aggression, he played against many legendary poker players: Jack Straus, Bobby Hoff, Little Red Ashey, Betty Carey and a cast of other colorful characters that illuminate fascinating stories from his past.

With his depth of experience and undeniable skill as a renowned tournament player, it surprised no one when T.J. was finally inducted into the Poker Hall of Fame in 2006. He was also declared *Card Player* magazine's Player of the Year in both 1998 and 2002. An amazing record of over 30 WSOP final tables is hard enough to fathom, but when you consider that four of those final tables were during the $10,000 main event, you start to understand what a formidable tournament player he is. Although T.J. has not yet won the main event, he came second on two occasions and was the first person to break the $1 million barrier for tournament winnings at the WSOP without ever taking first place in "The Big One."

In contrast to the Internet-driven propensity of many players to be overly aggressive with nominal hands, some would call T.J. Cloutier's approach traditional, but to suggest that he just waits for a good hand before playing would be a gross oversimplification. His strategy, developed through decades of play, places greater emphasis on quality starting hands than is favored by some of the newcomers to the game, but is also flexible enough to embrace lesser hands when appropriate. And bottom line, his record speaks for itself.

Let's hear what T.J. has to say…

T.J. CLOUTIER

THE MAKINGS OF A POKER WIZARD

Most top poker players are a fairly intelligent bunch, certainly more so than the average guy walking around the street, but they often have little quirks about them. One of the reasons they're so successful is that they recognize situations really well and get more money out of their winning hands than an average player. They also save more chips when they're behind in a hand. For example, if you were playing limit hold'em and there was a three-card flush on the board, a good player, up against a person who was firing at the pot, might make a bet knowing that the guy would call if he was on a draw. But he is also good enough to know that if his opponent already has his flush and reraises, he will be able to get away from the hand. A lot of average players will convince themselves that they have to call. Even though they think they're probably beat, they still call because of all the money in the pot. I think that's ridiculous. All the money that you save in those types of plays is money that you'll have available to double or triple up with later on.

The top players always get their money in with the right hand to try to stop others from drawing out on them. If an opponent calls and draws out on you, it happens, there is nothing more you can do about it! You want the other players putting all their money in, trying to do the drawing out, because that's where you can collect a lot of chips.

OIL RIGS, POKER AND SMOKY BACKROOMS

When I first started playing poker, I was just a kid and used to lose regularly. I paid my dues just like everybody else. I was working at a golf course in Daly City, California, and each time I finished carrying somebody's golf bag around for eighteen holes, I would come back after working hard and these guys would be waiting for me, wanting to play poker. They used to take all my hard-earned cash just about every time we played.

One day, one of the players had something called Lucky Bucks, which were certificates for $20 that you could use at Artichoke Joe's in San Bruno, California. If you put in $20 of your own and gave them the certificate, they would give you $40 in chips to play with. That was the first time I went to a real cardroom to play. I was just seventeen years old, but I got away with it because I was such a big kid. It was funny because I actually ended up playing the owner of the joint heads-up in draw poker and beat him.

I used to lose my paycheck regularly when I was a kid, because I usually ended up just playing against a bunch of old pros day after day, but then, in 1976, with only $100 to my name, I ended up moving to Longview, Texas to work in the oil fields. During my off- duty hours I learned how to play hold'em.

T.J. CLOUTIER

Eventually, I realized that I had a lot more talent for playing poker than I did for working in the oil fields.

In 1978 I quit working my day job altogether and moved to Shreveport, Louisiana to play around there and eventually started traveling all over Texas, Oklahoma, Arkansas and Louisiana playing in poker games. We used to call it "fading the long white line."

They were interesting times. I was once playing poker in a back room of what they called the Oil Well Club in Longview. Four guys came in with shotguns to rob the place. There was probably more money in the poker game than behind the bar at the time. We had a guy in the game who was a really big country type, he was so big, he even made me look small. He always wore overalls and would keep a pistol down the front pocket. When the robbers told us to stand up on the stools and keep our feet off the ground, this big guy got a little bit defiant with them so they whacked him across the chin and he decided to go for his pistol. Boy, they really gave it to him then and started hammering him across the head with the butt of a shotgun. He should have just given up his money like you're supposed to do when you're being robbed! You can always make more money.

They eventually found out that one of the managers was in cahoots with the guys who robbed the place. The person who owned the bar was called Jerry and he eventually went to jail for killing the manager, who had set up the robbery.

Back in those days you also had to be very careful what you said in a poker game. You could hardly say "boo" to somebody without getting yourself into trouble. Of course, things are very different nowadays. I always talk about Phil Hellmuth, whom I am very friendly with, and I enjoy saying that he wouldn't have lasted a week with his ego back in the old days in Texas. They would have probably found him buried somewhere out west.

That's why it's so good that we play in casinos now. You pay a rake or a time charge so that you're protected. It is much safer for the players and you don't get cheated. Not that some of that doesn't go on, but it is a very minor problem now compared to the old days.

Don't Play Poker With a Contract Killer

The funniest poker story of all from the old days was about George McGann, who was a stone cold contract killer from Dallas. George used to play poker with a guy called Tippy Toe Joe Shotsman. Joe knew how to play poker and would bust George just about every time they got together. On this particular occasion, they were heads-up and George got tired of losing all his money so he pulled out a gun and pointed it at Tippy Toe Joe. He said, "Joe, I want you to give me all the money you have in front of you and all the money in your pockets."

Tippy Toe Joe happened to have $10,000 in $100 travelers checks in his pockets at the time. George made him sign every last one of them in front of him. As he was signing them, Tippy Toe Joe looked up and had the nerve to ask George if he could borrow a couple of thousand dollars back to keep from going broke. Then, as they were walking down the stairs to leave, after being robbed at gunpoint, Joe said, "George, we aren't going to let this little incident ruin our game are we?" He knew that he would eventually get his money back if he could just keep the game going.

T.J. CLOUTIER

TOURNAMENT STRATEGY

The Importance of Observation

Learning how to observe other players at the table and absorb all their actions and mannerisms is perhaps the single most important lesson you can learn at the poker table. Knowing what everybody else is doing at the table and what they're capable of is very important. I already know what I have and what I can do. What I need to find out is what cards they have and what they're doing. You need to observe everything about your opponents and that includes betting patterns and physical tells. They're both significant.

Some people have certain physical mannerisms that they display in various situations and other people have different ways of making bets when they have certain cards. I know one player who raises less every time he has A-A than he will with J-J or Q-Q. He is afraid he is not going to get played with and wants to make sure he gets a call. I am an advocate of always raising roughly the same amount when you bet. For example, in a pot–limit game, if you're going to raise you should always raise the amount in the pot. That way you don't give away any information.

Instincts

Instincts are everything in poker. When you have played as long as I have, your first instincts are probably correct about 99 percent of the time. That's because your instincts are born out of all your practice and playing over the years.

Lots of players will sit there and try to rationalize what they should do in a given situation. They will be about to play a hand in a particular way and then question themselves saying, "I'd better do this; no I'd better do that." When they start thinking that way, they're usually wrong because they end up putting an opponent on a hand they can beat instead of playing the correct way for that particular situation. You have to listen to your instincts to play poker well.

Bluffing

A lot less bluffing goes on than people think. On the other hand, a lot of people are bluffing and don't even realize it. Layne Flack is a very good player who bluffs quite a bit, but if I played cards the way he does, I wouldn't last one hour. He plays a lot of hands that I won't even stand a raise with, but when it works, he does very well. I know of at least four occasions when he has arrived at the final table and had twice as many chips as the rest of the remaining players combined! It's pretty hard to lose a tournament when you have that many chips coming into the final table. That's his style and it works for him; I just don't play that way.

There are a number of players who will build a lot of chips early in the tournament or get knocked out trying. Layne Flack is one, Carlos Mortensen is another. Daniel Negreanu plays in a similar way, but he also moves in and out very well. Phil Hellmuth is a good player who plays a lot of pots, but who also gets dealt an amazing number of hands.

COMMON TOURNAMENT ERRORS

Overplaying Small Pairs in Early Position

One of the most common mistakes I regularly see is people overplaying small pairs in early position. Too many people go crazy with deuces, threes, fours and fives when they are sitting out of position. For the amount of times you are going to get paid off, it isn't worth it. My theory is that if you can't stand a raise you shouldn't put chips into the pot. That means that if you can't make a raise yourself or you're not willing to call a raise, you shouldn't enter the pot in the first place. Most pots are going to get raised at some point, so why limp in?

Wasting Too Many Chips Early

You want to be careful about not throwing chips away early in a tournament because the chips you preserve and don't give away then, are additional chips that you may be able to use later in the tournament when you have a good hand and can double up. A lot of people don't realize how precious chips are early on. They think they have to acquire all their chips early in the tournament. I don't play that way. If I have more chips at every break, I am happy as hell. I like to just keep cruising along when people are getting knocked out and get my chips later on when it counts.

Investing Too Much to Steal the Blinds

I also see a lot of mistakes made early in a tournament when everybody checks around and the player on the button or next to the button tries to steal the blinds. If there are no antes in the middle yet, the blinds are not worth all that much. A lot of people will sacrifice $900 or something just to pick up $200 or $300; it doesn't make a lot of sense to me. If I am going to bluff, I would rather bluff from a different position than the button so they won't think I am just trying to pick up the blinds.

Also, I still believe in the old theory: "If nobody in front of you has a hand, it increases the possibility that somebody behind you probably does." I am always wary of that possibility preflop when everybody folds around to me in late position.

Not Thinking About Your Opponent's Hand

A lot of amateurs and unsuccessful players share a big weakness: They only know what they have and don't spend enough time thinking about what other people have. In their mind, they will think up a scenario in which they have the best hand and end up putting in all their money when they shouldn't.

AGGRESSION

The top players use aggression at different times. Personally, I like to get deeper into a tournament before I start to open up. You can't win a tournament in the early stages. You win it at the end, but you have to get there first. I prefer to just keep growing my stack and not get too aggressive in the early stages. I want to have a chance to win the tournament, not blow it in the first hour.

I let other players do what they want to do; it doesn't bother me. That doesn't mean that I don't steal some pots. Sometimes you have to do that just to maintain the status quo. Lots of players try to steal the blinds, but I prefer to steal a pot when two or three people are in it for a raise and I can come back over the top of them. Then I've got enough chips to last about five times around the table. There is a big difference.

Dan Harrington once said, "T.J. Cloutier waits until he finds a crack in the wall and then attacks it like a Panzer division." Well, there is some truth to that comment. I do prefer to pick out certain players that I want to bluff and those are the people that I will work on. Somebody also once said that I am always just standing there at the end of the alley, waiting to attack. That simply means that you have to pick the right people to play against. You can't bluff an idiot.

I may see weakness in their play, how they bet a hand, or they may do something differently that will tell me they're weak. If you're observant, you'll pick up on that type of stuff and can use that information to your advantage. I have often said that if a wing fell off a gnat at the end of the table, I would see it. Just because I am talking doesn't mean that I'm not watching.

How to Defeat an Aggressive Player

The best way to defeat an aggressive player is to use his strength against him. I played Stu Ungar three times heads-up in tournaments and was fortunate enough to beat him all three times. Not that I consider myself a better player; he was an absolute genius when it came to poker. I just knew the best way to play him in a tournament setting. The times I beat him, I simply used his aggression against him. All I had to do was check to him twice when I had a good hand and he would do all the betting for me. He was out there swinging at the pot and I was just taking it back away from him. If I checked to him, he would always bet and I would come back over the top of him and take the pot back. He wasn't going to put a ton of money in the pot with nothing. On the occasions when he did call me, I was lucky enough to have a good hand.

> THE BEST WAY TO DEFEAT AN AGGRESSIVE PLAYER IS TO USE HIS STRENGTH AGAINST HIM.

Be Able to Change Gears

Ungar was a great player but he had one fault. When he was catching cards he played really fast and aggressive, and when he wasn't getting good cards he still played the same way. He never slowed down! He never changed gears.

My style of play changes all the way through a tournament. Initially, I start playing fairly tight, but I also adjust to how my opponents are playing. I am very aggressive at certain times during a tournament. At other times I will slow down a lot. When you're a couple of people away from the money and everybody else starts to tighten up, that is generally one of the times when I will loosen up. When you get close to the final table, the same thing happens. The other players all want to get on TV. You have to take advantage of those situations. Even though these opportunities are better known now than they were in the old days, a lot of people still don't take advantage of them.

STARTING HAND CONCEPTS

Unless stated otherwise, all of the situations discussed by the Wizards in the Starting Hand Concepts and Specific Hand Strategy sections are assumed to be at a full table, during the third level of a tournament. The blinds are $100/$200, and you have an average stack of around $11,000 in chips. It is also assumed that the players are displaying a moderate level of aggression and appear to be playing reasonably well.

Early Position

If you can't stand a raise with a hand, don't play it from an early position. In other words, if you will be unhappy if somebody behind you raises, you shouldn't bet. Always raise if you're first to enter the pot from an early position and usually play only premium hands.

The best hands to play, of course, are A-A, K-K, Q-Q, J-J, and A-K. I also will usually play A-Q and 10-10. In addition, if I am running good, and am sitting at just the right table, I may make an occasional raise with a smaller pair such as 9-9 or 8-8 to mix up my play and create some deception. I recommend staying away from pairs 7-7 and below. Hands like A-J, A-10, K-J or Q-J are trap hands that you should avoid playing up front.

Middle Position

Enter the pot with a raise if first to act with all the early position starting hands plus A-J, A-10, J-10, 7-7, 6-6, and occasionally,

10-9. Continue to avoid trap hands such as K-J and Q-J. And stay away from smaller pairs and suited connectors.

Late Position
You can raise with all the previous starting hands, plus K-Q, K-J, and K-10. In general, it is better to be the aggressor than the caller. If you're offered the correct odds, however, it is acceptable to see a cheap multiway pot with lesser hands, including medium pairs, and suited connectors. You can always throw your cards away if you don't flop a powerful hand.

SPECIFIC HAND STRATEGY

A-A
If you know you have the best hand preflop with something like A-A (or K-K) against what you're sure is an underpair, you have to be willing to put all your money on the line if the other player moves all in. There is no question about it.

If you end up getting your money in with a superior hand and get beat there is nothing you can do about it. If it happens it happens. I got knocked out of the WSOP one year in just that way. I had reraised the pot before the flop with A-A and a Frenchman called me. The flop came J-x-x with two hearts and we got all our money in. It turned out that he had the 7 ♥ 6 ♥ and had called my preflop reraise for nearly 30 percent of his chips with only a 7-high hand! He missed his flush, but ended up making a backdoor straight. He just got very lucky. There is nothing that a player with the best hand can do in that type of situation.

Suppose you have A-A in a preflop pot that has been raised and reraised. If a king or a queen comes on the flop, you have to consider the real possibility that the other player may have K-K or Q-Q in his hand and has flopped a set. You have a heck of a decision to make: You then have to play the player. If you think you're beat, you just have to throw your aces away.

Obviously, the ideal scenario with A-A is to get all the chips in before the flop against just one player. You can't do that very often, though, because if you move all in preflop, your opponents will just throw their hands away. Therefore, you often have to get the best of the flop as well to win with A-A.

Let me tell you about a situation that happened at the Bicycle Club a couple of years ago. I was in the small blind and looked down to find two red aces in my hand. A player I knew brought it in for a raise, and the button, who had been winning a lot of hands, moved all in. I was sitting just to the left of the button and loved the fact that he had moved all his chips in, so I sidled right up alongside him and called his all-in bet.

The first person who had bet was a good player and had two black kings in his hand. He knew that I would never jump the fence after there had been a raise and a reraise unless I had A-A, so he ended up throwing his K-K away. The player on the button had all his chips in with A-K of spades against my A-A. The flop came K-x-x with two spades. As it turned out, the first player would have flopped a set of kings.

The button ended up making his flush, so they both would have beaten me. But that's just the way it goes sometimes. You can't ask for much more than to get a lot of chips in with A-A against A-K! It is hard to be a bigger favorite than that.

K-K

Kings are probably the hardest hand to play in no-limit hold'em because it is the hardest to get away from. You can ask Doyle Brunson or any of the top players and they will probably agree with me. If there is a raise and a reraise, queens start to look like toilet paper and you can just throw them away. On the other hand, if you have K-K, what are you going to do with the hand? Are you going to be able to put one of the other people on A-A?

At times you have to be willing to lay down a big pair like K-K if you think you're beat. One year during the very early stages of the World Series of Poker main event, I made a small $200 raise and Mike Allen from Kansas City reraised me and made it $450 to go. I showed him my kings and then threw them away. He showed me A-A. About forty-five minutes later the exact same scenario occurred. I made a $200 raise and this time he made it $500. I showed my K-K and threw them away and he showed me A-A again. I had been playing with him for years and knew that the only hand he would ever reraise me with was A-A. I had to throw away my K-K because I knew I had the worst hand.

Pocket kings are a tough hand to play, especially given the fact that every time you get them, an ace seems to come on the flop. When you raise it up with the K-K preflop and the ace comes on the flop, what do you do? I played in a charity tournament recently, and as soon as it got down to the final sixteen, I found myself with pocket kings so I raised it up. The small blind called me, and the flop came A-7-3. When the small blind bet the pot, I just threw my kings away. It was as simple as that.

When you have a hand like K-K (or Q-Q) it always seems like there are a hundred aces in the deck. If you're at a table with a bunch of people you've never seen before, you just have to make the decision whether or not your opponent has A-A against your K-K. That is what poker is all about anyway— making the right decisions at the right time.

Q-Q
Do not slowplay queens from a front position because any ace or king that comes on the flop will put you in jeopardy. You

want to bring them in for a raise in order to get some money into the pot. In the early stage of a tournament, if a player reraises a substantial portion of his chips before the flop, pocket queens is not the type of hand that you want to take a stand with. You should release them in this scenario. You cannot take a lot of heat with queens before the flop. Making laydowns when it is correct to do so is just as important as making the right calls and raises.

If you hold queens in late position, especially on the button, and a few players have limped in front of you, your queens increase in value. The chances are that no one behind you (the blinds) has a bigger pair. Always raise with the queens. Then if you get a small flop, you can try to win the pot right there.

The major consideration with queens is not what you do with them when you have the best hand, but can you get away from them when you have the worst hand.

J-J

Jacks are much easier to play than queens or kings. You put in your raise preflop, and if the flop comes with overcards, you make your decision. If you are reraised with your J-J, whether or not you make the call depends on who you are up against. That is where the importance of observation comes in. It doesn't matter if you have J-J or even 9-9; if you put your opponent on overcards like A-Q and you want to go with the hand, you're an 11-10 favorite before the flop. But you always have to realize that any time you put your money in the pot, even if you're a favorite, you might be gone.

A-K*

What I do with A-K depends on a lot of factors, including my position, but I would certainly come in for a small raise

---

*The section below the first paragraph came from *Championship No-Limit & Pot-Limit Hold'em* by T.J. Cloutier and Tom McEvoy.

from the first few seats early in a tournament. I am not one for moving all my chips into the middle with just A-K. Ideally, you would rather see a flop with just one opponent, but if you get a couple of callers that's what you have to deal with. If the flop comes 9-10-J or something, where there are at least two cards to a straight or a flush, you would much rather play the pot against one person. Early in a tournament, I treat A-K very carefully. I am not going to invest a lot of money with it unless I get a good flop.

If somebody raises from the front when I am holding A-K in the back, the way I handle it largely depends on the player who is making the raise. There are times when I will just flat call the raise. There are times when I will try to win the money right then by reraising. And there are times when I will simply throw the hand away. It all depends on what I know about my opponent and how he is playing that day.

The purpose of moving all in with A-K is that you want to see all five cards. I'm not a move-in player, but in certain situations, especially short-handed and late in the tournament, you have to do it. Suppose that a player raises, you call with A-K and the flop comes 7-4-2. Your opponent makes a bet—now you have to give up the hand. If you make a decision to play A-K short-handed, you move in with it because you want to see all five cards.

More tournaments are won or lost with A-K against a big pair than any other hand. To win a no-limit tournament, you have to win with A-K and you have to beat A-K. You may not win or lose with them on the final hand, but it will usually be the deciding hand, the one that loses or wins the most chips for you. It is the biggest decision hand in a tournament.

Suited Connectors

I play suited connectors once in a while, as do players like Daniel and Doyle, but I don't play them a hell of a lot at a full table. Normally, it is not the type of hand that I go out of my way to play. If I'm short-handed, it is a different story. If I do decide to play with them and I am around back in one of the later positions, I am probably going to come in for a raise and try to win the pot right there. If I get called, at least I've got something that could make a hand.

I normally don't like to just call with that sort of hand unless I have a lot of chips and my opponent also has a lot. Then you can really win something, which may make it worth calling with suited connectors.

Flush Draws and Straight Draws

In a tournament, draws are death. I don't play many drawing hands in a tournament. You often end up wasting a lot of chips to draw to the river, and you may not even make your hand. I want the other person to be the one who is putting chips into *my* pot trying to draw out.

Everybody talks about the odds in tournaments, but a lot of the time, the odds go out the window. That is because if you're a 4 to 1 favorite you still have that one in five chance that you're going to bomb out of the tournament. You have to take that into consideration—it's not just a simple case of knowing that you're ahead. You may be a statistical favorite in many situations when the odds are calculated over a thousand hands, but you may not be ahead at that particular time. For example, if you have two overcards and a flush draw on the flop, you are a statistical favorite over a lot of hands at that point, but you could also be well behind. Even if you are the favorite, and you decide to move all in, you still have to get there. If you don't make your draw, you are out of the tournament.

One place where a lot of people make a huge mistake in no-limit hold'em is when they have a huge draw, the action is passed to them on fourth street and, instead of seeing a free card, they will bet the draw. If somebody makes a big reraise they will have to get away from the hand. If they're any good they will, because a good player is not going to risk all his chips on a draw, particularly with only one card to come. The correct play is to just take the free card.

SUCCESS IN TODAY'S TOURNAMENTS

Dealing With Young Aggressive Players

I have a lot of respect for the very aggressive, young players, but I don't fear them. Then again, I've never feared anything in my whole life anyway. I didn't even have any fear when I didn't know what I was doing!

There are some very good players that have spent a lot of time playing online, but it still isn't the same as looking somebody in the eye. An advantage that some of the older players have is that most of the big events are long and they have more experience at keeping their game together over those extended periods. One of the hardest things to do in poker is to bring your A-game with you every time you sit down and never make a mistake. It is very difficult to do that for five straight days. A lot of the new younger, aggressive players have trouble keeping their game together for long periods.

When Opponents See a Lot of Flops

I generally play fairly tight against those sorts of players. When I do come into the hand I make a good raise and see if they still want to play, put some pressure on them.

You just have to adapt to the style of the people you're up against. You are going to lose some pots to bad players who call raises with substandard hands, but in the long run you are going to be a winner. Playing better poker will make you the winner over the long term.

TELLS

One of the most common tells is when a player loads up before the action gets to him. He will be preparing to make a raise while the other players in front of him are still acting. If you're observant, you'll notice that type of thing. When you have a marginal hand and see a player loading up, you can fold because you know the player behind you is probably going to raise.

At other times people will look at their hand and then move closer to the table as if they're interested in playing. Noticing little things like that—which people do consistently—can give you a big edge in a poker game.

I can't give all the information away that I have learned over forty years of playing poker, but I will say that you can also learn a lot by closely watching how people bet and how they break their stack, how they put their money in when they raise or call. Mannerisms like that can tell you a lot—if you watch for them!

MONEY MANAGEMENT

I am the worst money manager in the history of poker, but luckily I have been married to Joy all these years and she is very good at it. Without her, I would be a pauper begging on a street somewhere.

I will say that there are very few players who have been consistently successful over the years playing tournaments. Nowadays, by the time you pay for the entry fees, accommodations and travel expenses to play the major events for a year, it probably costs around $500,000. If you don't win at least that much, you're behind, and it isn't easy to win that much money every year.

Be Prepared to Deal With Losses

You need to beat a lot of players to win tournaments, and the odds are really stacked against you. It doesn't just depend on how well you play. You must catch the right cards and find yourself in good situations if you are going to win. If you bust out, you just have to get up the next day, tell yourself that it is a different situation and try again. At the end of the year, the better players will be ahead.

Some people may have trouble dealing with getting knocked out of a number of tournaments in a row. It just doesn't bother me because I know I can play with anybody if I get my share of the cards. It is nice when you get lucky and get a lot of great cards, but if the cards break even on a given day I know I am going to win my share of the pots and am still going to be playing. I may not necessarily win the tournament, but I will have a good chance to win it. On the other hand, if you keep getting your money in with the best hand and lose because people draw out on you, there is nothing you can do about it.

I don't know what the greatest string of losses I have had is, but I do know that I can win tomorrow and the tournaments are worth so much nowadays that just one win can make your whole year. It is important to keep that in mind when you go through tough times.

PROUDEST ACHIEVEMENT IN POKER

The achievement that I am most proud of in my poker career is winning more than sixty major tournaments. I was also added to the Hall of Fame in 2006 and have six WSOP bracelets, all of which make me very proud. Winning the big one at the

Diamond Jim Brady tournament three years in a row was a big accomplishment as well. The first two years that I won, the buy-in was $10,000; the last year, it was lowered to $5,000.

I was the biggest money winner at the World Series of Poker until a few years ago, but now, with the huge increase in the number of players attending, all you have to do is win your first tournament and you are instantly the biggest money winner. Actually, since 1983, I have only had one losing year at the WSOP.

Nowadays, I am still out there trying to win them, especially since the purses are worth a lot more.

FINAL WORDS OF WIZDOM

Advice to Improve Your Game

Study as much as you can. Learn everything about the game. Read everything that you can that was written by credible players; you'll pick up something from every book you read. Even if there is one little sentence in a book that helps you, it makes it worthwhile buying.

Poker is like a job. If you want to be good at it, you have to work hard. Research the game, find out what works for you and what doesn't work—and take it from there.

WD: Internet poker has introduced a swath of young, aggressive players who will play with any two cards and are always frustratingly happy to put all their chips on the line with just a read and a prayer. With players duplicating the edited all-in short-handed final-table play that they see on TV, and trying to transport that style to full-handed deep-stack tournaments, the outcome can sometimes be explosive. Yet the proven, more traditional strategy of playing good cards, employing reason and patience still works, perhaps even more so now that there is such a wave of overly aggressive youthful players at the tournament tables.

This is not to say that T.J. can't become aggressive! He easily finds weakness in his opponents and can be relentless in his attack. However, his aggression is tempered with a large measure of common sense and patience, traits that are often lacking at many a poker table today. It is this deadly combination of talent, aggression and patience that instills fear in the minds of players when they see T.J. Cloutier walk toward their table.

MIKE SEXTON

The Ambassador of Poker

Career Tournament Earnings Exceeding $3,400,000

Winner, World Series of Poker Stud 8-or-Better, 1989

Winner, No-Limit Hold'em World Poker Finals,
Foxwoods Casino, 1992

Winner, No-Limit Hold'em Queens Summer Classic Championship, 1996

Winner, No-Limit Hold'em Queens Summer Classic Championship, 1997

Winner, European Hold'em Championship, European Finals of Poker, Paris,
2000

Winner, €5,000 Heads-up Championship, Paris, 2003

Winner, Speed Poker Invitational event, Crown Casino,
Australia, 2005

Winner, No-Limit Hold'em Tournament of Champions,
Las Vegas, 2006

More than 43 In-the-Money Finishes at the World Series of Poker

Author

Shuffle Up and Deal

Sitting Down With Mike

Often called "The Ambassador of Poker," Mike Sexton is probably the most visible personality on the poker scene. Well known to many as the public face of Party Poker, he has achieved even broader fame as the co-host of the internationally televised World Poker Tour. With Vince Van Patten as his partner, Mike delivers insightful blow-by-blow coverage of the final six players battling for the first place prize pool of over $1 million at each WPT stop around the world. Although he doesn't see the competitors' hole cards as they're actually playing at the WPT final table, Mike sees them during the editing and recording sessions at the studio where the "television" hands are chosen and narrated. This exclusive behind-the-scenes view and his depth of playing experience give Mike a special look at the hidden secrets to winning a big tournament in today's competitive environment, and bring his unique insight into the strategies of the top players to life in his commentary.

Sexton played professional poker for more than twenty-five years prior to teaming up with Party Poker and the WPT. He is also the author of a best-selling poker book, *Shuffle Up and Deal*. He started playing in World Series of Poker events in 1984, and has become one of the top ten players of all time for in-the-money finishes. Mike has received more than forty-three payouts from those tournaments alone, including the gold bracelet he won in 1989 in the Stud 8-or-Better event. In 2006, he won the WSOP Tournament of Champions event, earning a $1 million first-place payout. You can say that this man knows a lot about poker!

I first met Mike Sexton in January of 2004 during the Australian Poker Championships at the Crown Casino in Melbourne, Australia. Along with 107 other players who had won a $12,000 package to participate via online tournaments at Party Poker, I found myself sitting among 256 formidable contestants, including Mike, Scotty Nguyen, Mel Judah and Marcel Luske. They had come to compete for what was, at that time, the biggest poker prize pool in the southern hemisphere, a whopping $2,500,000 AUD.

Because of Party Poker's sponsorship of the event, Sexton was on hand to represent the online site and donate another five entries, with an offer to donate a matching amount to Tsunami Relief efforts for every dollar those players won. Unlike the WPT, where he is unable to play, Mike was able to sit at a poker table in the Land Down Under to once again prove his worth.

Mike made the money, finishing a very respectable 12th. It wasn't until I made a rather suspect call with an A-J against Mike's suited A-Q (he was all in with a short stack) that he departed the tournament when a jack came on the turn and he didn't improve. Mike got up from his chair and politely thanked everybody before walking to the rail. He seemed as happy in his rare moment of defeat as he is every time I have seen him since—a smile on his face, an air of confidence in his walk, and a stoic resilience that stand as his trademarks.

Let's hear what Mike has to say…

MIKE SEXTON

THE MAKINGS OF A POKER WIZARD

In the poker world there are many Damon Runyon-type characters and the most successful players are unique.* Most of today's best players are very bright people who would be winners in any line of business they pursued. Chip Reese could have been a multi-millionaire at anything he set his mind to; he was just so much smarter than the average person. You could also say that about Barry Greenstein or even Daniel Negreanu, a young player who has made millions playing poker.

A lot of players have won million-dollar prize pools over the last couple of years. However, before I grade a person as a truly great player they have to pass the test of time. If they're

---

* Damon Runyon was an author who spun tales of gamblers, petty thieves, actors and gangsters; few of whom went by "square" names. They preferred, or instead, were just known by, names such as "Nathan Detroit," "Big Jules," "Harry the Horse," "Good Time Charlie" and "Dave the Dude." —WD

still around ten years later winning tournaments, that's when I can start to define them as a great.

To Be One of the Best

I believe anybody can be a winning poker player if they're willing to make the effort. You certainly don't have to be anything near the greatest player in the world to make money playing poker. However, to succeed at the top level, to be in the top twenty or thirty on the World Poker Tour, for example, you must have natural ability. In addition to knowing the correct odds and basic probabilities involved in poker, you must have an uncanny feel for the game that helps you sense when your opponent is weak so that you can take the pot away from him. Instincts, a sixth sense, and a unique feel for the game separate the world's very best players from the rest of the pack. That's the difference between great players and average players

The Most Important Lesson in Poker

The biggest lesson you must learn to be successful is that you can never know it all. Poker is a never-ending learning process. As a result, some of the old-school guys who think they know everything about the game are being surpassed by the younger players. The young people that you see on the World Poker Tour winning millions of dollars literally live, breathe, eat and sleep poker twenty-four hours a day. They're constantly analyzing hands and asking themselves what they would have done in different situations. They never stop trying to improve their game. As soon as you think you don't need any more knowledge, you're probably about to go for a big downhill slide

I also believe with all my heart that every poker book out there has something to offer. I don't care who wrote it or what kind of slant somebody's put on it. You can learn enough from every book to make it worth the price you paid.

The requirement for constantly learning is also related to one of the most important aspects of being a winner, which is knowing your opponents. You should always be studying them, learning from their actions, trying to understand how they bet in certain situations and how they react to different types of players.

PAYING DUES AT AN EARLY AGE

I have loved poker ever since I was a kid. While I was in college and later on when I got out of the army, I played in cash games in North Carolina to supplement my income. I was very successful. Finally, after being a sales rep for three-and-a-half years, I discovered that I would rather play poker than get up at dawn and hit the road as a salesman.

Ironically, the guy who taught me how to play poker was Danny Robison. Danny was a world-class seven-card stud player. Many consider him the best seven-card stud player that ever lived. He and Chip Reese were partners when they first went to Las Vegas. They took $1,000 and turned it into more than $1 million in one summer. He and Chip were the dynamic duo of Las Vegas; they were the young guns who set the town on fire.

But before all that, Danny taught me how to play when I was in junior high school. I would get up before classes and deliver papers all week long on the paper route that he gave me. Back then, you collected from your customers every Friday night. I would get back home from collecting my money and Danny would be waiting for me on my porch ready to play some poker. He would then beat me out of my money every week. I think that was back in 1960. He was two years older than me, which gave him a big edge. At the time, I had no idea how good Danny was because he was the only guy I was playing. Unfortunately, he kept beating me.

"Don't keep playing with Danny; he's too good for you," my mom kept telling me. Every week the same thing would happen and I would come back with my chin on my chest. After several weeks, my mom looked at me and said, "You must be the dumbest kid in the world! If you're stupid enough to play with him every week and lose all your money after you've worked so hard, you don't deserve to have it!" She never forbade me to play with him, but would always remind me how foolish I was when I lost all my money. It was a great lesson for later in life.

Eventually Danny moved away and I went off to Ohio State where I played in other games and competitions. I realized at that time that I was a much better player than the people I was up against. Whether it was gin rummy or poker or any other kind of card game, I was winning most of the time. When I returned to North Carolina in the 1970s, I finally decided that I loved playing so much I had to try to become a professional poker player.

TOURNAMENT STRATEGY

In poker, it is vital to realize that playing people is much more important than just playing the cards you have. This means making your opponents think about what you have and getting a good read and feel for what they have. No-limit hold'em is really not about what cards you hold, but about what cards your opponent thinks you hold. And of course, it is about the number one skill in poker—being able to correctly put your opponent on a hand. Unlike average players, good players can recognize when their opponents are week and take the pot away from them. That's why they're so good.

> THE NUMBER ONE SKILL IN POKER IS BEING ABLE TO CORRECTLY PUT YOUR OPPONENT ON A HAND.

Early in a Tournament

When you first start a tournament, you are better off not getting too reckless or aggressive because the blinds aren't very big at that stage. Picking up those small blinds is not really going to help you that much. What's going to help more is sitting back and waiting and watching your opponents to see how they play. Get a feel for the game first, in the very early stage of the tournament. Also, it's important to know how long it's going to be before they break your table. If your table is going to be the first to move, you're going to have a different strategy than if you're expecting to be with those same players all day long.

Early on, most people play tight. Once you know your opponents well enough after a few levels, if they're not playing too fast, you can occasionally be aggressive, pick up pots, and start to accumulate chips.

Middle Stages

As the blinds increase (and certainly, once you start paying an ante), you need to become more aggressive. Usually around the third or fourth level, you should start taking over the game and raising pots. By the middle stage, there are more chips on the table to win, so you have more reason to play aggressively.

Later Stages

Right before people reach the money and just before they reach the final table, top players take tremendous advantage of the situation. On the World Poker Tour, since we play six at the final TV table, the pros can do a lot of damage and pick up many chips when there are nine players left. When they reach that final table of nine, they all want to make the TV show. The best players are raising constantly to build up their stacks so that when they get to the final six, they will have a lot of chips and a better chance to win.

I've seen several cases where there was no doubt in my mind that people won a tournament because they became aggressive when everybody was getting close to the money. One example that comes to mind happened during the World Series of Poker main event in 1992. I was sitting next to Hamid Dastmalchi, who eventually won the championship. Approaching the money he had about $60,000 in chips. There were 37 players left and it was the first time that they had ever paid 36 people, as the tournament had grown. They were playing hand-for-hand at every table and most of the players were just throwing their cards away hoping somebody else would go broke. Nobody wanted to play a pot. I'd like to bet that in the history of poker there has never been a tournament that took so long to go from 37 players to 36!

It took a couple of hours to lose one player. Dastmalchi just started raising every pot. He could see that nobody was playing. I was one of the guilty ones because I wasn't playing either. He built his stack up from $60,000 to $160,000 before we finally lost another player. That gave him enough chips to carry on and win the title.

If You Want to Win, Play to Win

It is important to realize that the percentage of times a good player makes the money is determined by how he plays. If you are just trying to get into the money rather than win, it's much easier to get paid.

If you're playing to come in first, you have a higher probability of getting knocked out early, but you're going to give yourself a much better chance of winning in the long run. You can't be afraid to play pots early in the tournament if you're trying to win. You have to accumulate chips so that if you make it to the final table, you'll get there as one of the chip leaders.

Most people have the mindset that they must make it to the money first. I used to think that the first priority in tournaments was survival. I had that mindset for a lot of years because, when you're putting up money to play, your first goal is to get that money back. Then you'll be on a freeroll for the big bucks. That's the way you think if you're a player out there trying to survive on the tournament circuit. You know you've got to make it to the money X number of times in a year to survive; otherwise you're not going to make it. Your bankroll is not going to hold up. I no longer believe this approach to be wise if you're trying to win.

So, how you play depends upon what your goal is, what you're trying to do. Honestly, most players do try to get to the money first and the final table second. Then they think about winning. The top guys like Gus Hansen, Phil Ivey and Daniel Negreanu are trying to win from the get-go. They're not worried about getting knocked out. If they get to the final table, they're going to get there with a lot of chips, which gives them a much better shot at winning.

On the World Poker Tour I've watched the great players and have seen what they do to win. To be successful you don't have to reinvent the wheel; all you have to do is watch the people that are successful and do what they do.

AGGRESSION

The ultimate aggressive player was Stu Ungar. With Stu, it didn't seem to matter what kind of players were at the table. He was fearless and it seemed as though he raised every pot. He became the table captain right away. He didn't back off from anybody. I get that same feeling from Phil Ivey and Daniel Negreanu. You also see Phil Hellmuth do it sometimes. Carlos Mortensen, Erick Lindgren and Antonio Esfandiari are all young guns who have that Stu Ungar style. When you are playing against them, it seems as if they're raising almost every pot, and they have been very successful at it.

Know Your Opponents Before You Become Aggressive

It's important to get to know your opponents at the table. You have to understand who the tight and loose players are. You should know which players are going to be defenders of their blinds. Many people will just lay their hand down at the first sign of aggression. Other people never want to give up their blinds. With those types of players you know they're going to play back at you, so you have to be prepared. In a tournament, you have to be able to pick up the blinds and antes to survive. In the later stages you have to do it at least once a round just to maintain the status quo. You see the good players doing it two, three or four times a round. And they often do it regardless of position.

Attacking the Blinds

Being aggressive enough to pick up the blinds every few rounds, particularly late in the tournament, can be very important if you want to survive with a small to medium stack. If you are the player trying to take the blinds and somebody reraises, you can't back off the next time. You've got to try a second and third time. Try to chop your money back out, so to speak. If your aggression fails on all of those occasions, you're going to be on a short stack before long, so you'll have to wait to pick up a hand before you try to do it again. I don't worry about percentages that much, but a rough estimate of how much of my stack I am willing to risk to pick up the blinds and antes would be around 20 percent, perhaps more.

You have to play hands when you get them and not be too afraid. It is important to pick up your fair share of blinds and antes in a tournament. If you don't, you are going to find yourself as the short stack.

Defending the Blinds

The best defense against somebody who is raising every pot and taking your blinds is to make a big reraise. If you don't, they'll just run over you. It doesn't matter if you have a hand or not. If a guy is raising your blinds every single time, you just have to come back over the top of him. That's your line of defense. That's the way you're going to stop him from doing it.

STARTING HAND CONCEPTS

> Unless stated otherwise, all of the situations discussed by the Wizards in the Starting Hand Concepts and Specific Hand Strategy sections are assumed to be at a full table, during the third level of a tournament. The blinds are $100/$200, and you have an average stack of around $11,000 in chips. It is also assumed that the players are displaying a moderate level of aggression and appear to be playing reasonably well.

Early Position

When first to act, I normally raise with all the premium hands such as A-A, K-K, Q-Q, J-J, A-K and even hands down to A-10 suited. It depends on who the players are to my left, but I will normally raise any pair 6-6 or better as well.

Middle Position

I play all the previous starting hands, but also include hands such as suited connectors and smaller pairs to try and pick up blinds, and in the later rounds, the antes. The hands you should play from middle and late position are dramatically influenced by the types of players sitting in the blinds. If they like to defend, your starting requirements have to be higher.

Late Position

Raise with cards as low as A-5 suited or better, K-J and K-10 suited and all the preceding hands. Call multiway pots with suited connectors and small to medium pairs. Be cautious limping in with hands such as A-9 or A-8 suited because they can get you into a lot of trouble in a multiway pot when you flop top pair.

SPECIFIC HAND STRATEGY

A-A

With A-A, you are generally better off just making a standard raise when you are the first player to come into the pot. It doesn't matter whether you have 6-4 suited or A-A, it's best to bet three to four times the big blind every time you come into the pot. If you bet consistently every time, nobody's going to be able to put you on a hand.

If you are a very tight player, it may make sense to occasionally slowplay your high pair. On the other hand, if you are perceived as an aggressive player, you should take advantage of that perception and make your standard raise of three to four times the big blind. In most cases, you should just make your standard raise.

If I raise with aces and a loose-aggressive player reraises and puts me all-in preflop early in the tournament, I'd gladly risk my entire stack to call him. In a real tournament where the money is at the top, I can't believe anybody would not want to put their money in with two aces before the flop. If you go broke, you go broke. You have the best hand going in. Poker is all about getting your money in the pot with the best hand.

With A-A, you have the best hand before the flop so you should put your chips in there. If they beat you, good luck to them.

The only time it may be correct to throw A-A away preflop would be in a situation such as a supersatellite with three players involved in a pot where two were likely to be knocked out, thereby assuring you a major result such as a seat in a main event. It is more important not to get unlucky, than it is to get lucky.

Hand Matchups

Probability of success if played to the river. Percentages are rounded to the nearest whole percent. Assume that all four cards are of different suits.

	Win	Lose
A-A versus K-K	81%	19%

I'll be honest with you; I wouldn't throw A-A away preflop no matter how many players were in the pot. Perhaps some math wizard will show me I'm not correct, but I promise you this, if four or five guys are in front of me and they're all in, I'm going to be right there with them with my two aces. They're just going to have to crack me.

Aces All-in Against Three Paired Opponents

Aces all in against three players holding kings, queens and nines has approximately a 47 percent chance of being beaten.

K-K, Q-Q

I generally play K-K and Q-Q the same as A-A before the flop; that is, I make a standard raise. What happens after the flop, or if you are reraised preflop, depends on who is doing the betting and how many chips you both have. Even if an ace comes on the flop, it is important to make a continuation bet most of the time to find out where you are in the hand. You have to find out whether you have the best hand after the flop.

Be aware that a number of other flops such as 9-8-7, 10-9-8 with two suited cards, or other high combinations that offer a lot of flush and straight possibilities, can be very hazardous to an overpair. You have to tread carefully.

A-K

I've probably lost more money with A-K than all the other hands put together. When people raise, or I raise and they reraise, it seems too easy to go all in with A-K. You should instead, probably be getting away from the hand. T.J. Cloutier plays A-K better than most players in the game because he lays it down a lot of the time. He says, "It's not a hand until you've helped it."

I like to raise with A-K coming in, and if somebody raises in front of me I usually come over the top of them most of the time. It's here that you're faced with a decision if they come back over the top of you. What do you do with it now? You should probably get away from it. Sometimes I get a little stubborn, go all in and soon find myself on my way to the rail. I think judgment comes into play, but A-K is not the kind of hand that's worth slowplaying; you've got to try to take the pot right there.

In a cash game, you're basically going to play A-K the same way as you would in a tournament. Yes, there are certain strategies that vary from cash games to tournaments, but in truth, it's all poker. Honestly, I've never played cash games much differently from tournaments. When I hear people say cash games are totally different from tournament games, I don't buy it. In my view, if you get a good hand, you play it, whether it's a tournament or a cash game.

J-J

I think you've got to raise with a hand like pocket jacks coming in if you're first to act; you can't limp with them and you can't throw them away. J-J is a premium hand, one of the top five in no-limit hold'em.

If a solid player with a larger than average stack raises from early position, you're usually better off if you reraise and get a feel for where you are. If the guy is a really tight player, you may want to just call the raise and take the flop to see what comes out. If it doesn't come 10-9-8, or if you don't flop a jack, you may want to get away from the hand if he bets again on the flop. Jacks are a pretty good hand in poker, but they also can get you into trouble.

Middle Pairs: 9-9, 8-8, 7-7

Some of the toughest hands to play in hold'em are the middle pairs. As a result a lot of people play them badly. The problem that comes with any middle pair is similar to that of J-J. If you call or raise before the flop and even one overcard comes out, then you have a problem. If your opponent bets, it is very hard to know what to do. That's the problem with playing middle pairs.

That's why I think you're usually better off reraising and taking the lead in the pot with those types of hands. I don't think there's anything more important in playing no-limit hold'em than being the person who is doing the betting.

Small Pairs

It's probably better to fold small pairs if a person raises ahead of you. It depends on how many chips you each have. Sometimes, playing small pairs can be worth it to try to flop a set, particularly if you think you can bust a person and take all his chips. It's the implied odds that you base your decision on. If a person has bet half his stack, you're going to either set him all in or not get involved to start with.

If the implied odds are good, it is not a bad play to occasionally call a preflop raise with a small pair. Say to yourself, "Okay, I'm going to play this hand and if I flop a set or another good hand, then I'm going to continue playing it. If I don't and the guy bets again on the flop, I'm going to give it up." If you have that kind of mentality, you shouldn't lose too much money.

If you decide to play a small pair and you're the first one to come into a pot, you should raise. If I have a small pair and a loose aggressive player raises in front of me, I would probably just call, but some good players like to reraise a lot. You'll see players who love to reraise with small pairs; in fact, that's Humberto Brenes' favorite play. Humberto will make an all-in reraise and force his opponent to either have a big pair or fold!

Suited Connectors 9-8, 7-6, 6-5

It's sometimes okay to play with weak cards such as 7-6 or 6-5 and similar hands. You can call a small raise with the thought that if you hit the flop, you can bust a guy. Once again, it is the implied odds that you're going for. You are not calling a raise because you think you have the best hand; you're hoping to catch a flop and bust somebody. That's what you see the great players doing. That's why they play the wide variety of hands that you see on the World Poker Tour. If they hit their hand on the flop, they're going to win a lot of chips.

Calling versus Raising

In poker, particularly in no-limit hold'em, your odds of success will keep going down as long as you're the one doing the calling before the flop. That's the first mistake many players make. You need to be the one doing the raising. You need to be doing the betting and taking the initiative in a pot. Look at how many hands in no-limit hold'em are won by the person who raises before the flop. In most cases, whatever comes out on the flop, if the preflop raiser bets again, the other guy throws his hand away. It happens time and time again. The person who takes the initiative often wins the pot, not the guy that's sitting there calling raises trying to catch a set.

I think that philosophy applies throughout the whole tournament. The guy that's doing the betting has got the edge, no question about it. The aggressor is going to be the victor in the end when it comes to playing no-limit hold'em.

BLUFFING

I've changed my approach to tournament poker after watching players like Daniel Negreanu and Carlos Mortensen, who are very successful on the World Poker Tour and the big buy-in tournaments. They're not sitting back waiting for A-A or K-K. They're bluffing at pots with regularity. Chips are power and you'll discover that it's the chip leaders who get down to the top spots most of the time. Bluffing is a very necessary part of the game if you want to accumulate a lot of chips.

The first tip I give anybody on bluffing is: Never bluff a weak player. They're not going to understand what hand you're representing, and they can't get away from their own hand if they hit something. Bluff the good player. Bluff the best player at the table. He's the one that will lay down a hand.

Bluffing Opportunities

Against the right type of player, a good bluffing opportunity occurs when your opponent raises before the flop, you call, and you both have a lot of chips. It doesn't really matter what you have, but for the purposes of this example, let's assume you have the 9♠ 8♠ and the flop comes K-6-4.

You   **Opponent**

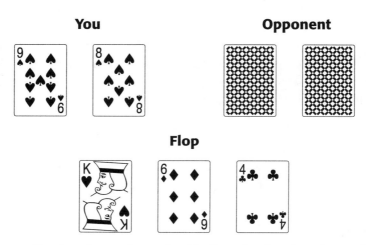

Flop

Generally, the player that raised before the flop is going to bet out again after the flop. When he bets on that kind of a flop, you have an opportunity to make a small raise even though you have nothing. When you reraise in that situation, you're sending a message that you have a king. If he has J-J, a hand such as A-Q, or any number of hands that are far better than yours, it's very difficult for him to call a raise when there's a king on the board. Essentially he must have a king in his hand to call you. It is an opportunity you can take if you have the heart to do it.

A Sophisticated Big Bluff

Let me describe a sophisticated bluff that you can make in the right situation. In this play, a player calls a preflop raise with nothing, and then calls a continuation bet on the flop. His intent is to make a large bet to steal the pot from the preflop raiser if the raiser checks on the turn. To illustrate, let's say that a guy raises preflop and you call with a 6-5 suited. The flop comes 10-9-2 and he makes a continuation bet.

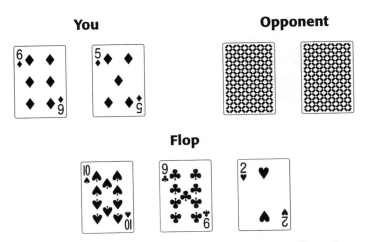

You **Opponent**

Flop

You call him and a card lower than a 10 comes off on the turn. He's probably going to check because he most likely has an A-K, A-Q, or two other big, unpaired cards. If he checks the turn, you can often take the pot away from him by betting.

You must have good instincts to make this play. It's such a difficult play to make that only the top players can pull it off. I'm talking about a play where you call on the flop with no hand and no draw, with the specific intent of taking the pot away from your opponent on the next round. You can only do this when you know that a player will only fire one shell into the pot. If he leads at the pot a second time you're not going to be able to make the play. Great players have the instinct required to make this sort of a move. They have a sixth sense that tells them when they can take a pot away from an opponent.

PLAYING FOR A LIVING

Cash Games versus Tournaments

Tournament poker is very tough on you. It's tough on you mentally because you're going to lose most of the time. You play for hours and hours and then get knocked out in some fashion and end up going home frustrated. It is very difficult to be able to deal with the poker world as a tournament specialist. You've got to have the right mindset to do it because you're going to be facing pain and frustration day in and day out.

I played the tournament circuit for fifteen years, long before the World Poker Tour was born. Tournaments helped me in my career because I had my share of success in them, and that success led me to other things. However, if you are not comfortable accepting the emotional hardship that goes along with playing tournaments, just play cash games. If you're a top-notch poker player, you're going to win seven out of ten times when you play cash games. Seven days out of ten you're going to go home happy and satisfied. The other three days you're not going to be upset because you know that poker is not just about what happened that day; it's about what happens over the course of the year.

Good players look at poker as a year-long game. Incidentally, that's the difference between the pros and amateurs. An amateur is normally all hung up about winning that day. A guy who thinks straight about poker doesn't really care what happens today. If the game is bad, even if he's losing a little bit, he will feel good about getting up and quitting and then coming back tomorrow. He has the discipline not to worry about losing today. The pro is looking at the bottom line over a longer period.

Still, I think that you really have to play the poker tournament circuit if you want to make it big in the poker world today.

Young players want to be seen on television, they want the whole world to know they're a player. They desire fame, fortune and recognition. People that haven't played tournaments for years are now coming out to compete in the World Poker Tour events. Like all of us, they have egos. They want to prove that they can play poker, and want all their friends and relatives to see them on national TV.

Dealing With a String of Losses

Even if you're a good player, you're not going to win many more than one in every forty or fifty tournaments you play. That's my guess. Theoretically, let's say that in a 100-player field, ten players make it to the final table and get a cash payout. Most tournaments pay about 10 percent of the field. That makes you a 10 to 1 underdog to make the money if you're an average player.

I figure good players are about 5 to 1 underdogs. They're getting roughly twice as much value as average players, but still only make the money about one out of every five times. Winning is still very, very difficult, even for the good players. The psychological hardship of defeat is tough and very frustrating. You need to make sure you have a good bankroll since you're knocked out most of the time.

TELLS

For the most part, the common tells are those that indicate when people are trying to look weak or strong. In other words, when their eyes are looking off to the side or trying to watch TV after they have made a big bet, generally they're strong. If they're trying to act strong, bang their chips onto the table or perhaps sit in a very rigid way staring you down, they're often weak.

Tells are much more subtle at the top level. They're very tiny indicators, maybe how a guy reaches for his chips or bets or peeks at his cards, just something that gives you a feel for the strength of his hand.

Tells really come into play in the lower stakes games. That's where you really pick up on them. Tells go along with your instincts. You just have a sense of who is a bit weak. Sometimes it is just the way your opponent looks or some small thing that he has done. Be observant and go with your instincts. When in doubt, go with your first instinct.

The simplest tell is the way that somebody stacks his chips. If he is meticulous, chances are he is going to be a solid type of player. If he is a bit messy, he is likely to be an aggressive, loose player.

Another obvious tell is when a couple of suited cards come out on the flop and your opponent looks down at his cards again. Most of the time he is looking to see whether he has a flush draw. If he just calls your bet, you can be fairly sure that he probably has the draw. And of course, at the lower levels you often see people almost light up like a Christmas tree when they hit their card on the river.

You have to be paying attention all the time to pick up tells, not just when you are involved in a pot. When you're not playing a hand, you may see something beneficial that you can use later. For example, a player often is bluffing when he bets quickly, and he usually has a good hand when he takes a long time to bet. You won't pick up this tell unless you are watching your opponents.

MONEY MANAGEMENT

Tournaments

If you're playing $1,000 tournaments, I recommend that you have *at least* $20,000 in your bankroll. There is, however, an old saying, "You only need one buy-in until you win the first one." Just remember that the average player will only cash in one out of every ten tournaments—assuming 100 players and payouts to the top 10 percent (ten players, in this example). The really good players make the money about two or three times out of ten.

Cash Games

One of the biggest mistakes I see with the newer players is that they try to play at limits that are too high for their skill level and bankroll. In the old days, all the players who were eventually successful as pros worked their way up through the respective levels. They played a year or two at $10/$20 or $15/$30 and then another year of $20/$40 or $30/$60 before moving up to the higher levels such as $60/$120 or $100/$200.

They paid their dues over a series of years to build up a bankroll and harness an ability to beat the competition. It doesn't matter what other people say, the truth is that, generally, the higher the limit you're playing, the higher the skill level of the competition. Every time you move up and play a different limit, you'd better believe you are going to be up against a tougher type of player.

If you want to learn how to play poker professionally, you have to swallow your pride. When you step up to a higher level and things don't go well, overcome your ego and drop back down to a level you *can* beat.

MY PROUDEST MOMENTS

The poker event that made me the happiest was when I won my first bracelet at the World Series of Poker. I don't think I will ever get a chance again to experience the same joy of victory that I felt when I won that first bracelet. At the time, the World Series was everything in the poker world. Certainly back then, to identify yourself as a great player, or to feel like a great player, you had to have a bracelet from the World Series of Poker. Also, the event that I won was the game I was playing every day of the week, which was stud 8-or-better. That was my Main Event. I think it was the most enjoyable tournament I have ever played because I don't remember making a single error the entire time and that was very satisfying.

It was also ironic that before the tournament started, a bunch of us got together and made a last-longer bet of $1,000 each. I won the $17,000 last-longer pool as well as the event prize money. The side bet was great fun and gave me even more inspiration to go on and win. That was certainly my happiest day playing poker.

First and foremost, I consider myself a poker player, but I am also very proud of my achievements away from the poker table. Creating the original Tournament of Champions, the PartyPoker.com Million poker tournaments, and leading PartyPoker.com from nowhere to being the biggest online poker site in the world have also been very satisfying achievements.

In addition, my long association with the World Poker Tour has been quite fulfilling. Make no mistake about it, the explosion of poker's popularity was caused by the creation of the World Poker Tour. It was the first poker show to be played in prime time on a weekly basis and, because of the WPT's success, ESPN expanded its coverage of the World Series of Poker. The network moved the WSOP from an early morning slot, when very few people even knew it was on, to mainstream TV. Eventually, Fox and NBC also started to run poker shows, but it all started with the popularity of the World Poker Tour. Also, it was partially due to my association with the WPT that I am considered an ambassador for poker. I am extremely happy and proud when people call me that.

FINAL WORDS OF WIZDOM

For Players Who Want to Turn Pro

The first word of caution I would pass on to new players is that being successful as a professional poker player is not as easy as it looks on TV.

Secondly, if you do manage to score a big tournament win, make sure you don't waste the money. You're going to have to keep a lot of it to help you survive until you make it to your next final table. If you burn up your money and let it slip away, you're going to discover that it isn't always as easy to get it back. It isn't even easy for the very best players in the world to make it to the top spots in the big tournaments. Be smart with your money if you want to be a professional poker player.

WD: Stoic is the word that comes to mind when one thinks about Mike Sexton. Both he and T.J. Cloutier have facial features that make you believe you are speaking to a living portrait or looking up at the impressive granite features of Mount Rushmore. During the course of our interview, it became apparent that Mike's rock solid facial features may be one of the reasons he has performed so well at the poker table over the years; he just doesn't provide those same elusive indicators of human behavior that many people hand you on a platter when you're sitting across from them. There is no flick of an eyelid, small tilt of the head or tightening around the corner of the mouth to give a deeper meaning or addendum to his words or actions.

Above all, Mike Sexton is a particularly interesting poker player to interview because he sees all the hands of the six players who reach the WPT final table. Viewers at home view only the cards that avoid the editor's cut so they get a very different view of the table dynamic and miss many of the hands that go uncontested. Particularly interesting is that, after twenty-five years of profitable play in tournaments, Mike has changed some of his core beliefs about the best way to play a tournament. Because of his special insight into the game he now believes that if you want to win the major tournaments, you can't just focus on survival as your primary goal. If you do, you'll rarely have enough chips on the final table to make a serious run for one of the top three spots.

It seems that Mike Sexton's years of experience and insights from the WPT are continuing to pay off. In 2006, he took home his first $1 million prize by winning first place in the No-Limit Hold'em Tournament of Champions in Las Vegas.

MEL JUDAH

"The Silver Fox"

Career Tournament Earnings Exceeding $3,000,000
Winner, World Series of Poker $1,500 Seven-Card Stud, 1989
Winner, Diamond Jim Brady Classic $1,000 Limit Hold'em, 1990
Second place, WSOP $1,500 Limit Hold'em, 1990
Winner, Diamond Jim Brady Classic $1,500 Limit Hold'em, 1991
Second place, WSOP $1,500 Omaha High-Low, 1991
Third place, WSOP Championship Event, 1997
Winner, WSOP $5,000 Seven-Card Stud, 1997
Third place, WSOP $5,000 Seven-Card Stud High-Low, 2000
Winner, WPT Legends of Poker No-Limit Hold'em Main Event, 2003
Second place, WSOP $5,000 Seven-Card Stud, 2003
Winner, Crown Australasian $2,000 limit Omaha High-Low, 2003
Winner, L.A. Poker Classic $1,000 Stud/Omaha Hi/Lo, 2004
Winner, Mirage Poker Showdown $3,000 Pot-limit Omaha, 2005
Winner, United Kingdom Open £1,250 No-Limit Hold'em, 2007

Sitting Down With Mel

His legendary prowess in seven-card stud often causes fear among competitors across the table. Mel Judah is also a world-class hold'em player and one of the very best all-around poker pros in the business. He holds two World Series of Poker bracelets for stud, a World Poker Tour trophy for no-limit hold'em, and multiple tournament titles in Omaha.

The general poker community knows him as the Silver Fox because of his white hair and the taciturn stealth with which he gathers chips at the table. I like to call him the "Aussie Battler" because he is a hard worker who has an accomplished yet understated way about him. You never see him stand up and yell, or partake in the seemingly ritualistic modern day frenzy to attract media attention. He has consistently turned down most requests for major interviews because he prefers to keep his theories private. If you don't know him personally or didn't see his photo on the cover of *Card Player* magazine a few years ago, you might easily sit across the table from him in a tournament and make the critical error of underestimating this very dangerous and extremely accomplished opponent.

Prior to immigrating to Australia in 1981, Mel Judah was a hairdresser in England who scrimped and saved to start his own salon. Eventually, he proved that with hard work, patience, experience and knowledge, you can make your way successfully in the poker world. For the last twenty years he has supported his family exclusively by playing tournaments and side games, winning nearly $3 million in prize money just from tournaments. When he is not playing in live games or tournaments on the professional circuit, you can often find him playing online at T6poker.com.

Let's hear what Mel has to say…

MEL
JUDAH

THE MAKINGS OF A POKER WIZARD

Self-control and Money Management Skills

Self-control and superior money management skills are the first ingredients you need if you want to move forward and improve as a poker player. It is also important to adapt your style of play to the type of opponents you are playing.

Knowledge

I believe the skill that distinguishes the very best players from the rest of the field is knowledge. It is an understanding of your opponents and ability to analyze hands so that you know when to defend, when to make a play, and when to get away from a hand. You also have to understand when you have simply been lucky. That level of understanding takes a lot of time and experience to achieve.

Many people think they have enough knowledge to play well and be successful long-term players because they have experienced some short-term success. The truth is that it requires a lot more experience than many people realize before they understand enough aspects of the game to execute them successfully over a long period of time.

Avoid Going on Tilt

A significant difference between an average player and a champion is the ability of the champion to avoid going on tilt. The better players are able to lose less when things are not going well. Minimizing your losses and maximizing your gains are key ingredients for success in poker. Anybody can play well when the cards are coming in their favor, but maintaining one's composure when the chips are down is critically important. After all, the money you don't lose is indirectly the same as the money you have won. The better players realize this and are very careful to play just as well when things are going badly.

Adapting to the Playing Environment

Adaptation is certainly one of the other strengths that good players have. It is an ability to analyze a given situation during a tournament and adapt accordingly. If a table is playing too tightly, a good player will start to take advantage of that and steal more blinds. If the other players are not aggressive enough, the good player will take advantage of that too, see a lot of flops cheaply and outplay opponents after the flop. He is constantly changing his play, based on the other players' actions and style.

Mentally Record the Actions of Your Opponents

Unlike a home game or a cash game with regular players, during the early stages of a tournament you don't have any prior knowledge of your opponents. You don't know who can lay down a hand or who will call a big reraise. You gain more knowledge and can make better decisions by diligently observing your opponents and using that information to make big decisions.

Are they the type of players who only make big bets with one of the very top hands preflop? Are they likely to be just making a value bet with a hand like A-J? It is a tremendous advantage to know which players overvalue certain hands and which don't. Are they calling stations? If so, you know they're going to give you some chips when you make a raise on the button with a big hand. Observing and mentally recording the actions and tendencies of your opponents is an absolute necessity if you want to be a long-term winner.

Limit versus No-Limit Hold'em

Many people see poker on TV and jump straight into no-limit hold'em when they first learn how to play. It then becomes very hard for them later to learn how to play limit hold'em effectively. I strongly recommend that players learn how to play limit hold'em successfully before they move up to no-limit. If you concentrate on limit hold'em first, it gives you a very solid foundation. Also, when you do make mistakes they're far less costly. There are a number of subtle yet significant differences between the two games.

In limit hold'em you are betting units and not putting your entire stack at risk. It allows you to put in more bets and take additional risk without hurting your stack too much. The betting is less about bluffing and more about strategic decisions such as getting in extra bets when it matters, deciding whether to raise on the flop or turn, raising to make a pot bigger with your straight or flush draw, or getting paid off when you have overcards.

Generally, you'll start with better hands in limit hold'em than you do in no-limit. Of course, your range of starting hands will depend on how loose or tight the game is and your position. If you are playing at a very tight table, you are not likely have a significant advantage over many of your opponents once they call you. If you raise and get called by people at a tight table you have to be very careful after the flop in limit hold'em.

If you are in a very loose limit game, you have a better chance of having an advantage over an initial raiser if you are able to isolate him. A lot of people call in a loose game, and you'll find that many loose players will raise with any two connected cards. If you have a hand such as A-J and a loose player to your right raises, you can reraise. That way, you'll stand a good chance of eliminating players to your left. In this example, you may be well ahead of the loose player who made the initial bet. In a tight game, that same opportunity is less likely to occur.

In no-limit hold'em, on the other hand, you can go broke at any time and have to be more aggressive in the way you play to protect your stack. No-limit allows you to create fear in your opponents so there tends to be more bluffing and greater use of position to win. You can also use position in no-limit to play small to medium pairs or suited connectors that will be paid off well if you hit the flop and your opponent has a premium hand, opportunities which are entirely different than in a limit game.

Playing People versus Playing Cards

On many occasions you have to go with your intuition when making decisions. Therefore, having a strong gut feeling can be very helpful. While it is important to get good cards and know how to play them, having a strong ability to read people is, at times, far more important than the cards themselves. All the great players who win large tournaments do so, in part, because they're able to read people well and make big calls or bets when they think their opponents are weak. They're able to analyze a situation and incorporate the tells from their opponents' body language to get a full picture. To be successful, you have to develop an ability to do both things well—play people and play cards.

MY START IN POKER

I first learned how to play poker by watching my father huddled around the kitchen table playing with his friends. He was a good player who gave me a very solid foundation on which to build. When I was older, I started to play in a few small home games, but it was not until I was about thirty years old and working as a hairdresser in London that I eventually played in my first casino poker game. My wife was away briefly with my son on a holiday and I had some spare time on my hands. I walked into a casino that had poker and found that I really loved the game. That very first night I met some serious players who invited me to a larger home game. I started to win most of the money in that game and was eventually barred for that reason. That is when my serious love for poker was born. I figured if I was good enough that people didn't want to play with me, perhaps I should do more of it!

Actually, over the course of my poker career I have been banned from a number of home games because I was winning too much. When that happens, you know you are probably doing something right. I played in a couple of other games around London for a few years while still running my own salon. Eventually my desire to visit Las Vegas became too strong to resist so, in 1981, I traveled there to check out the poker scene. I returned to Vegas in 1985 and won a satellite to the main event at the World Series of Poker and then did the same thing in 1987. In 1989, I won my first WSOP bracelet and since then, have never looked back.

TOURNAMENT STRATEGY

Avoid Common Tournament Errors

The biggest mistake I see new players making is playing too aggressively with average hands. They also bluff too much and are unable to lay down enough hands. They see the top players on TV at a final table and how much bluffing goes on, but don't see the lead up to the final table or hands that are thrown away. They conclude that it is correct to play very aggressively throughout the whole tournament, which is a false impression.

For example, I often see people limp in with a hand like Q-J early in a tournament, get raised by somebody to their left, and then move all in to steal the pot. Their opponent calls and turns over a hand like K-K—and all of a sudden, they're busted. If you limp in with average hands up front, you have to be willing to throw them away against a raiser. You are probably already well behind in the hand and will be playing out of position after the flop if you call.

> THE BIGGEST MISTAKE I SEE NEW PLAYERS MAKING IS PLAYING TOO AGGRESSIVELY WITH AVERAGE HANDS. THEY ALSO BLUFF TOO MUCH AND ARE UNABLE TO LAY DOWN ENOUGH HANDS.

To Win, You Can't Play it Safe

If you want to win a major tournament you have to take some chances and win a number of big hands along the way. Sometimes those opportunities are going to present themselves when you are on a draw. Especially today, because the average number of competitors has grown so much, reaching a final table is somewhat like walking through a minefield. You have to win over and over again, yet avoid a lot of traps along the way to be successful. On occasion you'll have to risk a substantial number of your chips as an underdog. For example, if you have a good flush draw on the flop and think you can get a good pot going or force your opponent to fold by making a substantial raise, sometimes it is necessary to take that risk. Winning that pot may give you the chips you need to have a substantial advantage later in the tournament.

When you take appropriate chances at the right time and are fortunate enough to build a reasonable stack, you have a substantial advantage over most of the smaller stacks later in the tournament because you can play more hands, perhaps see your flush draw to the river, and so on. The short stack has to risk all his chips at once. In some tournaments, you'll find that you are the short stack and have to make a move, or will be pot-committed in the big blind. If you are going to win a large tournament, you just have to get lucky in those situations.

Even when you do manage to build a large stack early in the tournament, playing is still hazardous. By the second or third day, the chip lead is constantly changing because things are so competitive. Because the blinds and antes are much larger by then, players with small to medium stacks have to become more aggressive just to stay alive. A lot of players start moving all in. You have to win most of those large confrontations to do well in the tournament and doing so requires a lot of risk. It is almost impossible to avoid the type of situation where you have Q-Q or J-J and a smaller stack moves all in with a hand like A-K or A-Q.

Years ago when the championship fields were much smaller, it was much easier to lay down a good hand even if you thought you were ahead because you knew that you would have plenty of time to let your advantage work for you. In today's events, where you are battling against a large number of players, you can't afford to lay down a big hand if you think you are well ahead, even if it means risking all your chips. You have to build a big stack if you want to make it to the final table.

Adapting to Different Tournament Stages

I don't go into a tournament with a set strategy of how I am going to play during the different stages. I am a fairly slow starter and like to get a good feel for the other players and then adjust my play accordingly. Nevertheless, the way my opponents play influences the way I play.

Many people play tighter and less aggressive poker during the **early stages** of a tournament. For the first two or three levels, this allows me to see a lot of fairly cheap flops and play more post-flop poker.

My play during the **middle stages** depends on the rest of the table and what they're doing. I am a fairly solid player, but if my table is fairly loose I'm forced to loosen up as well. If I am at a very tight table, and our relative chip stacks allow, I will take advantage of their tightness by raising the blinds more often. I know that they're unlikely to come back over the top of me without a premium hand.

During the **later stages**, when the limits move up, the tournament starts to dramatically change. Players become more aggressive and start moving all in if they have a small stack. During this stage you really have to wait for a situation where somebody wants to move all in and you have A-A or another dominant hand. Even then, a hand such as A-A is going to get cracked about 20 percent of the time in a heads-up situation.

As I stated previously, navigating your way through a tournament is a lot like traveling through a minefield. During the later stages of a tournament, when you have a lot of short to medium stacks moving all in, the best way to win is to make sure you only get involved with those players when you believe you are probably holding the best hand. You then have to be lucky enough to win the majority of those situations or you'll be out of the tournament. You can't pass up those opportunities or you'll never get enough chips to have a chance of winning.

Playing Short-Handed

When playing at a short-handed table of six or fewer players, the chance that more than one person is going to have a premium hand is a lot less than it is at a nine-handed table. With nine or ten players, it is normal to find three players involved in a pot, all with reasonable hands. That doesn't happen as much at a short-handed table. An average hand such as K-J has much more value when you are short-handed, particularly if a couple of people have already folded. You are likely to be well ahead against a random hand. Also, because there are likely to be fewer premium hands, there are more opportunities to steal the blinds.

The Role of Luck in Large Tournaments

Poker has changed a lot over the years. Many of the young Internet players who play today are super-aggressive and capable of making lots of moves. The live tournaments are not only more aggressive in nature, but also much larger. As a result, my game has had to change as well. In my opinion, the luck factor has increased by 30 to 40 percent due to the large number of players in the bigger tournaments. A lot of skill is involved in the earlier levels of a tournament, but in the later stages, luck plays a much larger role. With a small to average stack later in the tournament, you can easily find yourself in a situation where you raise the blinds with a good hand and run into something like K-K, but not be able to get away from the hand because you don't have enough chips.

Even though I still play fairly solid poker, because of this luck factor, there are times when I find it necessary to play looser than I did in the old days. If I have position, I will call some preflop raises that I wouldn't have previously called because many opponents are raising with lesser hands. On other occasions, depending on the stage of the tournament and my stack size, I will be more willing to gamble and commit my chips rather than let my stack become too small. If my stack gets down to three to four times the size of the big blind, I know that even if I double up, I will still be in a danger zone. I don't like my stack to fall below seven times the size of the big blind.

AGGRESSION

How to Counteract an Aggressive Player

Suppose you are out of position against an aggressive player who has raised or reraised you. It's late in the tournament and you think there is a good chance he may outmaneuver you after the flop. If you have a premium hand, moving all in is often the correct action, particularly at the final table with a short to medium stack. By moving in, you take away a lot of your opponent's moves and put the pressure back on him to make a decision.

When I have chips early in a tournament, I prefer to wait until I have position and a good hand before getting involved against an aggressive player. Unless I have A-A or K-K and am sure he will call a big reraise, I believe it is better to just call rather than reraise. This play allows me to build a larger pot, yet give no indication of the type of hand that I have.

In other words, if I have a good hand and position over an aggressive player, I am more likely to let him see a flop. However, if I am out of position with a premium hand such as A-A, I prefer to raise and win the hand preflop or make him pay to see a flop.

I will occasionally call a preflop raise from an aggressive player with an unexpected hand such as 7-8 suited if I am on or near the button. Most of the aggressive young Internet players are almost always going to make a continuation bet after the flop, regardless of whether they have a made hand. If you hit the flop, they will do the betting for you. If you have a tight image and have called preflop with a hand that they wouldn't expect, habitually aggressive players will keep betting all the way and, in many cases, give you most of their chips.

Bluffing

While bluffing is an important part of a successful strategy, opportune timing is actually far more important. A good sense of timing tells you when you can get away with a bluff. Many lesser players bluff too much at seemingly random times and have no true sense of when or against whom they're more likely to be successful.

For example, suppose another player and you both have A-K and see a flop that comes A-J-6. The other player will probably bet into you. If he is a good player, you may be able to come back over the top of him and force him to fold the hand. He will probably assume that you have a much bigger hand than A-K, possibly a set or top two pair. In the worst-case scenario, he will call and you probably will split the pot. Many average players wouldn't recognize that situation as an opportunity.

Sometimes, you just sense that your opponents are weak and can pick up the pot. On other occasions, you know that bluffing is the only way to win, so you are more or less forced to put in a bet. Overall, picking the right time to make the bluff is more important than the bluff itself. Stu Ungar had a tremendous ability to pick the right time to make aggressive plays and win large pots. He would be thinking two or three moves ahead and know exactly when to bet.

Bluffing is all about putting in the correct bet at the right time, not just making big bets to steal pots.

Online Players

In my experience, online players tend to play a fairly loose style of poker when they're playing live, certainly much looser than the full-time live-game player. Online, they have just a few seconds to act and don't know that much about their opponents, so they tend to play a larger range of hands with a lot less fear and a greater willingness to gamble. To beat them, you have to be willing to mix it up a bit. Wait for good hands and let them do the betting. Occasionally, play back at them if they're stealing your blinds too often.

STARTING HAND CONCEPTS

> Unless stated otherwise, all of the situations discussed by the Wizards in the Starting Hand Concepts and Specific Hand Strategy sections are assumed to be at a full table, during the third level of a tournament. The blinds are $100/$200, and you have an average stack of around $11,000 in chips. It is also assumed that the players are displaying a moderate level of aggression and appear to be playing reasonably well.

The size of your stack and the stage of the tournament are the primary factors that determine whether you play passively, aggressively or super-aggressively during a tournament. Just because you are dealt a good hand doesn't mean that you should always play the hand aggressively. Even though it is possible to generalize about how you play specific hands, you must remember that there is no set formula that always leads to success. The way I play will vary depending on the play of those people around me.

Early Position

As one of the first players to act with a reasonable stack, I don't recommend getting too fancy. Particularly during the earlier stages of the tournament, you still have a lot of playing time left, so stick to hands such as A-J suited, A-Q and all the premium hands: A-A, K-K, Q-Q, A-K and J-J.

Middle Position

The hands I play from middle position are influenced, to a larger degree, by the type of players who are in the big and small blinds and whether they're tight, aggressive or make a lot of calls. My action will also depend somewhat on my image. If I am getting respect because I haven't played many hands, my opponents will be more likely to lay down a better hand. If I have been making a lot of preflop raises, they will be more likely to call or reraise me.

Still, my advice is to wait for premium hands and don't be too creative. Occasionally, be willing to make a play with a hand such as J-10 suited, and all the hands that you would play from the earlier positions.

Late Position

My action in late position is dependent on the type of players in the blinds. I play all the hands that I have mentioned, and also loosen up somewhat from the button or next to the button, occasionally calling an early raise with medium connectors or a medium pair if the implied odds are attractive enough.

I will also make that type of a call from the big blind as well. If I have a tight image and call a raise from the button or big blind, my opponent is probably going to put me on a fairly big hand, not something like 5-3 suited. If I get a good flop, I have the potential to take most of my opponent's chips.

SPECIFIC HAND STRATEGY

A-A

When I am the first person to bet from early position and have A-A, I like to mix up my betting so that what I have is not obvious. I might raise three times the big blind or limp-in just to make people think about what I have. Most of the time I will come in with a raise, hoping that somebody will come back over the top of me with some sort of move.

K-K

With K-K and all the high pairs, I always make a standard raise of around three times the big blind. I don't want somebody to come into the pot and crack me with a weak ace.

Q-Q

I make the same standard raise preflop with Q-Q. If someone raises in front of me, I am more likely to just call and take a look at the flop. Whether to just call or reraise depends on the type of player who raised me and the relative size of our stacks. If I put my opponent on a smaller pair such as J-J or 10-10, I will reraise, of course.

A-K

At some stage during a tournament, you are probably going to have to gamble with A-K. Some players do that during the early stages of a tournament because they want to accumulate chips. Others prefer to play a waiting game to see how everybody is playing. Up front with A-K during the early stages of a no-limit tournament, I will normally make a small raise or limp in to build a pot. You have to accumulate chips, so it is necessary to play the good hands when you get them. On the other hand, you don't want to get rid of all your opponents. Ideally, you would prefer to see the flop with no more than two or three other players.

When you make a preflop bet with A-K and are raised, your actions should depend primarily on who raised and the size of that raise. In the early stages of a tournament, you can play more passively because it is often best to settle in and see how everybody is playing before you decide to commit too many chips.

In the later stages of a tournament, particularly with a smaller stack, you'll be far more likely to play A-K aggressively or hyper-aggressively and move all in when you are raised. If you have more chips, you can also decide to just call and see a flop. If you put your opponent on A-K and you have the same sort of hand, you can actually take the pot away from good players if an ace and a jack, queen or 10 come on the flop. When you push your chips in, some players will put you on top two-pair or assume you have flopped a set.

If you are short-stacked, moving all in is the correct action when you are raised holding a hand like A-K, even if you think your opponent may hold a hand as strong as J-J or Q-Q. If the blinds are still small, such as $25/$50, and I make a standard raise of $150 with a small stack of around $1,000 and somebody reraises to $300, I will be moving all in. However, if I have $10,000 in chips, I wouldn't necessarily make that move.

A-Q

I normally make a standard raise with A-Q from up front. If somebody in position reraises, my A-Q is probably not worth very much.

If I am on or near the button or in the big blind with A-Q and somebody bets, I have to consider all aspects of the hand before

I decide to call, reraise or move all in. A very important part of the decision-making process is considering which position he raised from. However, it is also important to keep in mind that just because he's raising from one of the later positions doesn't necessarily mean he's stealing. He may very well have A-K or better. What you do depends on the type of player making the raise. If he is aggressive and often tries to steal the blinds, the chances are that you actually have the best hand, so you should definitely reraise. However, if he doesn't play many hands, you have to be much more careful with A-Q.

J-J and 10-10

J-J is a little bit easier to play than 10-10. There are a number of different ways to play jacks. Limping in to see a cheap flop is not a bad idea. Alternatively, you can raise around two-and-a-half to three times the big blind and see if you get reraised.

If you are raised preflop, you can call and see the flop. After the flop, if you are first to act and no ace or king comes, the correct action is to bet. If you are raised again, you should probably throw the hand away. On the other hand, if you spike a jack on the flop and make your set, you can check and let the preflop aggressor do the betting for you.

What you shouldn't do with medium pairs, unless you are short stacked, is make yourself so pot-committed preflop that your opponent is going to end up seeing five cards. Many new players tend to overvalue medium pairs preflop and overcommit themselves. I would much rather see a flop before deciding what to do.

K-J, Q-10, Q-J, 10-9

These hands are much better played from good position near the button so that you can have control over the betting. From the early positions you can be easily dominated if raised. In other words, if you enter a pot from one of the first few seats and then call a raise, you can get yourself into a lot of trouble after the flop if you make a pair.

Small to Medium Pairs: 5-5 to 9-9

Some players like to raise with the small to medium pairs. Instead, I prefer to see a lot of cheap flops with them. However, the problem with not being aggressive is that the blinds will be able to get in pretty cheaply. As a result, when you do hit a flop and make your set, you have to be

> WHAT YOU SHOULDN'T DO WITH MEDIUM PAIRS, UNLESS YOU ARE SHORT STACKED, IS MAKE YOURSELF SO POT-COMMITTED PREFLOP THAT YOUR OPPONENT IS GOING TO END UP SEEING FIVE CARDS.

aware that somebody else may have made a straight or have a good draw to a straight or flush. I have been caught a number of times in that way. I remember one particular occasion when I limped in with 6-6 from the button, and the flop came 2-3-6. One player flopped a set of deuces, I made a set of sixes, and the player in the big blind had 4-5. Unfortunately, I lost most of my chips. That type of thing is going to happen from time to time if you let the blinds into the hand cheaply.

Early in a tournament, I will often just call with average pairs from up front to see a cheap flop and try to hit a set. If I'm raised by a player to my left, I will call if it doesn't cost too much relative to the size of my stack, then get away from the hand if I don't hit my set on the flop. When the stacks are big and the blinds are small, I know I can double my stack if I hit a set against a player who has a good hand.

Small to Medium Suited Connectors

You can play suited connectors if you want to, and many of the top players do just that, but the single most important word of advice I can give anybody is this: Don't fall in love with them.

Too many new players get involved with suited connectors and then bluff away all of their chips.

STATE OF MIND

Dealing With Downswings

When things have gone badly for a while, the best thing to do is take a break. Go back, look at your game and try to analyze objectively how you have been playing. If you find that you have been playing well, but are just having bad luck, you have to remember that eventually it will swing back the other way. If you get all your money in with A-A and get beaten by 6-6, there is nothing you can do. That's poker!

Periods of bad luck can go on for a long time, but it is important to remember that those are the situations in which you want to get your money in the middle. You want to get your money in as a favorite. Sometimes you are just going to be unlucky. You also have to recognize when you get lucky; don't confuse your good luck with superior skill. Alternatively, if you find that you have been playing badly, obviously you have to change your game.

It is also beneficial to remember the significant times when you have been lucky. They can make you feel a lot better by reminding you that the pendulum swings both ways. You can't always win with the best hand. When you get beat, it is nice to recollect the times you have been on the other end of the equation. I recall a particular WPT event in which I got very lucky against T.J. Cloutier. At the final table I was all in with K-J and he had A-10. I managed to spike a jack on the river to win a very big pot that gave me enough chips to go on and win the tournament.

TELLS

Good players will gather a tremendous amount of information from you at the table if you are not careful. I recommend speaking as little as possible and making a maximum effort to keep your actions consistent. If you are in a hand and somebody asks you a question, you are not obliged to answer. If they ask you how much the bet is, or how many chips you have, don't tell them—that's what the dealer is for. The minute you open your mouth, you give people free information that can be used to your disadvantage.

The way people put their chips into the pot is a fairly good tell that I often look for. Do they put them in with great force or very gently when they're strong? Do they bet quickly or slowly? As is the case with most tells, you have to remember what they have done in the past and be able to visualize those actions again for future reference.

Some people tend to reach for a drink when they're scared. Other people do it when they're confident. If you observe a player's behavior over time, you'll soon see if he demonstrates either tell.

Occasionally, players stare at you when they're weak. Others will do it and challenge you when they're strong so they can get a call from you. I believe people are less inclined to get into a staring match with you when they're weak. In either case, once you observe them do it a couple of times, the tendency becomes clear.

Some players talk a lot when they're nervous. It allows them to feel better by releasing nervous tension in order to stay in control.

Betting patterns often provide the most obvious information available to you at the table. Many people make a small bet when they're weak, others overbet when they're weak and make a smaller bet when they're strong. Have they just made a bet that makes them committed to the pot? If so, they're basically telling you that they're going to call if you bet. Although betting patterns are somewhat less reliable among the very bad players, keeping track of how a person bets can give you a real edge against reasonable players.

MONEY MANAGEMENT

In my opinion, if you pay your own way into tournaments today it is a losing proposition. There are so many people in the larger tournaments that even the very best players can go years without winning. To be able to afford all those tournaments, you either have to be sponsored, extremely wealthy, or win your way in through satellites.

One of the best ways you can manage your money well is to be very selective when it comes to deciding which tournaments to enter. Looking at the risk and likely return of the various tournaments is very important. For example, I would much rather enter a $5,000 buy-in event against 300 average players than enter an event with 50 very good players. My chances of having a big win would be greater in the larger tournament. You have to find the tournaments that best suit your financial situation.

To survive in the tournament business, you must have a reasonable win every now and then. It is nice to come first or second in a smaller $1,500 event, but the $30,000 that you win is only going to pay part of the bill for the larger tournaments. It is extremely costly to play the major events if you don't win your way in by playing the satellites. If I am going to invest my time in a long tournament, I prefer it to be one that has a substantial payout and a large number of intermediate players.

Play Satellites to Reduce Your Expenses

Let's say that a player has $25,000 in cash and wants to use it to play tournaments. I recommend taking around $4,000 of that money and investing it in satellites as a way of lowering overall cost.

Single table satellite events can be a very efficient way of keeping costs down. Even though they officially pay only one spot, the players usually make a deal when it gets down to two or three players.

Supersatellites are another way of reducing your tournament expenses. Unfortunately, in supersatelites, most people play well in the early rounds, but a lot of gambling goes on during the later stages because the blinds escalate so quickly. Also, supers can take up a lot of time and you may not get there. Overall, you have much less time to play your regular game. The blinds go up quickly on a single table satellite as well, but you are up against a smaller group of players and have a much better idea of the overall chip situation in the tournament. I find them a lot less time consuming.

Play Cash Games to Subsidize Tournaments

If you are a good player, cash games are the most consistent way of making money in today's poker environment. The best way to make money in no-limit hold'em cash games is to play consistently in one place so that you develop a good understanding of your competition. When you are traveling on the tournament circuit and sit down at a new cash game, you are always the outsider. You don't know who is tight, aggressive, reckless and so on. Nevertheless, cash games can be a good way to develop a significant source of income on the road.

Pot-limit and no-limit games tend to be far more volatile than limit games and can be very rewarding for skilled players who like to accept that volatility. Personally, I find that limit games provide a more consistent source of income and, overall, a greater edge for the better players.

Pro Expectation: Making the Money

The best players expect to make a final table one out of every fifteen or so tournaments and hope to win one out of every thirty. However, many good players can go through their whole career without winning a major tournament. Life can be very tough when you run badly for long periods of time. When things are bad you are consistently getting knocked out with the best hands and have terrible runs of cards. When that is happening, nobody knows or even cares about it except you. Then, suddenly, your luck turns around and you find yourself winning events back-to-back. If you are a good player, you must have patience—you'll eventually get your turn.

FINAL WORDS OF WIZDOM

If you are fortunate enough to be lucky and get some good breaks when you start playing poker, or if you play very well for a period of time and win some tournaments, don't become overconfident and start to think you know everything about the game.

Remember, we are all only as good as our last win.

> **WD:** The story of Mel Judah is interesting not just because of his numerous accomplishments, but also because, in many ways, he is the personification of a normal guy who competes day after day to make a living on the very tough professional poker circuit. He is the quiet achiever, the man who will tell you about the tough peaks and valleys of professional poker life, and the one just waiting in the wings to snatch another big win from the hordes of new players pumping Internet cash into the live tournament circuit.

MARC SALEM

How to Read People and Detect Lies

Author
Marc Salem's Mind Games
The Six Keys to Unlock and Empower Your Mind: Spot Liars & Cheats,
Negotiate Any Deal to Your Advantage, Win at the Office,
Influence Friends, & Much More

MARC SALEM

Sitting Down with Marc

Marc Salem, man of mystery, intellectual, entertainer and master of non-verbal communication, stands on the stage of yet one more packed-out theater. Under one of three Styrofoam cups a sharp knife points upward, poised to cut into Salem's hand if he picks the wrong ones when he slams his hand down to crush two of the three containers. His decision is based on the assistance of a volunteer from the audience who has unfortunately misunderstood his instructions. Salem misreads the man's minute mannerisms and clues, which were subconsciously supposed to indicate the location of the knife, and brings his hand down on the wrong cup. As the dagger slices through Salem's hand, blood spurts to the ground and a wave of shock suddenly flows over the crowd.

On this particularly unusual day the audience gets to see one of Marc Salem's few errors. Ironically, that error and its very visible result has proved to the audience that the show is certainly no sham. Further, it has underlined the great confidence with which Salem is normally able to read the non-verbal tells of those around him. Since 1997, when he finally decided that there was more benefit in entertaining people with this mastery than educating them with a pen, Professor Salem has been using his unique skill as an expert in kinesics, commonly referred to as body language, and his uncanny understanding of the mental process to fascinate audiences around the world. Even though he spends a lot of time on the stage, he is also in great demand as a public speaker and continues to educate lawyers, politicians and public servants in the minute nuances of voice and movement that reveal our thoughts to those around us.

Salem holds a Doctorate in Education from New York University and a Ph.D. in Developmental Psychology from the University of Pennsylvania. He has been on the faculty of NYU, UP, Manhattan College and Marymount College. He was also a Director of Research at the Children's Television Workshop for over nine years, studying and understanding the nature and development of the mental process.

Salem worked for four years directly with Ray Birdwhistell, the founder of kinesics. Intrigued by the way people unconsciously pass on information through facial expressions, posture and eye movements, Birdwhistell, who passed away in 1994, published a major work called *Kinesics in Context*, which is still considered the preeminent work on the subject of non-verbal communication.

Fortunately for those who play poker on a regular basis, Marc Salem has avoided taking up the game because of his self-confessed compulsive behavior and a hectic schedule that wouldn't allow the time for another area of focus in his life. However, for *Poker Wizards*, he has agreed to share some of his knowledge and understanding of the most obvious ways to perceive truth and deception, an invaluable skill in one's search for mastery of the game of poker.

Let's hear what Marc has to say…

READING TELLS AND DETECTING DECEPTION

In our day-to-day lives, and specifically when we are involved in a game such as poker, most of us don't absorb the majority of the information that is available to us. No matter how good an opponent is, there will always be some leakage of information given off by the body. If there is an attempt to hold it in somewhere, it will escape somewhere else. According to Alton Barbour in his well-known work *Louder than Words*, published in 1976, human communication can be broken down as shown in the box on the following page.

Human Communication
7 percent verbal (words)
38 percent vocal (volume, intonation, rhythm, and so on)
55 percent body language (facial expression, posture, gestures, and so on)

The numerous interactions that go on around us often don't even enter our field of understanding. If we train ourselves to let them in, and then correctly interpret the information that is available, we can gain a tremendous advantage over the opposition.

Learning How to Read People and Detect Deception

There are three basic mind-tool areas in learning how to read people and detect deception. They are:

1. **Observation**

   Watching closely for the visual ingredients of deception and learning how to recognize facial expression, body language and gestures. Reading your environment every chance you get.

2. **Listening**

   Listening effectively for what normally goes unheard. Developing a system for picking up vocal tones, sudden changes, unconscious sounds, word choices, and silences. Imagine your ears as funnels picking up all the audio clues coming to you. This visualization actually works because we can control what we hear as well as what we see.

3. **Interpretation**
   Comparing current behavior to what you have seen and heard before. Finding inconsistency in an action is the challenge and the key. The inconsistency is often more significant than the action itself.

OBSERVATION

In today's busy world, people need to retrain themselves to pay closer attention to their environment because there is a tendency to be lazy and filter out information that is not required. If I were to ask you what is on the center of the back of a one-dollar bill, I'll bet your answer would be incorrect. Even though we have all handled such a bill thousands of times, I rarely find anybody who can tell me it is the word "one."

A very simple way that people can immediately start to pick up more information, particularly at a poker table, is to look at things outside their normal field of vision. If you make an effort to perceive movement out of the side of your eyes—that is, events that are in your peripheral vision—you instantly start to pick up more cues.

Another great way of picking up a vast array of additional information is to watch poker recordings in fast motion. The discrepancies start to jump out and you see a whole breadth of tics and movements that you would never have seen in slow motion. In fact, that is also a great way to uncover your own mannerisms and tells. Just have a friend film you playing poker for a while, and then replay it at high speed. You can also experiment watching television with the sound off, and not just the WPT or WSOP—you can watch almost anything that involves human interaction.

You don't have to be at a poker table to improve your observational skills. Just as you can enhance your physical health with regular exercise, you can sharpen your powers of observation by exercising that faculty. For starters, watch people while they're talking. You should practice studying people in conversation everywhere—at work, at a party, in a restaurant, on a plane, or in the park. You are looking for the variations possible in different mannerisms and silent signals.

How many kinds of smiles do you see and how would you evaluate them? How about frowns, smirks, finger pointing, dry coughs and toe tapping? While I will provide a full gamut of silent signals below, you must put in the work of noticing and cataloging them. Does the computer salesperson appear confident about his merchandise? Does his pitch convey any doubts? If he's good, it won't. He wants to send out only the signals that will make you buy. Observe mannerisms and try to assess what the subject is doing and why. Soon, you'll become a collector of mannerisms. It's not only easy to do, there is a considerable amount of stimulating entertainment in putting the overt behavior of others under the scrutiny of your own private magnifying glass. As a side benefit, you also become more sensitive to the signals of those around you.

Several well-known criminal lawyers have developed this skill for use in situations where even the slightest edge gives them an advantage. Police, therapists, teachers, clergy and Fortune 500 CEOs have all attended my programs, often with the specific purpose of sensitizing themselves to the actions of others. Actors and politicians (often one and the same) have also taken advantage of this knowledge. I myself appear regularly on Court TV to analyze cases as they happen.

Gradually, your increased observational abilities will pay off. In a week you'll be considerably more observant than you are today. After two weeks you'll be alert to nuances that seem elusive now. In a month, with little effort, you'll be an observational superman or woman. You'll be able to pick up each of the mannerisms being displayed almost constantly by friends, strangers and your opponents at the poker table.

LISTENING

At a poker table, you often see players trying to engage their opponent in conversation in the hope that they will gain a critical advantage, a hint or guidance of some type that will help them decide how to proceed at critical junctures. Even though most players know that they should try to gain information by listening to their opponents, they don't really know what to listen for.

Achieving a level of proficiency at focused listening and its subtleties, and an ability to decipher what is really being said, also takes practice. When you are at the poker table and in everyday life, force yourself to summarize what you hear and how it is being said, how the words are being used, and which words are emphasized. It is not simply the tone or sound itself that matters. Just as with observation, it is the context of the action that is most important.

Tone becomes most important when it is inconsistent, discordant, jarring to the ears. An automobile engine rattles before gaining power, the computer grinds upon start-up. A baby cries for a brief moment in the night. A stairway creaks in an empty house. These sounds stand out because they're inconsistent. If you hear an inconsistent sound when someone is talking, you should listen more closely. Vocal tones vary from person to person, but each individual usually speaks with a steady tone. What becomes significant is the moment when the steadiness varies, creating a tonal distortion, even if only for a split second. Prolonged distortions like screaming, sobbing and high-pitched hysteria are easy to hear, and the reason for the sound is usually obvious.

When you are practicing your listening skills, momentary changes are what you should concentrate on. Listen for the brief distortions that serve as the most critical signals.

INTERPRETATION

The major work in non-verbal communication, *Kinesics in Context*, by Birdwhistell, is a great source for interpreting human behavior, Kinesics is the original term for body language, but the word "context" is really the key to understanding and interpreting what body language is all about.

When you start to absorb more information, certain actions become more significant because you are able to place them in context. Because you are working hard on your observational skills, you may see somebody draw his chair closer to the table, but it may not mean anything other than the fact that he wants to get closer to the table! If, on the other hand, you have done your job, you may have noticed that it is not something he does every hand, rather he does it with a degree of regularity prior to making a big play. If so, it suddenly becomes an action that has a far greater significance because you have placed it in the context of his normal behavior. A tell like that may seem simple, but it may be well outside your normal field of perception if you haven't trained yourself to absorb more of the detail of what is constantly going on around you.

THE IMPORTANT THING IS CONTEXT, THAT IS, WHAT PEOPLE DO IN THE CONTEXT OF NORMAL BEHAVIOR AND WHAT THEY DON'T.

The first thing you have to do when trying to decipher tells is to establish the player's normal behavior patterns, then see where those patterns are broken. Often, people will say something like, "When he touches his nose, he is lying." Well, that may be true, unless he happens to have an itchy nose that night! It is vitally important to observe that person first and see what his normal patterns are. The fact that he touched his nose the last time he was bluffing may be absolutely meaningless if you haven't established what his normal behavior is.

UNMASKING TELLS

Identifying Deception
When trying to uncover deception, you need to look for a sense of discomfort, which shows itself through a deviation from the way a person has been normally acting.

In poker, you want to find out who is telling the truth, who is lying, who is misrepresenting the value of his hand, and who is not. Determining an opponent's level of discomfort is key to unraveling the code of tells. Even with A-A, a person can become uncomfortable when risking a lot of chips, but discomfort is much more obvious when a normal person is lying.

Observation is an intricate part of the process because you not only have to pick up the fact that people are uncomfortable, but also must observe and remember how they were playing before the discomfort flag was raised. If you have seen them make big bets without displaying discomfort and then show down the best hand, but now they're making a big bet and are obviously quite uncomfortable, they're clearly telling you something!

If you see any of the following, it often indicates a high level of discomfort.

High Levels of Discomfort

1. Someone who generally speaks a lot, but is suddenly silent.
2. Someone who normally speaks quickly, but is now speaking slowly.
3. Someone who is normally motionless, but is now agitated and moving around a lot.
4. Someone who is suddenly still when he normally moves about a great deal.
5. Someone who starts touching his face for the first time.
6. Someone who demonstrates any number of irregular indicators that deviate from normal behavior.

After you have uncovered a level of discomfort, one's skill and interpretation as a poker player become important. You have to figure out what that discomfort means. In many cases it means that the player is lying. In other cases, it can mean that the player has A-A and is uncomfortable because he fears his opponent has made two pair or a set. If you watched the last time that player showed a bluff or a great hand, deciphering the discomfort will be a lot easier.

The Body's Secret Language

Body language is just like any other language; very few of the words mean anything unless they're tied to other words. A player putting his hands behind his head doesn't mean much unless it is tied to other events, different cues, and your past observation of that person. You're looking for relationships in the indicators, what I call a "packet of signals." You're not looking for just one thing. It is far easier to be able to say, "That person is lying when he leans back," or "He's confident when he touches his nose," and so on, but it doesn't work that way.

The information you get is just a piece of a larger language. Has he done it before? Does he do it regularly when strong or weak? What else is he doing that may confirm that read? These are all questions that have to be answered to correctly interpret the information you gather. If you can build up a dictionary of the individual behaviors that your opponents display, your ability to understand the language of tells will be much stronger.

PHYSICAL COMMUNICATION

Palms and Hands
How open somebody's hands are is very often a reliable indicator of how open and honest the person is being. Someone sitting with palms up and open is more likely to be open and honest with you. Of course, the reverse also applies: People who suddenly clench their hands into a fist with palms facing downward are more likely to be lying or have something to hide. The clenching and unclenching of one's hands is a very strong indicator of discomfort as well.

Hand Over Mouth or Face
Again, one has to observe how often these actions occur and in what context. A person covering his mouth with a hand could mean that he just has bad breath or is uncomfortable with his smile. It could also mean that he is uncomfortable with what he is doing and is lying. Observe him for a while first to make sure that it's not normal behavior whenever he bets. If it is truly a change in behavior, the movement of a hand to cover the face often indicates that the person is trying to hide something and does not want you to get the true message.

Steepling of Fingers

When people place their hands together with fingers leaning against each other and facing upward, as if in prayer, it is often a sign of perceived superiority. If they seem to be doing it subconsciously and it is not something they do regularly, it probably means that they have a good hand.

Feet and Legs

When a person suddenly crosses his feet or arms, and has not previously been doing so, the action often represents a more defensive posture. Although they are hard to see under a poker table, a person's feet carry a lot of information. You can often see the upper body moving or a small vibration of clothing above the table when there is a jiggling of the foot or leg.

The tapping of toes, tightening of legs, and crossing and uncrossing of the ankles are all important things to look for. Identify the normal behavior and then watch to see how it changes when a player bets. Does he stop tapping his feet when he bluffs? Many people have a tendency to become still and discontinue normal behavior when scared or under a lot of stress. Try casually leaning back in your chair and then glancing down at your lap, using your peripheral vision to see what the players on either side of you are doing with their feet the next time they're in a hand.

Smile

A fake smile comes on quickly and disappears quickly because the muscles that cause a smile are very hard to control. On the other hand, a real smile arrives and fades slowly and usually crinkles up the side of the face all the way to the area above the eyes.

Pupil Dilation

When people become excited their pupils become larger. People may be excited because they have a terrible hand and are bluffing, or because they have just made the nuts. It helps substantially to have a base line to help with your decision, or to pick up other cues as to whether or not they are bluffing. For example, if his pupils get larger while showing a quick, insincere smile, it probably means that he doesn't have such a great hand. However, if his pupils dilate when he makes a big bet, but he's clearly relaxed and leaning forward, or if he answers a question in a normal tone of voice with a natural smile, there is no way you are going to risk a lot of chips by calling!

Blocking visual access to the pupils is one of the reasons why some people wear sunglasses when playing poker. Another reason is to be able to put people on edge and watch their actions without their knowing it.

The Fight or Flight Reflex

A well-known physical reaction is one's natural desire to flee in the face of danger. People tend to shift backward when wanting to flee or lean forward when ready to fight or engage—but these reactions are not always the case. Many people lean back when very satisfied, or when they intend to play.

It is important to watch your opponent for a while to see what he normally does. The flight reflex does not have to be as obvious as leaning back to have a substantial meaning. Pulling back one's chin is often far more subtle, but can still indicate fear. The most famous example was when President Bill Clinton said, "I did not have sexual relations with that woman." As he said the words, Clinton, with a small movement of the head and neck backwards, moved his chin closer to his chest.

If somebody is in the middle of talking to you and his shoulders suddenly move back, it may be what is called a "micro-shove," which can have the same meaning. Actually, the micro movements are often more reliable because they're involuntary.

The more overt movements such as leaning back are much easier to fake and are also likely to mean other things. If somebody leans back and puts his hands behind his head, it is generally a sign of smugness. However, in poker when you have a good hand, it wouldn't be normal for a person to show off his smugness in such an obvious way so it would be far more likely to be the action of somebody wanting to look confident when he really isn't. Therefore, it would be much more likely that the person is bluffing.

Forehead

A lot of people crinkle their forehead when in thought. A distinctly different look is crinkling the forehead in a way that goes from the eyes up and indicates surprise. Surprise is a very natural and normally uncontrollable display of expression that is easy to spot if you are paying attention. It usually manifests itself in eyes that open wider and the forehead moving up from the eyebrows. As a good poker player, you have to interpret what that surprise reaction means.

Swallowing, Gulping

When somebody lies or is very uncomfortable with what he is saying or doing, a biochemical reaction occurs during which the throat dries up. It is physiological and cannot be controlled. Again, go back and take a look at the tapes of President Clinton being grilled in the Senate hearings about Monica Lewinsky. During the questioning, he drank an unusually large amount of soda. It wasn't just the hot lights that caused his need for liquids; it was a physiological need caused by a high level of anxiety. If somebody makes a large bet and then tries to look casual by drinking some water, it may make a lot of sense to question the validity of his bet.

Obviously Casual

A pretty good rule of thumb is that whenever you see somebody obviously trying to look casual, he probably isn't relaxed. Taken in context with other indicators, this type of behavior can be a big help to the observant player. For example, if your opponent check-raises you, then leans back and gives you a quick but insincere smile and drinks some water, doing his best to look smug and casual, you can be pretty sure that the reverse may be true. He may not be smug and casual. He may be extremely weak.

Staring Straight Into One's Eyes

It is not normal for a person to stare directly into your eyes for a long period of time when making responses. When that occurs, it often means that he is trying to hide something. The traditional response is to say something while looking at you, then look away, look at you again, look away and so on.

Closing of the Eyes

When people are lying they tend to close their eyes or blink rapidly. This is considered to be a form of behavior that goes back to their childhood habit of closing their eyes so it cannot be seen that they're lying. Even though it is very childlike behavior, a lot of us still do it in adulthood. It may manifest itself as more of a rapid blinking of the eyes, but is still a very common indicator.

Eyes Looking Up to the Left or Right When Talking

While scientific opinions on the subject vary, there is a reasonable body of evidence to suggest that different functions of the left and right brain cause different responses. If you are right-handed and are trying to recollect something that is factual, you look up and to the left. If you are trying to visualize something you have never seen before, you look up and to the right. In the latter case you are more likely to be making something up. The opposite indicators apply if you are left-handed. Although often helpful and quite obvious, these tells can be tough to work with at times. They are somewhat unreliable because the differences between remembering, reconstructing and creating are very narrow for some people.

Nostril Flare
More often than not, flaring of the nostrils shows excitation, good or bad, which normally occurs when a person is pleased by something or when he is very angry. The perfect visual of the nostril flare under anger is that of the angry bull.

Tight Lips
When you see people move their lips so that they suddenly appear to be thinner, it is often a sign that that they're misrepresenting what they're saying. It is a micro movement of the lips rolling back that causes them to look thinner. In doing so, people are trying to close off their means of communication.

Tongue and Wetting of the Lips
The action of wetting one's lips with the tongue is connected directly to the biological element of the throat drying up. It comes from the fact that we really do experience a physiological reaction when we are uncomfortable or lying. Keep in mind that people don't always have to be lying to be uncomfortable.

Distinct from the wetting of the lips, slightly sticking out one's tongue has an unusual connection with working on a problem. It usually indicates a person who is in a period of uncertainty, not so sure about the cards he holds or how to bet his hand.

VERBAL COMMUNICATION

How often do you listen in an average day? It is certainly more than you speak, but much less than you think you do. Listening is not merely hearing. It is an active approach, an attitude, a way in which you relate to the world. To be good at it, you must make it a part of the way you live. Once you have a base line on how a person usually talks, you can gain a lot of information from a person's voice. Of course, it is not what he says that is important, but the way it is said. The force, tone and rhythm of a person's voice can be very important.

Vocal tones vary from person to person, but each individual usually speaks with a steady tone. What becomes significant is the moment when the steadiness varies, creating a tonal distortion, even if only for a split second. Prolonged distortions like screaming, sobbing and high-pitched hysteria are easily distinguished, and the reasons for these outbursts are obvious. However, with most tonal changes, you have to listen for the subtleties—they aren't going to hit you over the head.

Pitch

The higher the pitch a person's voice rises during a conversation, the more anxious that person is becoming. Listen for a rise or fall in pitch or register, especially if the speaker quickly corrects it. For example, when a voice changes from low to high and then back to low again, something's probably wrong with what is being said.

Force

Force as it relates to the strength applied to a single word or phrase can be very important. It often conveys more meaning than the speaker intends, because emphasis is usually unconscious.

Cracking Voice

It is usual for the voice to crack during conversation as the throat dries up due to stress or discomfort. You have to listen for it very carefully, as it may just be a brief rasp that occurs in one word. When you pick it up, that rasp or crackling sound is often a very distinct sign of uneasiness.

Non-Verbal Sigh

Expulsion of breath may just indicate a sense of relief as you release tension. It can also indicate a genuine sense of disappointment. Unfortunately, a sigh is very easy to fake so it can also be used to create a false sense of disappointment. Humans have a tendency to take in more oxygen to feel energized, but panic also involves heavy breathing, so people sigh for many reasons. A sigh can be a really hard tell to decipher. Unless you can put this it into some sort of context through previous observation, sighs can have too many meanings to be definitive all by themselves.

FINAL WORDS OF WIZDOM

Understand Gut Feeling

Are you in tune with your body and smart enough to recognize your gut feelings when you get them? If so, you have an advantage at the poker table. Your gut feelings come about through a culmination of your life's experience, and can tell you far more than you can logically figure out. It is my belief that gut feeling will beat logic most of the time. If you're faced with a tough decision between an option that appears logical and a seemingly lesser choice, and somewhere deep inside, your gut feeling tells you to take the lesser of the two, go with your gut feeling. Often, it will be the correct choice.

MARC SALEM

Remember the Importance of Context
All the mannerisms, actions and behavior you observe are meaningless unless you understand the context of past behavior and current circumstances. A word in any language, particularly the language of the body, achieves far greater meaning when it is supported by the context of the words that surround it.

Recommended Reading
The Silent Language by Edward Hall
The Memory Book by Harry Lorayne
The Relaxation Response by Herb Benson
The Mind by Bill Moyers
Kinesics in Context by Ray Birdwhistell
Telling Lies. by Paul Ekman
Detecting Deception from the Body or Face. Journal of Personality and
    Social Psychology, 29(3), 288-298.
Six Keys to Unlock and Empower Your Mind by Marc Salem
http://www.agricola.umn.edu/Library/facialexpressions.htm
http://www.psiresearch.org/
http://www.MarcSalem.com

WD: Not only has Marc entertained people all around the world with his own stage shows, so wondrous is his understanding of human communication and the workings of the mind that he has been featured on numerous television shows, including *Sixty Minutes, CNN, Rosie O'Donnell, Maury* and his own TV special, *Marc Salem's Mysterious Mind.* He has also authored two successful non-fiction books: *Marc Salem's Mind Games* and *The Six Keys to Unlock and Empower Your Mind: Spot Liars & Cheats, Negotiate Any Deal to Your Advantage, Win at the Office, Influence Friends, & Much More.*

WARWICK DUNNETT

Wizard Wizdom
Summary

THE MAKINGS OF A POKER WIZARD

> "Nobody is that much better than anybody else at the big table. They have different styles, different ways of doing things. But everybody gets the same cards."
>
> Robert Duval in *Lucky You*

While writing this book I watched the movie *Lucky You*, and this quote jumped out at me because it so aptly reflects the sentiments of the Poker Wizards. One of the points they consistently emphasized during our conversations was the importance of diligent observation and focus.

Every player pointed to the ability to observe and assimilate information as a principal trait of a successful player. Although you'll find an occasional weak player or two at your table when playing in today's professional tournaments, any one player's ability to dramatically outperform his opponents is somewhat limited. The bulk of today's players are better educated and substantially more experienced than the average player was ten years ago. The pros view good observation skills as the single biggest edge you can quickly gain over your opponents.

When focused, you are more aware of your surroundings. That is where you get your edge in a poker game. As Harrington pointed out, poker is generally a zero-sum game less commissions. We all get the same cards over the long term. It is what we do with those cards that will determine whether our play will be profitable. The best players just make better decisions than the average ones.

How do the good players consistently make better decisions? Some people call it "feel." The players who have a good feel for the game and make the best reads are the ones who are paying attention at the table. They focus on the following things.

Betting Patterns

All the pros consider betting patterns to be far more important than physical tells. How a player bets in given situations is an invaluable predictor of the cards he holds, and how he may act in similar situations later in the game.

Physical Mannerisms and Actions

Salem pointed out that actual words account for only 7 percent of human communication. Fifty-five percent of the way we communicate is via body language, and another 38 percent of the available information can be gained from vocal indicators such as volume, intonation and rhythm.

Watch how other players act and what they do when they're worried, bluffing or strong, and look for the mannerisms that Marc Salem talks about in his chapter. Another tell that is very reliable is people quickly glancing down at their chips after a good card comes out. As the cards are coming out, watch the players and their eyes, not the cards.

Verbal Mannerisms and Tells

If you are also lucky enough to be up against a player who is talking to you during the hand or is willing to answer questions, even if you totally disregard the meaning of his words and just focus on volume, intonation, tone and rhythm, you can receive an additional 38 percent of the information that he is giving off. That is why listening to and observing other players is so important. One of the best times to do this is when you are *not* in the hand. You then have much more time to focus and absorb all the information that is available to you.

Pay attention to tonal distortions, changes in volume, and emphasis. Also, listen to what a person says when commenting on other hands. You can gain information about how he is likely to play in the future. Daniel Negreanu likes to find out what type of person his opponent is by asking what he does for a living. Does he read a lot of poker books? Is he likely to be predictable or deceptive?

Stack Size

Be constantly aware of your stack size, the stacks of other players at the table, the average stack size in the tournament, and how those amounts relate to the blinds and antes.

Cloutier sums up the need for paying attention with one of his well-known comments: "Even if a gnat's wing fell off at the other end of the table, I would know about it. Just because I'm talking to somebody doesn't mean I'm not paying attention."

DISCIPLINE AND EMOTIONS

The need for discipline commences well before you sit down at the table to play. Luske and Negreanu both stress how important it is to be physically and mentally prepared for a tournament. Once you have decided that you are in good shape to play, utilize sound judgment and money management skills to stop yourself from risking more than you can afford. Personal discipline is the key.

When You're at the Table

When you're at the table, you start to use your discipline to wait for good opportunities and get away from bad situations. As Negreanu says, you have to use a lot of emotional discipline to avoid playing differently when you have taken a bad beat.

When It's Time to Stop

In a tournament, there is no doubt as to when it is time to stand up and leave! However, when you're way down in a cash game, or even well ahead, it sometimes takes a huge amount of discipline to get up from the table. To be a good player, you have to force yourself to put your ego aside and walk away a loser—for the time being, of course.

You need to discipline yourself to objectively analyze what went wrong when you lost and why you were successful when you won. Don't just credit your negative performance to bad luck or assume you were skillful when you won. Continually attempt to educate yourself and improve. All the good pros do!

Dealing With Downswings

Unless you are an amazing player who never makes incorrect decisions and always has luck on your side, you are going to go through losing periods in your quest to become consistently profitable at the end of every year.

It is important to learn how to deal with the financial downswings and the sometimes psychologically crippling disappointments that occur in tournament poker. Not only do you have to avoid running out of money by playing at appropriate levels and not overextending yourself, you also have to maintain a state of mind that keeps you playing well. Dropping down to play at lower levels, if necessary, and building up your bankroll again, or gaining some solace from winning against lesser opponents, is a highly recommended way to get back on track.

Avoid Playing Badly When You're Losing

When thinking of gambling in general, but specifically with regard to the inconsistent and huge swings that a player faces in tournament poker, I like to visualize what a sinkhole in outer space would look like. Playing poker is, so to speak, like flying around the circumference of this very dangerous void. If you get too close to the edge, you can easily find yourself being dragged in. When you lose, it is too easy to find yourself playing badly, which in turn can cause more losses until you suddenly find yourself in a place where the losses don't seem to matter any more! Like quicksand, the harder you try to get out of the hole, the faster you sink into it. This is the stuff of nightmares, but represents a situation you consistently need to avoid if you want to be a successful player.

All the pros admit that they have gone through some pretty long losing streaks, but instinctively recognize that losing is just part of the game. They detach themselves very effectively from the unsatisfactory outcomes that they occasionally face by looking at it from a mathematical point of view and recognizing that bad beats and consistent periods of loss in tournament poker are going to happen. They agree that if you want to be successful, you can't take it personally and let it affect your game. On the other hand, it is critical that you analyze your game to make sure that the downswing wasn't actually caused by bad play on your part. If that is the case, it is imperative that you change the way you are playing.

Chip Reese, who was regarded as one of the best players in the world, once made a comment that I have never forgotten: "Everybody gets bad beats in poker; it is how they play after a bad beat that separates the good players from the bad."

Find Personally Satisfying Games

People who don't want to deal with long periods of losses may find that playing one-table tournaments with a generous payout structure is more rewarding than playing big multitable tournaments. Even though the payout is a lot less, I enjoy the increased regularity of return that single table sit-and-gos offer since roughly 30 percent of the players make the money. If you're good at playing that type of tournament, you're in the money nearly half of the time, a much more rewarding outcome for people who desire more consistent returns.

Another option for players who enjoy a regular flow of self-gratification is to look for multitable online satellites that reward a high percentage of players. On many online poker sites, the tournament satellite entries that you win can then be converted and used to enter regular cash tournaments. Inversely, most non-satellite tournaments offer a big return for a small buy-in, so only a small percentage of participants are paid a substantial amount.

The most obvious option for players who desire a regular cash flow is to become a proficient cash game player. On the other hand, if you prefer going for glory and the biggest payouts, make multitable tournaments your forte.

Don't Play When Tired

Getting a lot of rest and having a sharp mind are more important than many people realize. When most people have been awake for more than fifteen hours, they start to experience a dramatic reduction in cognitive reasoning skills. I find my own play deteriorates dramatically after six to eight hours at a poker table.

> GETTING A LOT OF REST AND HAVING A SHARP MIND ARE MORE IMPORTANT THAN MANY PEOPLE REALIZE.

Lyle Berman confirms a similar theory in his interesting autobiography, *I'm All In*. When younger, he states that one can play for longer periods, but when older, one's ability to concentrate and make great decisions is dramatically reduced without adequate rest. We older folk, it seems, need a regular afternoon nap! Even Harrington admits that he has decided to consciously switch off for limited periods of time during tournaments just to stay sharp over the long run.

Even though some players can stay up all night and then all day playing cards, most people who have been playing for an extended period start to give money away, make increasingly worse decisions, and play in a way that they would not even have considered fifteen or twenty hours earlier when they started. According to a 2000 study published in the *British Scientific Journal*, the impairment of ability in people who had been awake for more than seventeen hours and then tried to operate a motor vehicle was greater than that of people who had a blood alcohol level of .05 percent.

If you have tracking software for your online play, you may find a distinct correlation between the time of day and success rate. During the daytime hours in the United States, I find that I win far fewer single-table tournaments than I do during the early hours of the morning when, presumably, most of the players have been up all day and night. Of course, I make sure that I am well rested to take advantage of the crazy play that occurs when online players are tired and try to quickly win back the money they have lost during the night.

During daytime hours, I have found that the online play from U.S. players reaches a higher standard. It is my belief that there are very large contingents of serious players in America who make their living from online poker during the day. It would not surprise me if many of those players were at-home moms or others who are unable to take on full-time jobs, but can afford a few hours of online play to bring dollars into the household. And I'm sure many are players who have decided to play poker for a living and keep reasonable hours of work.

Maintaining focus after long periods of play is a problem for most players. For many, their earning rate often goes way down after about eight hours. It is easy to find yourself in a hole and struggling to play your way back profitability—but that doesn't always work. If you are down because you have been playing badly, have made aggressive, risky moves that just didn't work out, or have taken bad beats while playing well, falling back into a more solid mode often is more practical. Even though your ability to make good decisions has declined, at least you will be playing better cards that are easier to play before and after the flop, and require less finesse. Nevertheless, even good cards require good decisions after the flop. If you are overly tired, you are normally better off calling it quits for the night.

When tired, I am rarely able to sense tells in the same way as when I'm rested. When fresh, I will often sit down at a table and within a few minutes pick up great tells that just become obvious to me. If I have been playing all day, I have no idea what other players are holding based on their physical characteristics or actions. So, I have to base almost all of my decisions solely on the cards. That is not the optimal way of playing no-limit hold'em. So many additional factors go into the game, particularly ones that come from being observant.

To Win, Your Mind Needs to Be in the Right Place

Negreanu summed it up very nicely when he stated that your emotional state of mind is everything in poker. Luske likes to meditate and exercise before he goes to a big tournament, and just about every Wizard agrees that emotional well-being was definitely one of the most important contributors to success in poker.

The pros represented in this book have learned to avoid going on tilt, but everybody is subjected to daily stresses, both at and away from the table. Not all players are burdened with the financial and emotional realities associated with paying a mortgage, bringing up kids, or trying to keep a marriage together. But everybody has issues and problems that can easily affect their game if they allow it to happen.

STRATEGIC IDEAS

Selective Aggression

Just about everybody knows that you must be aggressive if you are to be successful at poker. Viewers see it every time they watch a WPT or WSOP final table on TV. Unfortunately, what they see on TV is not a true representation of what they really need to be doing to be successful through the bulk of a tournament.

If you ever have the opportunity to watch a player like Dan Harrington or Chris Ferguson you'll be amazed at how few hands they sometimes play. They aren't necessarily in there at every opportunity trying to make something happen. They wait for the right opportunity before being aggressive. As Ferguson said, "You have to be aggressive, but everybody says that! At the same time you have to be able to lay down a big hand and it is very hard to find people that can do both of those things successfully. Just being aggressive is not going to do it. It is picking your spots. It is being aggressive at the right time that is important."

Ferguson adapts his level of aggression to make his opponents play a style of poker that is uncomfortable for them. Harrington discussed in depth how one's level of aggression should change based on the

GOOD PLAYERS MAKE ADAPTATIONS IN STRATEGY AND CHANGES IN THEIR LEVEL OF AGGRESSION. THEIR PLAY IS BASED ON THEIR OPPONENTS' PLAY.

stage of the tournament, the size of the blinds, and the size of one's stack relative to the rest of the stacks at the table.

Based on the ever-changing environment of poker, good players make adaptations in strategy and changes in their level of aggression. Their play is based on their opponents' play. None of the wizards who contributed to this book are consistently aggressive throughout a tournament. Some of them are known to be extremely aggressive players—just not *all* the time.

Understanding the Mathematics of Poker

Of all the qualities you need to be a good player, understanding poker math is probably the easiest to acquire. It is not difficult to understand hand values, the probabilities that certain hands will occur, and to calculate the odds that you are being offered or are likely to achieve. Countless resources are available that will allow you develop an understanding of the salient points, including many online poker calculators that will assist you with this task. Acquiring a solid foundation is really a question of putting in a few hours of study and doing post-game analysis. Further, countless online discussion groups are available for those who wish to seek feedback on particular hands and strategic philosophies. Certainly, there is no shortage of people willing to comment on your play.

Some players take their understanding of the math in poker to another level. Ferguson has a comprehensive knowledge of game theory that helps him decide how many times and when it is correct to bluff, call, bet, raise, reraise, check or fold. It also helps him understand the impact that those actions will likely have on his opponents.

All the pros have a comprehensive understanding of the odds involved in poker, but they don't use that knowledge alone to determine which hands to play. They all use the statistical probability of success to a certain degree in their strategy, but a lot of other factors also affect their decisions.

Playing People, Not Just Your Cards

When most people decide that they seriously want to learn how to play poker, they buy some books or DVDs and try to obtain an understanding of all the basic principles and probabilities that make up the game. They develop their knowledge of recommended starting hands and figure out when it may be correct to call or raise, depending on pot odds and position. Often they will start playing limit hold'em and, with persistence and a little luck, become a moderately profitable player.

At some stage, a player who wants to break through to the next level must move beyond rote formulas and strategies and be able to make strategic decisions based on an opponent's character and actions, not simply his own cards. Everybody who plays poker eventually gets the same cards. But unless a person is able to bring some value-added advantage to the table and make good decisions based on something other than just the cards he receives, he may have years of enjoyable poker time, but not make much money. Most of those value-added decisions will be based on what he has observed about an opponent's behavior.

In tournaments, being able to steal pots when you believe your opponents are weak is a matter of pure survival. You have to make those plays regardless of the cards you hold. On many occasions you'll have to call a big bet on the river with only an average hand when it looks as if your opponent has missed his flush draw. To win a large tournament, you may have to check-raise bluff when you know that you're up against a player who has an overpair, but can be forced to lay down a hand. Over the term of a successful poker career, good players make a multitude of decisions based purely on what they think of their opponents' actions.

Of course, it goes without saying that everybody would prefer to have great cards, but that is not always going to happen. Even when you do get good cards, you still have to make critical decisions that are based on your opponents' past actions rather than what you hold. At times, the top players don't even have to look at their cards to beat an average player.

Playing your opponents, not just your cards, is a major requirement for profitability stressed by all of the Poker Wizards. You would think that this would be obvious, but it is surprising how many players give no thought to what their opponents have. The best players not only consider what their opponent is likely to hold, they take it to another level by adapting their play to what they think their opponent believes they have. To be a really good player, it is imperative to take your thought process to the third level, not just the second.

Individual Style

"If you go with the herd, you get hit by the herd." Aptly said by Luske, he means that if you play the same as the others, you're going to achieve the same level of success they achieve. Sexton put it another way when he referred to the top players in the world as being Damon Runyon-type characters with very individual personalities.

If you want to be really successful at poker, you must develop an individual style that is in keeping with your own personality. Understand the mathematics involved in the game, but don't try to follow a set formula for success or you'll just end up like all the other people following the same formula. To be comfortable with your decisions, they have to be your own, not somebody else's.

Some people are just aggressive by nature. That is the style that works best for them. Others are incredibly patient and analytical, while still others prefer to make spur-of-the-moment decisions based purely on feel. Many people never become psychologically comfortable in handling the long losing periods that a hyper-aggressive strategy likely brings between big wins; they need to get into the money more often to feel good about themselves.

By all means, cherry-pick different philosophies from the players or perhaps, after reading *Poker Wizards*, decide that you like one style or another and adapt that player's insights to your own natural style of play.

Should You Risk All Your Chips With A-A Preflop?
A pair of aces is roughly a 4 to 1 favorite against another pair if played to the river. That means a lower pair has about a 20 percent chance of winning against aces. Though some old-school players dislike giving up their long-term advantage early in a large tournament, none of the Poker Wizards said they would throw away aces preflop. The majority of the younger, more aggressive players would savor any opportunity to push all their chips forward even in a coin-flip situation.

When I first took up poker, I read an interesting article that suggested it was wrong for players with superior skill to jeopardize the advantage they have over the course of the tournament by engaging another player in an all-in situation during the early stages. As a result, I was driven to pose this question to the pros: "Would you ever lay down aces preflop to an all-in raise?" The answer was a unanimous "No!"

The truth is, the advantage that the good players have over the rest of the field in the big tournaments would never justify giving up a hand where a player was a 4 to 1 favorite. The edge that the better players enjoy is just not great enough. It would be unusual for a player to get anywhere near a final table unless he had faced and won a number of all-in situations. Certainly, there is no better situation to be all-in before the flop than heads-up with A-A.

Early in the Tournament: The Big Debate

Luske enjoys being aggressive early in a tournament and is willing to take the risks necessary to build a chip advantage before the antes and blinds become too large. If successful, his stack gives him the freedom to tighten up in the middle stages and become more selective. He seems to be almost cheerful about the fact that as a result of his strategy he is knocked out early on a regular basis, giving him the time he wants to do other things with his life. The majority of players who are more risk-averse spend a lot more time sitting in tournaments, yet end up on the rail anyway; it just takes a lot longer!

Most Poker Wizards advocate the need to take advantage of the weaker players that abound earlier in a tournament, and to take the risks necessary to build a big stack. That doesn't mean that they all go crazy; they just look for opportunities to potentially double or triple up early.

T.J Cloutier suggests a more conservative strategy in the early stages of a tourney. He believes that every chip you save gives you one more that can be doubled up later on when the pots are bigger.

Because the blinds are so small relative to the average player's chip stack early in a tournament, traditional wisdom and mathematical probability confirm that it is not profitable to risk a large stack unnecessarily in a confrontation over a small pot. On the other hand, a growing school of thought suggests that one should play lots of pots early while it is not expensive to do so. There is no doubt that many good players will be more willing to throw away a hand such as J-J or Q-Q early against a large reraise, because they fear getting busted by a bigger hand or getting committed to a coin flip for most of their chips. The same players may not be as quick to make the fold later in the tournament when the pot is larger and the time available to look for premium hands is running out.

When a player's financial commitment to a pot is greater relative to his stack size, the pot odds often make it more profitable to call or reraise all-in with a high pair. Remember, if you are going to try to move a player off a premium hand early in a tournament, you have to risk a large number of chips to do so and risk becoming short-stacked very early. When playing aggressively, trying to steal pots or attempting to move somebody off a hand, it is extremely important that you know your opponent is *capable* of folding.

MONEY MANAGEMENT

The Wizards make it clear that if you can't manage your financial resources, you just won't make it as a long-term profitable poker player. The need for money management skill is more pronounced when it comes to tournament poker, but even the best cash game players go through extended periods where they can't seem to catch good cards. Too often, when hours of patient play are finally rewarded, a great hand is suddenly rendered worthless on the flop or beaten by a lucky opponent who makes a terrible play yet hits a three-outer on the river. You may have a set of aces and be beaten by a straight, or flop the nut straight and have an opponent hit two consecutive cards to make a flush. Torturous things happen to good players in poker because they will always be subjected to bad beats from less-skilled players.

If you're a cash game player and reasonably proficient, there is no doubt that you'll have far fewer negative days than does a tournament player. And unless you are having a really bad run, or are your own worst enemy, or are playing when tired or under the weather, there is a pretty good chance that you'll be ahead at the end of most weeks.

On the other hand, if you play tournaments for a living, you could easily go for months without getting a major return on the hours you have invested at the table. One of the questions that I asked the pros was what sort of a bankroll they would recommend for a player who was starting out and wanted to play $1,000 tournaments for a living. The answers ranged from $20,000 to $200,000. The most analytical players of the group recommended at least $100,000 as an appropriate bankroll for an above-average player who wants to play the smaller buy-in events and satellites on the tournament circuit. If you expect to be playing the major $10,000 events, you had better come with a bankroll of between $500,000 and $1,000,000 to weather the expenses and inevitable dry spells of tournament life. Either that, or find a very good sponsor.

Ironically, this would seem to rule out almost everybody, yet the fields are still growing in the large buy-in events because of all the recreational players and people who win seats through qualifying events.

Negreanu made another important point that needs to be considered by anybody who wants to play tournament poker professionally: "If you're a bad player, all the money management in the world isn't going to help; eventually you're going to lose it all." In other words, make sure that you're a good enough poker player before you drop your regular day job.

MORE POKER WIZDOM

Intelligence

To be a successful poker player over the long term, one has to be reasonably intelligent, understand the math, know how much to bet, remember how people have previously bet, and understand equity. A player typically has to make those decisions under some duress. All the Poker Wizards I talked with were obviously very bright. I agree with Mike Sexton that they're the type of people who could be successful at whatever they set their minds to do. They have something "more" that allows them to excel.

To be a truly great player, you have to also have what Daniel calls "street smarts." Being street smart relates to understanding your surroundings, the people you're up against, and assessing the best way to deal with them. It has nothing to do with the type of college degree you hold. If you are street smart, you also have the raw intelligence and mental toughness to make good decisions when things are going bad, and smart enough to make as much money as possible when the good situations occur.

Being able to recognize and take advantage of opportunities is not necessarily a gift you are born with. It is often developed from the thousands of hands, tormented losses and joyful wins that make up your poker history. Players like Brunson and Cloutier gained that experience traveling across the country from town to town playing poker in backroom bars and clubs.

Today, people can gain much of the same experience and savvy in a substantially shorter period by playing online.

Online Poker – Playing Multiple Tables

Ferguson was the most enthusiastic Wizard about the benefits of playing online, and was particularly enamored with the advantages of playing multiple tables. He often plays multiple lower-limit tables online at Full Tilt purely for the benefit of viewers and players on that site. The ability to play multiple tables, however, is not something that everybody can handle.

People who play more than two tables simultaneously are often reduced to playing only solid hands without considering how other players are likely to react; therefore, profitability sometimes goes down. Another big drawback for relatively new players is that they have less time to study the texture of the board or think about how opponents have bet earlier in the hand, potentially missing a lot of the information needed to make the best decision. Nevertheless, as Ferguson points out, if you're looking for action and want to play solid hands, but don't have the patience to wait for them on a single table, multiple tables may be the way to go.

If you are going to play multiple tables, first become comfortable with your single table strategy and then work your way up one table at a time, finding the game and number of tables that works best for you. Above all, continue to keep track of your winnings or losses by using Poker Tracker or some other software that allows you to properly assess whether your multiple-table strategy is making money for you.

In no-limit Texas hold'em, an understanding of where you can bluff or think that other players may be bluffing is easier to achieve if you have time to focus on all of your opponents and their actions. When playing multiple no-limit tables, the average person loses much of his ability to study and record what other players are doing.

Let Your Style and Skill Level Evolve

The Wizards stressed that if you really want to improve your game, you need to occasionally try new strategies, styles and moves. If you find yourself going down a road that becomes a bit too rough, you have to turn around and return to the basic philosophies that have worked in the past. Mistakes are part of the learning process in poker; you won't grow without them. If new approaches don't work, be sure to analyze your strengths and weaknesses so that you can fall back on the part of the game that has worked for you in the past.

After speaking with Negreanu, I tried to take a more aggressive approach to poker, playing more pots, being less predictable, and trying to instill fear in my opponents. Inevitably, I found myself playing more pots after the flop with marginal hands. Without the depth of skill that the top players bring to the table in their post-flop play, I found myself becoming a less profitable player. It wasn't until I worked my way back to a more conservative strategy, using Cloutier's books as a mainstay, that my play became profitable again.

Trying to play like Daniel allowed me to win an occasional large pot when I would flop two pair with my 9-7 suited, but most of the time I would end up with a medium pair or a weak flush draw and be forced to make a lot of tough decisions after the flop, which is not my strong point. However, if your post-flop play is really good, the Negreanu style may be much more profitable for you in the long run.

Developing a style that suits *your* strengths and weaknesses is vitally important. If you're aggressive, love to play people with large bankrolls after the flop, and consider yourself a sharp decision maker with a lot of post-flop savvy, you might try to play like Negreanu. Sexton certainly believes that a more loose-aggressive style is the way to go if you want to win tournaments in today's environment. If not, perhaps the more traditional approach that Cloutier or Liebert recommend, sprinkled with just a few loose raises to confuse your opponents, will work better.

Life as a Poker Pro: The Reality

The viewing public sees the top players on TV, but does not realize how many tournaments the professionals on the circuit actually play before they reach a final table. Many days are filled with disappointment as they get knocked out of the majority of the events they enter well before reaching the final table.

Most tournament players lose with great regularity. My image of the top player's lifestyle was shattered when I saw one famous player huddled for thirteen hours in a rear seat in the economy section of our Qantas flight back to the United States from Australia, shoulder to shoulder with other mere mortals in that class. His trip to the Aussie Millions on that occasion had lacked any substantial financial return.

Losing is an ironic yet necessary part of the winning process because luck plays such a major part in the game of poker. Notwithstanding, being a consistent winner at tournament poker also requires a great deal of skill. You have to combine both luck and skill on an ongoing basis. Your position at each table, your opponents' level of skill, the cards you get and when you get them—these things and more play a huge role in determining your success rate. Given all these factors, even the most brilliant players go through long periods when they don't make it to a final table or even to the money. Understanding this relationship and maintaining a level of self-confidence during the losing periods seems to be a character trait that all the good tournament players share.

Luck and its Role in Poker

Harrington emphasizes that luck and, as a result, volatility, play a large role in poker, particularly within the realm of tournament poker. Because of the luck factor, it is easy for us to misinterpret results over the shorter period. In other words, your poker results (or investment results) have to be evaluated over a great number of years before you can determine whether you're truly skillful or simply lucky.

Once you come to terms with the fact that results over the short term are dramatically impacted by luck, you are faced with another very tricky question. Are your results the product of a playing style that is likely to be profitable (or unprofitable) over a long period, or just the product of the immense short-term impact of luck?

To fully understand the role that luck can play in success and how it can relate to poker, Harrington recommends reading Nassim Taleb's, *Fooled by Randomness*, which provides readers with a fascinating, yet contrarian, approach to the significant but often hidden impact that chance plays in our daily lives. Taleb published another popular book in 2007 called *The Black Swan*, which also deals with the impact of highly improbable events on our lives. Taleb's views predominantly run opposite to mainstream philosophies, often mocking the normal perception that we are ruled by a mathematical probability, which guarantees a set result if a set strategy is followed. His suggestion is that life, and in turn the marketplace, are subject to a far greater number of improbable events than would be expected, and that the impact of those events is greater than perceived. Because of this, many people over the short term are handed either very beneficial or ruinous results that actually bear no direct correlation to probable long-term performance.

How does all of this relate to poker? Most people who play poker seriously have some understanding of the fact that bad beats and extended periods of luck are statistically going to occur. Unpredictable results are part of playing poker and, if accepted rationally, allow the player to go on, play well and not be affected psychologically. What most people don't fully appreciate is that any particular outcome in poker is not guaranteed to follow the statistically probable bell curve that most books suggest. Yes, the opponent who is on a flush draw should only make the flush and beat you roughly once every three times, but that statistic is only a probability generated over the long term. If you play poker regularly, particularly online where you see a lot more hands, you'll notice that most predictable outcomes are anything but predictable—other than the possible prediction that what is statistically probable often seems to be the least likely outcome.

In addition to a statistically insignificant situation during a poker session and the impact of luck, you have to throw in the irrational and unpredictable actions of other players. This almost guarantees a greater volatility than would be expected using traditional models of probability. People who want to play successful poker over a long period have to come to terms with this fact. They need to develop a strategy that is likely to work, possess a bankroll that will carry them through the difficult times, and have a tough mental attitude that takes into account the large impact that luck can have on a person's results over the short term.

You're statistically likely to be dealt aces once in every 221 hands, but may play 1,000 hands and never get aces. For substantial periods, just about every pair you get will miraculously turn into three of a kind on the flop even though it is only supposed to happen roughly once in every eight times. Alternatively, you might play a thousand hands and not see three of a kind once. The point is that over the short term, luck plays a much larger role in the outcome than many players perceive. Add the often unpredictable behavior of your opponents, and the outcome of a poker hand cannot be effectively correlated to statistical expectations over the short term. Because of this volatility, having a proper bankroll is much more important than most players realize, particularly if you're primarily playing tournaments.

Bad Players Lose too Much with Big Hands

As a result of the coaching I received from the Wizards, I started to look at hands differently. My play improved substantially and the way I viewed opportunities, possibilities and flops changed dramatically.

I also learned something else. In the game of poker, you run a greater risk of losing your chips when you have a good hand than when you have an average hand. When good players make a set, middle straight or something like a king-high flush on the flop or turn, they're far more aware of what is going on around them than are the bad players. That is why they're able to make more money in the good situations and lose less when it looks like they may be beaten.

When a bad player flops a middle straight, it suddenly becomes "the nuts." Adrenaline rushes to his brain and that's all he sees. He often won't recognize the fact that if somebody plays back at him, there is a real possibility that his opponent has a higher straight draw with a possible flush draw as well, or perhaps two pair or a set. Of course, those are the types of situations that you really want in poker, but the seasoned veteran will lose a lot less on the hand if it looks as if his opponent has a better hand.

When you Win, Just Take Your Chips and be Quiet

Hopefully, after you have read this book and practiced some of its strategies and philosophies, you'll find yourself dominating your regular poker game and taking everybody's chips. When that happens, whatever you do, don't say anything after you have taken your opponents' money other than "sorry" or "bad luck." Even if they abuse you, laugh or ridicule your play, you don't need to respond. Bad players won't understand your explanation anyway and it will just make them more upset. If an unfortunate argument develops, you may have to give up playing in that game and thus put a real dent in your annual bottom line!

Recently, during what used to be my very lucrative home game, the following hand occurred. It demonstrates this lack of perception by bad players, and serves to remind me that after you win a big pot, it is best to just sit there and shut up!

During one of the last hands of the evening, the following situation developed. I was sitting in the big blind and was able to see a good-sized multiway flop holding 7♦ 9♣. After a great flop of 6♠ 8♥ 10♠, I checked.

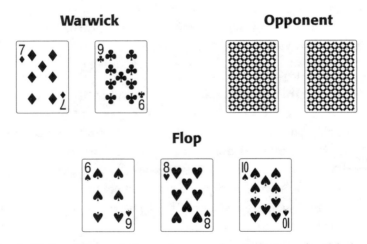

Warwick

Opponent

Flop

The initial preflop raiser made a moderate bet, and a third very loose-aggressive player with a large stack reraised all in.

I had the largest stack at the table at the time, but wasn't happy that I was going to be risking all of the night's hard-earned winnings on one hand so close to the end of the evening. After all, the pot now exceeded the amount that I earn in a week as an airline captain. I knew I was ahead on the flop with the middle straight, but there was a higher straight draw and a flush draw out there waiting to kill me.

I also had to decide whether to try to keep the initial raiser (and his probable overpair) in the hand by just calling, or reraise all in and not be greedy. After a bit of Hollywooding and a certain amount of genuine displeasure that I had to risk a huge amount of money against an obvious draw or a set, I chose the later option and moved all in, forcing out the player to my left.

Normally, against better players in this situation, the opponent who moved all in could easily have a hand like 9♠ J♠, giving him a high straight draw and a flush draw, which would make me a slight underdog (47 percent versus 52 percent). Even if the all-in player had a pair such as 8♠ 8♣, giving him three of a kind and a backdoor flush draw, he still had about a 39 percent chance of beating me by the river. As you can see, the odds of winning are not necessarily as good as you might imagine when you first realize that you've flopped a middle straight.

The all-in player, a crazy guy with a lot more money than poker sense, turned over 10-3 offsuit for a below-average top pair, and I won a substantial pot. After the hand was over, everybody was upset that I had indicated displeasure about having to move all in when I had flopped a straight. Even though he wasn't involved in the hand, a wealthy restaurateur, probably the worst player at the table, was leader of the pack. Insulted that such a bad player was lecturing me, I then made my most costly poker mistake of the year—I tried to explain my actions. Needless to say, unfortunately, I no longer play in that once very profitable home game!

Gut Feeling

The pros recognize that gut feeling is really a signal sent by one's inner self and born of years of experience that would be perilous to ignore. Most of the Wizards believe that when faced with a tough decision, it is often better to go with your gut rather than try to rationalize your actions. Ferguson in particular prefers to intellectualize those feelings before acting on them. The pros also pointed out that many players tend to overanalyze situations and end up discarding their first instinct in favor of a more rational conclusion. More often than not, the Wizards believe that you are better off going with your first instinct because it comes from all your years of experience and a certain level of subconscious observation that may not be obvious at the time.

If you have spent much time watching Negreanu play poker on television, you'll hear him remark that, on occasion, even he doesn't understand why he is making a particular play. He simply has a very strong voice inside that is telling him to make it. He recognizes that voice as an internal mechanism based on hundreds of thousands of hands and past experiences that help him decide what to do. As a result, he sometimes calls, bets or folds at apparently illogical times.

Really great players make better decisions more regularly than players of more average ability. Of course, there are many reasons why successful players make better decisions, but in part, it is because they're able to connect more closely with those constructive subconscious feelings and signals we refer to as "gut feeling."

Ironically, it was the master of non-verbal tells himself, Marc Salem, who gave me the most insightful piece of indirect information. When I asked him about the significance of the inner voice, he pointed out that gut feeling has tremendous significance "if you are smart enough to recognize it." It wasn't until later when I listened to the recording that I realized how rare he thinks it is for a person to actually connect with his true gut feeling. That begs the question: Is that little voice that says "Call!" your gut feeling, or is it perhaps driven by other inner desires such as your need to win or your desire to prove your superiority? Or could it be a more complex, self-destructive urge that tells you to call when you know you shouldn't? The better players understand the differing internal signals they're getting and know which ones to heed and which to ignore.

FINAL WORDS OF WIZDOM

Finally, after absorbing the wisdom of the Wizards, I realized that if everybody played poker in the same way, they would eventually achieve the same results. However, the reality is that people make different playing decisions and that's what makes poker so interesting and unpredictable. It is the quality of your decisions that determines whether you will ultimately be successful.

This book has provided various strategies that you can follow to make sure you are heading in the right direction. My main intent has been to give you insights into the complex thought processes that champion players employ in their winning journey along the tournament trail.

The Wizards of Poker have each developed a unique style of play that works best for them. Now it's up to you to develop your individual style. Let their magic work for you!

About the Author

As a Boeing 747 captain with a large U.S.-based cargo company, Warwick Dunnett travels the globe looking for adventure, new challenges and conquests. For the last five years, he has found those challenges not only in the exotic countries he visits, but also inside his constant companion, a small grey laptop computer.

On an auspicious day in 2003 Warwick discovered the tough world of competitive poker. Perhaps it was the training he received as a futures trader earlier in life or the professional pilot's mathematical reasoning that allowed him to adapt so well. In any case, he found that long periods of observation intertwined with brief moments of adrenalin-pumping exhilaration were familiar territory—and he fell in love with poker. After a couple of months of play, he won a major limit hold'em tournament on an online site, then later won a $13,000 entry package into the Australian Poker Championship Main Event.

By 2005 his prize winnings from poker rivaled his income as a professional pilot when he won $85,000 (Aus.) for a 6th place finish in the Aussie Millions, and then went on to acquire a package entry to the World Series of Poker main event worth $13,000 and an additional three more entries to the 2006 and 2007 Australian Championships in Melbourne, valued at $33,000.

Born in Australia, Warwick now resides in San Francisco with his wife and two young children. When not away flying, he stays close to home and avoids the rigors of the tournament circuit, preferring to primarily play online and in local cash games so he can spend as much time as possible at home with his family. Fueled by a desire for a greater understanding of poker and a deep passion for the game, Warwick sought out answers to a selection of poker's most difficult questions—questions that are now answered by some of the world's best players in Poker Wizards.

GLOSSARY

The glossary is extracted from the poker dictionary, *Poker Talk*, courtesy of Avery Cardoza, Cardoza Publishing.

all in: When a player has all his chips committed to a pot.

big blind: 1. The larger of two forced blind bets in hold'em posted by the player two seats to the left of the button before the cards are dealt. Compare to small blind. 2. The player occupying this position.

bubble: In a tournament, the point at which all remaining players will win money except for the next player to get eliminated. For example, with 37 players remaining and 36 places paid, that 37th place is the *bubble*.

button: 1. The player occupying the dealer position who, in games with blinds, goes last in all rounds except the first. 2. The physical disk, often plastic and labeled "dealer," that indicates the dealer position.

come over the top: 1. Raise or reraise. "When Billy raised my bet on the turn, I came over the top for all my chips."

connectors: Two or more cards in sequence, such as 5-6 or J-Q.

cutoff seat: The position to the right of the button.

equity: 1. The amount of money invested in a hand or in a game. 2. The amount of money in a pot a player would expect to win if the hand were played out over the long run, for example, if the player had a one-third chance of winning a $120 pot, his *equity* would be $40.

flop: The three cards that are simultaneously dealt face up upon completion of the first round of betting and can be used by all active players.

gutshot straight: See Inside straight.

implied odds: The amount of money that can potentially be won (assuming opponents will make additional bets) compared to the cost of a bet. For example, if a player is contemplating calling a $10,000 bet, and he figures that $90,000 more will be put into the pot, he has implied odds of 9 to

GLOSSARY

1—that is, he is betting $10,000 to possibly win $90,000.

inside straight: 1. A straight draw consisting of four cards with one "hole," such that only one rank can complete the hand, for example, 2-4-5-6, in which only a 3 can complete the straight. Compare to an open-ended straight.

in the hole: 1. Cards held face down by a player. 2. To be losing and having a long way to go to break even.

kicker: The highest side card to any hand of one pair, two pair, three of a kind, or rarely, four of a kind hand. For example, in hold'em, A-J against K-J on a flop of J-Q-3-J-4 would be won by the A-J hand, the three jacks with the ace kicker beating the three jacks with the king kicker.

last longer bet: A wager between two or more players on who will go further in a tournament before being eliminated, the winner being the last active player among the participants who has not yet busted out.

limper: A player who makes the minimum permitted bet as a way to enter the pot.

loose: 1. A player who plays many hands and enters many pots. 2. When applied to a game, a collection of players who play many pots.

loose-aggressive player: A player who not only plays many hands but plays them aggressively with frequent bets and raises.

make the money: In a tournament, to finish among the top players and win cash.

marginal hands: Hands that are borderline profitable, with long-term expectations of about break-even when played, thus being about equally correct to play as to fold.

moves: Fancy plays: bluffs. "Watch out for B-Man; he's got lots of moves."

muck: 1. Fold. "He bet and I mucked." 2. The place on the table where discarded cards are placed. "Throw that piece of cheese in the muck."

nuts: The best possible hand given the cards on board; usually expressed as *the nuts*.

on tilt: A player who has lost control of his emotions due to a bad loss or succession of losses and is playing recklessly.

one out of the money: In a tournament, the point at which all remaining players will win money except for the next player to get eliminated. For example, when there are 37 players remaining and only 36 places are paid. Also bubble.

open-ended straight: Four consecutive cards to a straight, such as 8-9-10-J, such that a card on either end will make a straight, as opposed to an inside straight.

outs: Cards that will improve a hand that is behind enough to win a pot. For example, a hand of 7-7-9-9-K has four outs against a completed straight, the two remaining sevens and nines, which will make a winning full house, while a player who needs to complete a four card flush draw to win, has nine outs, the remaining suited cards in the deck.

overcard: A hole card higher in rank than any board card. For example, if a player holds A-10 and the flop is K-J-6, the ace is an overcard.

overpair: A pocket pair that is larger than any open card on the board. For example, Q-Q on a flop of J-10-6.

positive equity: A hand that is mathematically favored to win in the long run.

pot: The total of all bets placed in the center of the table by players during a poker hand and

push somebody off a pot: To force a player to fold by aggressive betting and raising.

put a player on a hand: Deduce an opponent's hand by his betting and playing actions.

river: The fifth and last community card dealt or its betting round (or both considered together).

set: Three of a kind.

sit-and-go: A one-table tournament that begins as soon as a table is filled; there is no scheduled starting time. Cash prizes are typically paid to the top three places. Also, *sit 'n' go, SNG.*

small ace: An ace accompanied by a low side card, such as a 3 or 7.

small blind: 1. The smaller of two forced blind bets in hold'em posted by the player immediately to the left of the button before the cards are dealt. Also called *little blind.* Compare to big blind. 2. The player occupying this position.

stack: 1. The total amount of chips a player has on the table. 2. In a tournament, the relative number of chips a player has compared to other players.

stone cold nuts: The best possible hand, given the situation.

suited connectors: Cards that are of consecutive rank and in the same suit, such as 8 9.

tell: An inadvertent mannerism or reaction that reveals information about the strength of a player's hand.

tight player: A player who plays only premium hands and enters few pots.

trap hand: A hand that, if played, has a high risk of incurring big losses.

trips: Three of a kind.

turn: The fourth community card.

under the gun: The first player to act in a round of poker, particularly the first betting round.

up front: In early position.

weak-tight player: A player who plays few hands, but when he does, he plays them weakly.

where you are at in a hand: To know one's relative hand strength compared to opponents.

POKER PRODUCTS TO IMPROVE YOUR GAME

GREAT CARDOZA POKER BOOKS
ADD THESE TO YOUR LIBRARY - ORDER NOW!

DANIEL NEGREANU'S POWER HOLD'EM STRATEGY *by Daniel Negreanu*. This power-packed book on beating no-limit hold'em is one of the three most influential poker books ever written. Negreanu headlines a collection of young great players—Todd Brunson, David Williams. Erick Lindgren, Evelyn Ng and Paul Wasicka—who share their insider professional moves and winning secrets. You'll learn about short-handed and heads-up play, high-limit cash games, a powerful beginner's strategy to neutralize professional players, and how to mix up your play and bluff and win big pots. The centerpiece, however, is Negreanu's powerful and revolutionary small ball strategy. You'll learn how to play hold'em with cards you never would have played before—and with fantastic results. The preflop, flop, turn and river will never look the same again. A must-have! 520 pages, $34.95.

POKER WIZARDS *by Warwick Dunnett*. In the tradition of Super System, an exclusive collection of champions and superstars have been brought together to share their strategies, insights, and tactics for winning big money at poker, specifically no-limit hold'em tournaments. This is priceless advice from players who individually have each made millions of dollars in tournaments, and collectively, have won more than 20 WSOP bracelets, two WSOP main events, 100 major tournaments and $50 million in tournament winnings! Featuring Daniel Negreanu, Dan Harrington, Marcel Luske, Kathy Liebert, Mike Sexton, Mel Judah, Marc Salem, T.J Cloutier and Chris "Jesus" Ferguson. This must-read book is a goldmine for all serious players, aspiring pros, and future champions! 352 pgs, $19.95.

POKER TOURNAMENT FORMULA 2: Advanced Strategies for Big Money Tournaments *by Arnold Snyder*. Probably the greatest tournament poker book ever written, and the most controversial in the last decade, Snyder's revolutionary work debunks commonly (and falsely) held beliefs. Snyder reveals the power of chip utility-the real secret behind winning tournaments-and covers utility ranks, tournament structures, small- and long-ball strategies, patience factors, the impact of structures, crushing the Harringbots and other player types, tournament phases, and much more. Includes big sections on Tools, Strategies, and Tournament Phases. A must buy! 500 pages, $24.95.

OMAHA HIGH-LOW: How to Win at the Lower Limits *by Shane Smith*. Practical advice specifically targeted for the popular low-limit games you play every day in casinos and online will have you making money, and show you how to avoid losing situations and cards that can cost you a bundle—the dreaded second-nut draws, trap hands, and two-way second-best action. Smith's proven strategies are spiced with plenty of wit and wisdom. You'll learn the basics of play against the typical opponents you'll face in low-limit games—the no-fold'em players and the rocks—and get winning tactics, illustrated hands, and tournament tips guaranteed to improve your game. 144 pages, $12.95.

TOURNAMENT TIPS FROM THE POKER PROS *by Shane Smith*. Essential advice from poker theorists, authors, and tournament winners on the best strategies for winning the big prizes at low-limit rebuy tournaments. Learn proven strategies for each of the four stages of play—opening, middle, late and final—how to avoid 26 potential traps, advice on rebuys, aggressive play, clock-watching, inside moves, top 20 tips for winning tournaments, more. Advice from Brunson, McEvoy, Cloutier, Caro, Malmuth, others. 160 pages, $14.95.

NO-LIMIT TEXAS HOLD 'EM: The New Player's Guide to Winning Poker's Biggest Game *by Brad Daugherty & Tom McEvoy*. For experienced limit players who want to play no-limit or rookies who has never played before, two world champions show readers how to evaluate the strength of a hand, determine the amount to bet, understand opponents' play, plus how to bluff and when to do it. Seventy-four game scenarios, unique betting charts for tournament play, and sections on essential principles and strategies show you how to get to the winners circle. Special section on beating online tournaments. 288 pages, $24.95.

GREAT CARDOZA POKER BOOKS
ADD THESE TO YOUR LIBRARY - ORDER NOW!

HOW TO WIN AT OMAHA HIGH-LOW POKER *by Mike Cappelletti.* Clearly written strategies and powerful advice shows the essential winning strategies for beating Omaha high-low poker! This money-making guide includes more than sixty hard-hitting sections on Omaha. Players learn the rules of play, best starting hands, strategies for the flop, turn, and river, how to read the board for both high and low, dangerous draws, and how to beat low-limit tournaments. Includes odds charts, glossary, and low-limit tips. 304 pgs, $19.95.

THE BIG BOOK OF POKER *by Ken Warren.* This easy-to-read and oversized guide teaches you everything you need to know to win money at home poker, in cardrooms, casinos, and on the tournament circuit. Readers will learn how to bet, raise, and checkraise, bluff, semi-bluff, and how to take advantage of position and pot odds. Great sections on hold'em (plus stud games, Omaha, draw games, and many more) and playing and winning poker on the internet. Packed with charts, diagrams, sidebars, and detailed, easy-to-read examples by best-selling poker expert Ken Warren, this wonderfully formatted book is one stop shopping for players ready to take on any form of poker for real money. Want to be a big player? Buy the Big Book of Poker! 320 oversized pages, $19.95.

WINNER'S GUIDE TO TEXAS HOLD'EM POKER *by Ken Warren.* New edition shows how to play every hand from every position with every type of flop. Learn the 14 categories of starting hands, the 10 most common hold'em tells, how to evaluate a game for profit, the value of deception, the art of bluffing, eight secrets to winning, starting hand categories, position, and more! Includes detailed analysis of the top 40 hands and the most complete chapter on hold'em odds in print. Over 500,000 copies sold! 224 pages, $14.95.

KEN WARREN TEACHES TEXAS HOLD 'EM *by Ken Warren.* This is a step-by-step comprehensive manual for making money at hold'em poker. 42 powerful chapters teach you one lesson at a time. Great practical advice and concepts with examples from actual games and how to apply them to your own play. Lessons include: Starting Cards, Playing Position, Raising, Check-raising, Tells, Game/Seat Selection, Dominated Hands, Odds, and much more. This book is already a huge fan favorite and best-seller! 416 pages, $26.95.

WINNER'S GUIDE TO OMAHA POKER *by Ken Warren.* Concise and easy-to-understand, Warren shows beginning and intermediate Omaha players how to win from the first time they play. You'll learn the rules, betting and blind structure, why you should play Omaha, the advantages of Omaha over Texas hold'em, glossary, reading the board, basic strategies, Omaha high, Omaha hi-low split 8/better, how to play draws and made hands, evaluation of starting hands, counting outs, computing pot odds, the unique characteristics of split-pot games, the best and worst Omaha hands, how to play before the flop, how to play on the flop, how to play on the turn and river, and much more. 224 pages, $19.95

CHAMPIONSHIP TOURNAMENT POKER *by Tom McEvoy.* Enthusiastically endorsed by more than five world champions, this is a *must* for every player's library. McEvoy lets you in on the secrets he has used to win millions of dollars in tournaments and the insights he has learned competing against the best players in the world. Packed solid with winning strategies for 11 games with extensive discussions of 7-card stud, limit hold'em, pot and no-limit hold'em, Omaha high-low, re-buy, half-half tournaments, satellites, and includes strategies for each stage of tournaments. 416 pages, $29.95.

HOW TO WIN NO-LIMIT HOLD'EM TOURNAMENTS *by McEvoy & Don Vines.* Learn the basic concepts of tournament strategy and how to win big by playing small buy-in events, graduate to medium and big buy-in tournaments, adjust for short fields, huge fields, slow and fast-action events. Plus, how to win online tournaments. You'll also learn how to manage a tournament bankroll and get tips on table demeanor for televised tournaments. See actual hands played by finalists at WSOP and WPT championship tables with card pictures, analysis and useful lessons from the play. 376 pages, $29.95.

Order now at 1-800-577-WINS or go online to: www.cardozabooks.com

GREAT CARDOZA POKER BOOKS
ADD THESE TO YOUR LIBRARY - ORDER NOW!

CRASH COURSE IN BEATING TEXAS HOLD'EM *by Avery Cardoza.* Perfect for beginning and somewhat experienced players who want to jump right in on the action and play cash games, local tournaments, online poker, and the big televised tournaments where millions of dollars can be made. Both limit and no-limit hold'em games are covered along with the essential strategies needed to play profitably on the preflop, flop, turn, and river. The good news is that you don't need to memorize hands or be burdened by math to be a winner—just play by the no-nonsense basic principles outlined here. 208 pages, $14.95

INTERNET HOLD'EM POKER *by Avery Cardoza.* Learn how to get started in the exciting world of online poker. The book concentrates on Internet no-limit hold'em, but also covers limit and pot-limit hold'em, five- and seven-card stud, and Omaha. You'll learn everything from how to play and bet safely online to playing multiple tables, using early action buttons, and finding easy opponents. Cardoza gives you the largest collection of online-specific strategies in print—more than 6,500 words dedicated to 25 unique strategies! You'll also learn how to get sign-up bonuses worth hundreds of dollars! 176 pages, $9.95

HOW TO PLAY WINNING POKER *by Avery Cardoza.* New and completely updated, this classic has sold more than 250,000 copies. Includes major new coverage on playing and winning tournaments, online poker, limit and no-limit hold'em, Omaha games, seven-card stud, and draw poker (including triple draw). Includes 21 essential winning concepts of poker, 15 concepts of bluffing, how to use psychology and body language to get an extra edge, plus information on playing online poker. 256 pages, $14.95.

POKER TALK: Learn How to Talk Poker Like a Pro *by Avery Cardoza.* This fascinating and fabulous collection of colorful poker words, phrases, and poker-speak features more than 2,000 definitions. No longer is it enough to know how to walk the walk in poker, you need to know how to talk the talk! Learn what it means to go all in on a rainbow flop with pocket rockets and get it cracked by cowboys, put a bad beat on a calling station, and go over the top of a producer fishing with a gutshot to win a big dime. You'll soon have those railbirds wondering what *you* are talking about. 304 pages, $9.95.

OMAHA HIGH-LOW: Play to Win with the Odds *by Bill Boston.* Selecting the right hands to play is the most important decision to make in Omaha. This is the *only* book that shows you the chances that every one of the 5,278 Omaha high-low hands has of winning the high end of the pot, the low end of it, and how often it is expected to scoop all the chips. You get all the vital tools needed to make critical preflop decisions based on the results of more than 500 million computerized hand simulations. You'll learn the 100 most profitable starting cards, trap hands to avoid, 49 worst hands, 30 ace-less hands you can play for profit, and the three bandit cards you must know to avoid losing hands. 248 pages, $19.95.

KEN WARREN TEACHES 7-CARD STUD *by Ken Warren.* You'll learn how to play and win at the main variations of seven-card stud (high-low split and razz—seven-card stud where the lowest hand wins), plus over 45 seven-card stud home poker variations! This step-by-step manual is perfect for beginning, low-limit, and somewhat experienced players who want to change their results from losses to wins, or from small wins to bigger wins. Lessons include starting cards, playing position, which hands to play to the end, raising and check-raising strategies, how to evaluate your hand as you receive every new card, and figure out what hands your opponents likely have. 352 pages, $14.95.

Order now at 1-800-577-WINS
or go online to:
www.cardozabooks.com

GREAT CARDOZA POKER BOOKS
ADD THESE TO YOUR LIBRARY - ORDER NOW!

HOLD'EM WISDOM FOR ALL PLAYERS *By Daniel Negreanu.* Superstar poker player Daniel Negreanu provides 50 easy-to-read and right-to-the-point hold'em strategy nuggets that will immediately make you a better player at cash games and tournaments. His wit and wisdom makes for great reading; even better, it makes for killer winning advice. Conversational, straightforward, and educational, this book covers topics as diverse as the top 10 rookie mistakes to bullying bullies and exploiting your table image. 176 pages, $14.95.

MILLION DOLLAR HOLD'EM: Winning Big in Limit Cash Games by *Johnny Chan and Mark Karowe.* Learn how to win money consistently at limit hold'em, poker's most popular cash game, from one of poker's living legends. You'll get a rare opportunity to get into the mind of the man who has won ten World Series of Poker titles—tied for the most ever with Doyle Brunson—as Johnny picks out illustrative hands and shows how he thinks his way through the betting and the bluffing. No book so thoroughly details the thought process of how a hand is played, the alternative ways it could have been played, and the best way to win session after session. *Essential* reading for cash players. 400 pages, $29.95.

THE POKER TOURNAMENT FORMULA by *Arnold Snyder.* Start making money now in fast no-limit hold'em tournaments with these radical and never-before-published concepts and secrets for beating tournaments. You'll learn why cards don't matter as much as the dynamics of a tournament—your position, the size of your chip stack, who your opponents are, and above all, the structure. Poker tournaments offer one of the richest opportunities to come along in decades. Every so often, a book comes along that changes the way players attack a game and provides them with a big advantage over opponents. Gambling legend Arnold Snyder has written such a book. 368 pages, $19.95.

HOW TO BEAT SIT-AND-GO POKER TOURNAMENTS by Neil Timothy. There is a lot of dead money up for grabs in the lower limit sit-and-gos and Neil Timothy shows you how to go and get it. The author, a professional player, shows you how to reach the last six places of lower limit sit-and-go tournaments four out of five times and then how to get in the money 25-35 percent of the time using his powerful, proven strategies. This book can turn a losing sit-and-go player into a winner, and a winner into a bigger winner. Also effective for the early and middle stages of one-table satellites.176 pages, $14.95.

HOW TO BEAT INTERNET CASINOS AND POKER ROOMS by *Arnold Snyder.* Learn how to play and win money online against the Internet casinos. Snyder shows you how to choose safe sites to play. He goes over every step of the process, from choosing sites and opening an account to how to take your winnings home! Snyder covers the differences between "brick and mortar" and Internet gaming rooms and how to handle common situations and predicaments. A major chapter covers Internet poker and basic strategies to beat hold'em and other games online. 272 pages, $14.95..

I'M ALL IN: High Stakes, Big Business, and the Birth of the World Poker *Tour by Lyle Berman with Marvin Karlins.* Lyle Berman recounts how he revolutionized and revived the game of poker and transformed America's culture in the process. Get the inside story of the man who created the World Poker Tour, plus the exciting world of high-stakes gambling where a million dollars can be won or lost in a single game. Lyle reveals the 13 secrets of being a successful businessman, how poker players self-destruct, the 7 essential principles of winning at poker. Foreword by Donald Trump. Hardback, photos. 232 pages, $24.95.

7-CARD STUD: The Complete Course in Winning at Medium & Lower Limits by *Roy West.* Learn the latest strategies for winning at $1-$4 spread-limit up to $10/$20 fixed-limit games. Covers starting hands, 3rd-7th street strategy, overcards, selective aggressiveness, reading hands, pro secrets, psychology, and more in an informal 42 lesson format. Includes bonus chapter on 7-stud tournament strategy by Tom McEvoy. 224 pages, $19.95.

DOYLE BRUNSON'S EXCITING BOOKS
ADD THESE TO YOUR COLLECTION - ORDER NOW!

SUPER SYSTEM *by Doyle Brunson*. This classic book is considered by the pros to be the best book ever written on poker! Jam-packed with advanced strategies, theories, tactics and money-making techniques, no serious poker player can afford to be without this hard-hitting information. Includes fifty pages of the most precise poker statistics ever published. Features chapters written by poker's biggest superstars, such as Dave Sklansky, Mike Caro, Chip Reese, Joey Hawthorne, Bobby Baldwin, and Doyle. Essential strategies, advanced play, and no-nonsense winning advice on making money at 7-card stud (razz, high-low split, cards speak, and declare), draw poker, lowball, and hold'em (limit and no-limit).This is a must-read for any serious poker player. 628 pages, $29.95.

SUPER SYSTEM 2 *by Doyle Brunson*. The most anticipated poker book ever, SS2 expands upon the original with more games and professional secrets from the best in the world. Superstar contributors include Daniel Negreanu, winner of multiple WSOP gold bracelets and 2004 Poker Player of the Year; Lyle Berman, 3-time WSOP gold bracelet winner, founder of the World Poker Tour, and super-high stakes cash player; Bobby Baldwin, 1978 World Champion; Johnny Chan, 2-time World Champion and 10-time WSOP bracelet winner; Mike Caro, poker's greatest researcher, theorist, and instructor; Jennifer Harman, the world's top female player and one of ten best overall; Todd Brunson, winner of more than 20 tournaments; and Crandell Addington, no-limit hold'em legend. 672 pgs, $34.95.

CARO'S GUIDE TO DOYLE BRUNSON'S SUPER SYSTEM *by Mike Caro*. Working with World Champion Doyle Brunson, the legendary Mike Caro has created a fresh look to the "Bible" of all poker books, adding new and personal insights that help you understand the original work. Caro breaks 36 concepts into either "Analysis, Commentary, Concept, Mission, Play-By-Play, Psychology, Statistics, Story, or Strategy. Lots of illustrations and winning concepts give even more value to this great work. 86 pages, 8 1/2 x 11, $19.95.

ACCORDING TO DOYLE *by Doyle Brunson*. Learn what it takes to be a great poker player by climbing inside the mind of poker's most famous champion. Fascinating anecdotes and adventures from Doyle's early career playing poker in roadhouses are interspersed with lessons from the champion who has made more money at poker than anyone else in history. Learn what makes a great player tick, how he approaches the game, and receive candid, powerful advice from the legend himself. 208 pages, $14.95.

MY 50 MOST MEMORABLE HANDS *by Doyle Brunson*. This instant classic relives the most incredible hands by the greatest poker player of all time. Great players, legends, and poker's most momentous events march in and out of fifty years of unforgettable hands. Sit side-by-side with Doyle as he replays the excitement and life-changing moments of the most thrilling and crucial hands in the history of poker: from his early games as a rounder in the rough-and-tumble "Wild West" years—where a man was more likely to get shot as he was to get a straight flush—to the nail-biting excitement of his two world championship titles. Relive million dollar hands and the high stakes tension of sidestepping police, hijackers and murderers. A thrilling collection of stories and sage poker advice. 168 pages, $14.95.

ONLINE POKER *by Doyle Brunson*. Ten compelling chapters show you how to get started, explain the safety features which lets you play worry-free, and lets you in on the strategies that Doyle himself uses to beat players in cyberspace. Poker is poker, as Doyle explains, but there are also strategies that only apply to the online version, where the players are weaker!—and Doyle reveals them all in this book.192 pages, illustrations, $14.95.

BOBBY BALDWIN'S WINNING POKER SECRETS *by Mike Caro with Bobby Baldwin*. The fascinating account of 1978 World Champion Bobby Baldwin's early career playing poker against other legends is packed with valuable insights. Covers the common mistakes average players make at seven poker variations and the dynamic winning concepts needed for success. Endorsed by superstars Doyle Brunson and Amarillo Slim. 208 pages, $14.95.

MIKE CARO'S EXCITING WORK
POWERFUL BOOKS YOU <u>MUST</u> HAVE

CARO'S MOST PROFITABLE HOLD'EM ADVICE *by Mike Caro.* When Mike Caro writes a book on winning, all poker players take notice. And they should: The "Mad Genius of Poker" has influenced just about every professional player and world champion alive. You'll journey far beyond the traditional tactical tools offered in most poker books and for the first time, have access to the entire missing arsenal of strategies left out of everything you've ever seen or experienced. Caro's first major work in two decades is packed with hundreds of powerful ideas, concepts, and strategies, many of which will be new to you—they have never been made available to the general public. This book represents Caro's lifelong research into beating the game of hold em. 408 pages, $24.95

MASTERING HOLD'EM AND OMAHA *by Mike Caro and Mike Cappelletti.* Learn the professional secrets to mastering the two most popular games of big-money poker: hold'em and Omaha. This is a thinking player's book, packed with ideas, with the focus is on making you a winning player. You'll learn everything from the strategies for play on the preflop, flop, turn and river, to image control and taking advantage of players stuck in losing patterns. You'll also learn how to create consistent winning patterns, use perception to gain an edge, avoid common errors, go after and win default pots, recognize and use the various types of raises, play marginal hands for profit, the importance of being loved or feared, and Cappelletti's unique point count system for Omaha. 328 pages, $19.95.

CARO'S BOOK OF POKER TELLS *by Mike Caro.* One of the ten greatest books written on poker, this must-have book should be in every player's library. If you're serious about winning, you'll realize that most of the profit comes from being able to read your opponents. Caro reveals the the secrets of interpreting *tells*—physical reactions that reveal information about a player's cards—such as shrugs, sighs, shaky hands, eye contact, and many more. Learn when opponents are bluffing, when they aren't and why—based solely on their mannerisms. Over 170 photos of players in action and play-by-play examples show the actual tells. These powerful ideas will give you the decisive edge. 320 pages, $24.95.

CARO'S FUNDAMENTAL SECRETS OF WINNING POKER *by Mike Caro.* Learn the essential strategies, concepts, and plays that comprise the very foundation of winning poker play. Learn to win more from weak players, equalize stronger players, bluff a bluffer, win big pots, where to sit against weak players, and the six factors of strategic table image. Includes selected tips on hold 'em, 7 stud, draw, lowball, tournaments, more. 160 pages, $12.95.

CARO'S PROFESSIONAL POKER REPORTS

Each of these three powerful insider poker reports is centered around a daily mission, with the goal of adding one weapon per day to your arsenal. Theoretical concepts and practical situations are mixed together for fast in-depth learning. For serious players.

11 DAYS TO 7-STUD SUCCESS. Bluffing, playing and defending pairs, different strategies for the different streets, analyzing situations—lots of information within. One advantage is gained each day. A quick and powerful method to 7-stud winnings. Essential. Signed, numbered. $19.95.

12 DAYS TO HOLD'EM SUCCESS. Positional thinking, playing and defending against mistakes, small pairs, flop situations, playing the river, are just some sample lessons. Guaranteed to make you a better player. Very popular. Signed, numbered. $19.95.

PROFESSIONAL 7-STUD REPORT. When to call, pass, and raise, playing starting hands, aggressive play, 4th and 5th street concepts, lots more. Tells how to read an opponent's starting hand, plus sophisticated advanced strategies. Important revision for serious players. Signed, numbered. $19.95.

Order now at 1-800-577-WINS or go online to: www.cardozabooks.com

THE CHAMPIONSHIP SERIES
POWERFUL INFORMATION YOU <u>MUST</u> HAVE

CHAMPIONSHIP NO-LIMIT & POT-LIMIT HOLD'EM *by T. J. Cloutier & Tom McEvoy.* The bible for winning pot-limit and no-limit hold'em tournaments gives you all the answers to your most important questions: How do you get inside your opponents' heads and learn how to beat them at their own game? How can you tell how much to bet, raise, and reraise in no-limit hold'em? When can you bluff? How do you set up your opponents in pot-limit hold'em so that you can win a monster pot? What are the best strategies for winning no-limit and pot-limit tournaments, satellites, and supersatellites? Rock-solid and inspired advice you can bank on from two of the most recognizable figures in poker. 304 pages, $29.95.

CHAMPIONSHIP HOLD'EM *by T. J. Cloutier & Tom McEvoy.* Hard-hitting hold'em the way it's played *today* in both limit cash games and tournaments. Get killer advice on how to win more money in rammin'-jammin' games, kill-pot, jackpot, shorthanded, and full table cash games. You'll learn the thinking process for preflop, flop, turn, and river play with specific suggestions for what to do when good or bad things happen. Includes play-by-play analyses, advice on how to maximize profits against rocks in tight games, weaklings in loose games, experts in solid games, plus tournament strategies for small buy-in, big buy-in, rebuy, add-on, satellite and big-field major tournaments. Wow! 392 pages, $29.95.

CHAMPIONSHIP OMAHA (Omaha High-Low, Pot-limit Omaha, Limit High Omaha) *by Tom McEvoy & T.J. Cloutier.* Clearly-written strategies and powerful advice from Cloutier and McEvoy who have won four World Series of Poker Omaha titles. You'll learn how to beat low-limit and high-stakes games, play against loose and tight opponents, and the differing strategies for rebuy and freezeout tournaments. Learn the best starting hands, when slowplaying a big hand is dangerous, what danglers are (and why winners don't play them), why you sometimes fold the nuts on the flop and would be correct in doing so, and overall, how you can win a lot of money at Omaha! 296 pages, illustrations, $29.95.

CHAMPIONSHIP HOLD'EM TOURNAMENT HANDS *by T. J. Cloutier & Tom McEvoy.* An absolute must for hold'em tournament players, two legends show you how to become a winning tournament player at both limit and no-limit hold'em games. Get inside the authors' heads as they think their way through the correct strategy at 57 limit and no-limit starting hands. Cloutier & McEvoy show you how to use skill and intuition to play strategic hands for maximum profit in real tournament scenarios and how 45 key hands were played by champions in turnaround situations at the WSOP. Gain tremendous insights into how tournament poker is played at the highest levels. 368 pages, $29.95.

CHAMPIONSHIP HOLD'EM SATELLITE STRATEGY *by World Champions Brad Dougherty & Tom McEvoy.* Every year satellite players win their way into the $10,000 WSOP buy-in and emerge as millionaires or champions. You can too! Learn the specific, proven strategies for winning almost any satellite from two world champions. Covers the ten ways to win a seat at the WSOP, how to win limit hold'em and no-limit hold'em satellites, one-table satellites, online satellites, and the final table of super satellites. Includes a special chapter on no-limit hold'em satellites! 320 pages, $29.95.

HOW TO WIN THE CHAMPIONSHIP: Hold'em Strategies for the Final Table, *by T.J. Cloutier.* If you're hungry to win a championship, this is the book that will pave the way! T.J. Cloutier, the greatest tournament poker player ever—he has won 60 major tournament titles and appeared at 39 final tables at the WSOP, both more than any other player in the history of poker—shows how to get to the final table where the big money is made and then how to win it all. You'll learn how to build up enough chips to make it through the early and middle rounds and then how to employ T.J.'s own strategies to outmaneuver opponents at the final table and win championships. You'll learn how to adjust your play depending upon stack sizes, antes/blinds, table position, opponents styles, chip counts, and the specific strategies for six-handed, three handed, and heads-up play. 288 pages, $29.95.

POWERFUL WINNING POKER SIMULATIONS
A MUST FOR SERIOUS PLAYERS WITH A COMPUTER!
IBM compatible CD ROM Win 95, 98, 2000, NT, ME, XP

These incredible full color poker simulations are the best method to improve your game. Computer opponents play like real players. All games let you set the limits and rake and have fully programmable players, plus stat tracking, and Hand Analyzer for starting hands. Mike Caro, the world's foremost poker theoretician says, "Amazing... a steal for under $500... get it, it's great." Includes free phone support. "Smart Advisor" gives expert advice for every play!

1. TURBO TEXAS HOLD'EM FOR WINDOWS - $59.95. Choose which players, and how many (2-10) you want to play, create loose/tight games, and control check-raising, bluffing, position, sensitivity to pot odds, and more! Also, instant replay, pop-up odds, Professional Advisor keeps track of play statistics. Free bonus: Hold'em Hand Analyzer analyzes all 169 pocket hands in detail and their win rates under any conditions you set. Caro says this "hold'em software is the most powerful ever created." Great product!

2. TURBO SEVEN-CARD STUD FOR WINDOWS - $59.95. Create any conditions of play; choose number of players (2-8), bet amounts, fixed or spread limit, bring-in method, tight/loose conditions, position, reaction to board, number of dead cards, and stack deck to create special conditions. Features instant replay. Terrific stat reporting includes analysis of starting cards, 3-D bar charts, and graphs. Play interactively and run high speed simulation to test strategies. Hand Analyzer analyzes starting hands in detail. Wow!

3. TURBO OMAHA HIGH-LOW SPLIT FOR WINDOWS - $59.95. Specify any playing conditions; betting limits, number of raises, blind structures, button position, aggressiveness/passiveness of opponents, number of players (2-10), types of hands dealt, blinds, position, board reaction, and specify flop, turn, and river cards! Choose opponents and use provided point count or create your own. Statistical reporting, instant replay, pop-up odds high speed simulation to test strategies, amazing Hand Analyzer, and much more!

4. TURBO OMAHA HIGH FOR WINDOWS - $59.95. Same features as above, but tailored for Omaha High only. Caro says program is "an electrifying research tool...it can clearly be worth thousands of dollars to any serious player. A must for Omaha High players.

5. TURBO 7 STUD 8 OR BETTER - $59.95. Brand new with all the features you expect from the Wilson Turbo products: the latest artificial intelligence, instant advice and exact odds, play versus 2-7 opponents, enhanced data charts that can be exported or printed, the ability to fold out of turn and immediately go to the next hand, ability to peek at opponents hand, optional warning mode that warns you if a play disagrees with the advisor, and automatic mode that runs up to 50 tests unattended. Tough computer players vary their styles for a great game.

6. TOURNAMENT TEXAS HOLD'EM - $39.95

Set-up for tournament practice and play, this realistic simulation pits you against celebrity look-alikes. Tons of options let you control tournament size with 10 to 300 entrants, select limits, ante, rake, blind structures, freezeouts, number of rebuys and competition level of opponents. Pop-up status report shows how you're doing vs. the competition. Save tournaments in progress to play again later. Additional feature allows quick folds on finished hands.

Order now at 1-800-577-WINS or go online to: www.cardozabooks.com

FREE BOOK!
TAKE ADVANTAGE OF THIS OFFER NOW!

The book is **free**; the shipping is **free**. Truly, no obligation. Oops, we forgot. You also get a **free** catalog. **And a $10 off coupon!!** Mail in coupon below to get your free book or go to www.cardozabooks.com and click on the red OFFER button.

WHY ARE WE GIVING YOU THIS BOOK?

Why not? No, seriously, after more than 27 years as the world's foremost publisher of gaming books, we really appreciate your business. Here's our appreciation back! Take this free book as our thank you for being our customer; we're sure we'll see more of you!

THIS OFFER GETS EVEN BETTER & BETTER!

You'll get a **FREE** catalog of all our products—over 200 to choose from—and get this: you'll also get a **$10 FREE** coupon good for purchase of any product in our catalog!

Our offer is pretty simple. Let me sum it up for you:
1. Order your **FREE** book
2. Shipping of your book is **FREE!***
3. Get a **FREE** catalog (over 200 items—and more on the web)
4. You also get a **$10 OFF** coupon good for anything we sell
5. Enjoy your free book and **WIN!**

*U.S. customers only. Sorry, due to very high ship costs, we cannot offer this outside the U.S. However, we still have good news for foreign customers: Spend $25 or more with us and we'll include that free book for you anyway!

CHOOSE YOUR FREE BOOK

Choose one book from any of these books in the Basics of Winning Series (15 choices): Baccarat, Bingo, Blackjack, Bridge, Caribbean Stud Poker and Let it Ride, Chess, Craps, Hold'em, Horseracing, Keno, Lotto/Lottery, Poker, Roulette, Slots, Sports Betting, Video Poker.

Or choose from these five books: Internet Hold'em Poker, Crash Course in Beating Texas Hold'em, Poker Talk, Poker Tournament Tips from the Pros, or Bobby Baldwin's Winning Poker Secrets.

When you order by Internet, enter the coupon code **WIZARDS** to get your free book

---

HURRY! GET YOUR FREE BOOK NOW!
USE THIS COUPON OR GO TO OUR WEBSITE!

YES! Send me my **FREE** book now! I understand there is no obligation whatsoever! Send coupon to: Cardoza Publishing, P.O. Box 98115, Las Vegas, NV 89193. No phone calls on free book offer.

Free book by website: www.cardozabooks.com (click on red OFFER button)

Shipping is FREE to U.S. (Sorry, due to very high ship costs, we cannot offer this outside the U.S. However, we still have good news for foreign customers: Spend $25 or more with us and we'll include that free book for you anyway!)

WRITE IN FREE BOOK HERE _____

Name _____

Address _____

City _____ State _____ Zip _____

Email Address* _____ Coupon Code: WIZARDS

*Get our FREE newsletter and FREE email offers when you provide your email. Note: Your information is protected. Privacy Guarantee: We do NOT and never have sold our customer information in 27 years. Your information remains private. One coupon per address or per person only. Offer subject to cancellation at any time.